The Client
Who
Changed Me

The Client Who Changed Me

Stories of

Therapist Personal

Transformation

Jeffrey A. Kottler and Jon Carlson

Routledge
Taylor & Francis Group

NEW YORK AND HOVE

Published in 2005 by
Routledge
Taylor & Francis Group
270 Madison Avenue
New York, NY 10016

Published in Great Britain by
Routledge
Taylor & Francis Group
27 Church Road
Hove, East Sussex BN3 2FA

© 2005 by Taylor & Francis Group, LLC
Routledge is an imprint of Taylor & Francis Group
Formerly a Brunner-Routledge title.

Printed in the United States of America on acid-free paper
10 9 8 7 6 5 4 3 2 1

International Standard Book Number-10: 0-415-95107-0 (Hardcover) 0-415-95108-9 (Softcover)
International Standard Book Number-13: 978-0-415-95107-4 (Hardcover) 978-0-415-95108-1 (Softcover)

Library of Congress Cataloging-in-Publication Data

Catalog record is available from the Library of Congress

Taylor & Francis Group
is the Academic Division of T&F Informa plc.

Visit the Taylor & Francis Web site at
http://www.taylorandfrancis.com

and the Routledge Web site at
http://www.routledge-ny.com

CONTENTS

ABOUT THE AUTHORS

JEFFREY A. KOTTLER is one of the most prolific authors in the fields of psychology and education, having written 55 books about a wide range of subjects. He has authored a dozen texts for counselors and therapists that are used in universities around the world, and a dozen books each for practicing therapists and for educators. Some of his most highly regarded works include *On Being a Therapist*, *The Imperfect Therapist*, *Compassionate Therapy*, *Finding Your Way as a Counselor*, and *Making Changes Last*. He has also written several highly successful books for the public that describe complex phenomena in highly accessible prose: *Beyond Blame*, *Travel That Can Change Your Life*, *Private Moments*, *Secret Selves*, *The Language of Tears*, and *The Last Victim: Inside the Minds of Serial Killers*.

Jeffrey has been an educator for 25 years. He has worked as a teacher, a counselor, and a therapist in preschool, middle school, mental health center, crisis center, university, community college, and private practice settings. He has been a Fulbright Scholar and senior lecturer in Peru (1980) and Iceland (2000), and has worked as a visiting professor in New Zealand, Australia, Hong Kong, Singapore, and Nepal. Jeffrey is currently chair of the Counseling Department at California State University, Fullerton.

JON CARLSON, Psy.D., Ed.D., is distinguished professor of psychology and counseling at Governors State University, University Park, Illinois, and a psychologist with the Wellness Clinic in Lake Geneva, Wisconsin. In addition to serving as the longtime editor of *The Family Journal*, Jon is the author of 35 books in the areas of family therapy, marital enrichment, consultation, and Adlerian psychology. Some of his best-known works include *The Intimate Couple*, *The Disordered Couple*, *Brief Therapy with Individuals and Couples*, *Health Counseling*, *Theories and Strategies of Family Therapy*, and *Time for a Better Marriage*.

Jon has developed and produced more than 200 commercial video-tapes that feature the most prominent leaders in the field (including the professionals featured in this book) demonstrating their theories in action. These videos are used to train the next generation of practitioners.

Together, Jeffrey and Jon have collaborated on four other books: *American Shaman* (with Bradford Keeney), *Bad Therapy*, *The Mummy at the Dining Room Table*, and *Their Finest Hour*.

Chapter 1

FROM CLAY TO FIRE
A Mythological Tale

Myths are central to the core of human experience in all cultures and contexts. They are, in the words of Joseph Campbell (1991), "public dreams" in the same sense that dreams are merely private myths. They provide a window into a culture, whether that viewpoint looks at matters of cosmology, sociology, or a profession such as psychotherapy. Without myths, Rollo May (1992) argued, a society will rupture just as clients' own search for meaning will collapse unless their search for "truth" involves replacing limited stories with other myths that provide a new foundation on which to stand.

Throughout human history, there have always been myths and cultural stories related to godlike figures who provide guidance and nurturance for vulnerable mortals. The stories of Zeus, Neptune, Thor, Buddha, Jesus, Mohammed, Moses, and others all portray super ordinary beings who work on behalf of human beings, who often cannot manage their own affairs without some divine intervention. It was even said that the gods invented humankind as a source of entertainment, just as the novelist Tom Robbins once commented that water invented human beings as a means for transporting itself from one place to another.

In all their interactions with human beings, gods were almost never changed by these encounters—the influence moved in only one direction. The gods, by definition, were immutable, as constant as the stars. Their job was to change others while remaining impervious to change themselves.

Contemporary therapists might find these points relevant to their own training. We are taught from our very first courses that we are to avoid meeting our own needs at all costs, that we are to remain objective and detached. We are instructed to enforce clear, consistent, and impenetrable boundaries that prevent possible "boomerang" effects in which we might be inadvertently changed for the worse. It is as if, like the ancient gods, we are supernatural beings who, through training, supervision, and supreme

1

self-restraint, are able to remain above the fray that affects mortal beings. Any possible counter-transference effects, or personal reactions, can thus be worked through to the point that we return to the position of clarity. We have been warned that the consequence of letting one's guard down can be disastrous, not just for our clients, but also for ourselves.

Prometheus was one god of ancient Greece who was credited with no less than the birth of humankind. It was Prometheus who first created mortals out of clay figures. These were beings who led lives without even the most basic necessities—they were helpless and vulnerable, cold and hungry, without even the most basic means to take care of themselves. In other words, human beings were flawed, miserable, and without hope.

Prometheus saw himself as the champion and advocate for mortals, a voice of compassion and caring. He lobbied on their behalf and attempted to help them take care of themselves. Zeus, the Lord of all gods, refused to assist in this matter. In fact, he specifically forbade Prometheus to fool around with humans, and ordered him to attend to the more important celestial business. Moreover, he was suspicious and annoyed by Prometheus, who had powers to see the future but refused to share what he had foreseen.

But Prometheus became more than a little attached to his "clients," these mortal beings who were so interesting and unpredictable. When lobbying on their behalf failed to persuade Zeus to permit divine intervention, Prometheus decided to take matters into his own hands. There are times, after all, when a helper must trust his own heart, even when this path may conflict with the wishes of one's supervisor.

Prometheus discovered an unguarded gate into Olympus—a back door, so to speak —that gave him secret access to the fires that burned at the portal to the sun. He stole some burning embers and delivered them to humans in order to provide them with warmth and light.

Not surprisingly, this enraged Zeus, who did not take kindly to upstarts who challenged his authority. A certain degree of altruism could be tolerated, but not when it went against his explicit desire. Prometheus was therefore taken, in chains, to be taught a lesson he would never forget, and would also provide a lesson to others who might consider disobeying orders. Prometheus was chained in the Caucasus Mountains, where he was to be tortured by the same ritual every day: an eagle would attack him and eat his liver. By the next day, the prisoner would have recovered, only to be attacked again and again, for all eternity.

If the story were to end here, this would hardly be a very encouraging lesson for therapists who allow themselves to become overinvolved in their quest to help people and who, in turn, became affected by this helping journey. If anything, this would be another in an endless series of stories we are told to warn us against such efforts. Our clients, who feel as if they are made of clay, may cry and plead for deliverance, and we should do all we can to help them (short of stealing fire), but never, we are told, should we allow them to penetrate our core. Bad things happen under such circumstances—that is how we are supposed to get the sort of compassion fatigue that feels as if our livers are being eaten every day for a thousand years.

Zeus felt some pity for Prometheus. Or, if not pity, then he still wanted the prophecy about his own future that only his captive could know. Yet even with the offer of his freedom, Prometheus refused to tell Zeus who would be the mother of his child. Again it seems that this would have a very unhappy ending for those who stick to their ethical convictions, even with dire consequences.

Prometheus' actions were so highly admired by humans and many gods alike, that a few volunteers came forward to sacrifice themselves so that he might regain his freedom and continue to work benevolently on behalf of mortals. We learn from his actions several important lessons:

1. People need "gods" or advocates to bring "fire" in order to move beyond a claylike existence.
2. If we are to allow ourselves to truly care for our clients, and to act as courageous advocates for their rights, we, too, may suffer pain and loss of sleep. Prometheus actually had this to say about doing therapy: "It is easy of him who keeps his foot free from harm, to counsel and admonish him who is in misery" (Aeschylus [525–456 B.C.], 1926).
3. Myths and stories may be told in very different ways, implying quite different lessons; Prometheus may be viewed as benevolent, heroic, and altruistic, or as narcissistic, oppositional, and arrogant.

Naturally, there are limits on our applying the myth of Prometheus to the work and lives of contemporary therapists. In this postmodern era, we are hardly "gods" or supreme beings whose job is to deliver fire to figures of clay. We are as much partners in a journey, or perhaps guides who have familiarity with the territory, contour maps of the terrain, and some experience exploring the trails in the vicinity. Ideally, we don't have to "steal" fire from others, or provide it for those who are helpless; rather, we teach clients to build their own fires so they can survive on their own.

FROM MYTHS TO REALITIES

Changes associated with doing therapy are very often framed in negative terms. Practitioners are thus admonished to monitor carefully the toxic effects that can result from getting too close to their clients' issues.

Freud (1910) warned that such counter-transference reactions can pollute the relationship as well as diminish the clinician's ability to remain objective. Others have written about the sort of burnout and compassion fatigue that can infect therapists who allow themselves to overpersonalize their work. A pervasive message is often communicated to beginners in the field: "Be very, very careful, or you will become 'infected' by the negative energy of your clients. You can end up another casualty if you allow them to get to you."

Yet like any changes that take place as a result of some transformative experience, they can be for better or for worse. It is certainly true that therapists (and their clients) can suffer terribly if certain boundaries are collapsed. It is also the case that the personal and professional aspects of our lives can become so fused that it is difficult to maintain a healthy balance. Carl Rogers (1972), for example, describes how he lost his sense of self in a relationship with a particular client to the point that he teetered on the brink of a nervous breakdown. Dozens of other volumes present similar cases of situations in which therapists were irrevocably changed—mostly for the worse—because they didn't maintain their detachment. They were punished as Prometheus was punished for stealing fire.

What has so often been ignored, however, are those times when therapists are changed for the better. Some of the earliest psychoanalytic revisionists, such as Carl Jung and Harry Stack Sullivan, recognized the times when therapists and clients actually reverse their roles. Irv Yalom, known for his frankness about the intimacy he has experienced in some therapeutic relationships (Yalom, 1989), also reveals how he has been helped by his clients. He even describes the therapist and client as "fellow travelers"—both on a journey of discovery together (Yalom, 2002, p. 8). Taking an even more extreme position, the great family therapist Carl Whitaker once claimed that all the therapy he did was for himself. He felt that unless he had potential, and interest, in growing as a result of his interactions with a family, he wasn't interested in working with them. He believed that if clients couldn't help him to grow, he couldn't do much for them either. Therapy, to Whitaker, was always reciprocal.

When we attempt to help clients deal with personal struggles, we often end up helping ourselves with similar issues. When we heal others' pain, we heal our own. We find ourselves talking in sessions, preaching lessons to our clients, and then realize, suddenly, that we are really talking to ourselves. We end up taking the advice that we offer to others when we tell them such things as the importance of living more in the present moment, or spending more quality time with loved ones, or behaving in more fully functioning ways.

Then there are the things we learn from our clients every day. With each conversation we are pressed to examine themes that we may have ignored, challenge our most cherished beliefs, and explore our own most vulnerable areas. In a sense, when doing this type of work, there is nowhere to hide. Clients bring to sessions all those forbidden subjects and secrets that are rarely discussed anywhere else. And with each session we conduct, we become more knowledgeable about people and more wise about the world.

There are times when we come home from work positively bursting with new lessons we can't wait to share with loved ones. "You won't believe what I learned today!" is such a common refrain that our families give us amused looks. Of course, then they also give us their attention because they, too, can't wait to hear about some new insight or understanding.

These are rather small, if interesting, lessons that might accrue each day or week. There is always some new refinement of technique that develops, just as there are advances in our understanding of what we are doing and how we are doing it. Goldfried (2001), for example, collected a series of "clinical events" that precipitated conceptual revisions among well-known theorists. There is constant learning with regard to the nature of the human condition. We are always adding to our knowledge base about different cultural groups, individual differences, and the infinitely creative ways that people cope during adverse conditions.

What we are interested in are the really big changes that therapists have undergone as a direct result of their work. We are talking about once-in-a-lifetime transformations that therapists are still working to integrate into their lives.

In spite of prohibitions to the contrary, and a reluctance to speak about this almost forbidden topic in public, there are a lot reasons why this phenomenon of reciprocal changes in therapy could so easily occur, perhaps the most significant of which is the heavy and intense feelings circulating in the room.

No matter how placid we pretend to be on the outside, there are times when we are just as emotionally activated as our clients. At times we feel scared, if not terrified. It is not uncommon that we may feel frustrated or even angry, even as we work hard to stay neutral. The conversations are often steeped in confusion, complexity, and ambiguity. There is drama (and entertainment) in the sessions that rivals any of our favorite films or plays. There is authentic intimacy in the relationships, built on many hours spent talking about the most personal things imaginable. When things are going well, there is a kind of transcendent empathy when it feels as if we can feel the client's heart beating and the soul speaking. How could we not be affected by such an intense level of engagement?

In *On Being a Therapist*, Kottler (2003) speaks about the ways that clients, as distracted and disoriented as they may be, as amateurish as they may be in their efforts, are still powerful change agents in our lives, for better or for worse. "Whenever we enter a room with another life in great torment, we will find no escape from our own despair. And we will find no way to hold down elation we feel as a witness to another person's transformation—just as we are the catalyst for our own" (pp. 256–257).

It might be more accurate to amend this quote by adding that the client can be the catalyst for our changes. Just as we say and do things that are deliberately and strategically designed to influence people in desirable directions, so, too, are clients doing the same thing. They are working just as hard to win our approval and recruit us over to their worldview. They do this not just because they want support for their positions but also because they are just as convinced as we are that they are right and others are mistaken or misinformed. Eventually, we usually win the battle of wills, but this is mostly because of our training and experience. But that's not to say that clients don't get a few licks in along the way.

Then there are all the inadvertent and unintentional ways that clients trigger our growth and learning, all without having the slightest idea about the fireworks going on inside us. In a book about changes that experienced therapists undergo (Kahn & Fromm, 2001), Spiegel (2001) speaks of the ways he has been changed by the cancer patients he has worked with over the years, how their struggles to come to terms with their impending deaths have caused him to live his own life more intensely. Rather than feeling despair working with dying people, he reports how inspired he feels.

A client brings up an issue and we realize, as we are responding, that it is one that we have not yet fully resolved. We talk about finding meaning in life and discover new meanings for ourselves. We confront a client about some action taken, and soon realize that we were talking as much to ourselves as to the client. A particular conversation comes back to haunt us, gripping us in a way that we can't let go of unless we face the underlying issue. New decisions in our lives are based, in part, on dialogue we have had with clients. On and on the parallel process continues, every week, day, and hour.

Finally, there are the unconscious changes that we experience as a result of work in the trenches. Over time, the ways we look at the world, the ways we interact with others, the ways we see ourselves shift gradually as a consequence of our encounters with clients. We may be seen by the public as the gurus, the wizards, the healers, the oracles whom pilgrims visit in order to seek enlightenment, but it is one of our most closely guarded secrets how much we gain from such helping encounters.

SOME AMAZING STORIES

In the stories that follow, you will have the opportunity to hear from the most prominent therapists in the world. These are the theorists, scholars, researchers, and clinicians, from a wide variety of orientations and contexts, who have most shaped contemporary practice. They are the professionals who have written the classic texts and conducted the most significant research in the field. Each of them has logged tens of thousands of hours, seeing people for a variety of reasons and presenting complaints. They have spent a significant part of their lives in the company of others in excruciating pain.

Among all those people these therapists have seen and helped, we wondered which client, or even which particular session, changed them the most. As they think back on their illustrious careers, who (or what) stands out as their most significant transformative experience that occurred while they were helping someone else? This could have been a seminal case that helped shape their conceptual ideas, but more likely it was an intensely personal transformation that changed them forever.

Each of our participants was interviewed and asked to tell his or her own story. We pressed them for details and fleshed out the context of the experiences so as to present them in a way that puts you, the reader, right there in the room with them. It is our belief that contained within these narratives are the keys to transformative and lasting changes, the kind that endure throughout a lifetime. If we can understand better how this phenomenon occurs in the lives of those who help others for a living, we may very well develop a clearer framework for how to initiate such changes more effectively in the future.

Chapter 2

JEFFREY A. KOTTLER
About Last Night

Like many therapists, I joined the profession not only to help others, but also to help myself. It seemed to me that spending one's life talking to people about their most intimate secrets, their most pressing problems, and their most disturbing behavior was an excellent way to make me feel more normal. It also seemed like great theater to have access to people's innermost thoughts and secrets. So, from the very beginning, I fully expected to be changed by doing this sort of work; I considered it part of the job.

It has been over 30 years since I saw my very first client as an intern (described in our previous book, *The Mummy at the Dining Room Table*), but suffice it to say that this case so impacted me that I can reproduce, almost verbatim, everything that took place between us. The client certainly changed me, if for no other reason than that he firmly cemented my passion to understand why people do the strange things they do, and what they get out of behavior that, at first, may seem incomprehensible. Dozens of books later, I am still trying to answer the same questions, but one thing I do know for sure: there is no way one can sit with people in the throes of crisis, the depths of despair, or an advanced state of madness without being profoundly changed by the experience.

With the best of training, and the most careful self-monitoring and supervision, countertransference reactions may certainly be kept reasonably at bay. Yet some clients still invade our dreams, visit our fantasies, intrude in idle thoughts, and simply become significant "occupants" of our conscious and unconscious lives. Spending hour after hour, week after week, being with people in the most intimate conversations imaginable, there is no way we could ever truly avoid being changed by these interactions. We see people emotionally "undressed" every day. We are offered access to secrets and life stories that have never been shared before—with anyone. We are privy to life events that are almost never spoken about in public, sometimes never even admitted to oneself. We are exposed to the most horrific, most tragic, most heart-wrenching stories imaginable. We

talk about the most personal, the most significant, and the most meaningful subjects that are possible. And as if that is not enough, we are
specially trained to be reflective, analytic, and scrupulously honest about
innermost thoughts and feelings. Thus, a more accurate questions might
not be "When have therapists been transformed by their clients?" but
"How does this occur?"

RECIPROCAL INFLUENCE

Even though we had the presumption, if not the gall, to expect our contributors to come up with a single case that represents their most dramatic transformation, I feel somewhat hypocritical in that I cannot do the
same. Try as I might, I just can't think of one session, or even one client,
who changed me significantly as a result of our work together. That is
not to say that I don't experience such personal upheaval when doing
therapy. On the contrary, I think that every client changes me, and every
therapy relationship impacts me almost as much as it does my clients.

I find it endlessly fascinating to explore the ways that the therapeutic
process wields its power and magic in ways that are so unexpected—not
only for clients, but for their therapists as well. The session ends, and
sometimes both partners in the process leave the encounter with their
heads spinning.

This happens so often that it is hard for me to recall a single incident
that stands out from all the rest. Instead, there was a three-month inter-
val in my early training days when my work with several clients changed
me forever. Even how I behave and react this day, this hour, 30 years
afterward, is the direct result of my interactions with the people I helped
during a focused internship experience.

LEARNING SELF-TALK

Helplessness was a big theme in my early life. My mother was depressed
and actively suicidal throughout much of my childhood. As an adolescent,
and into early adulthood, I also struggled with depression, or at least emotional volatility that masked a deeper sadness. I felt like a victim of those
around me—the boss who didn't appreciate me, the girl who didn't respond
the way I wanted, the friend who didn't understand, my father, who didn't
support me the ways I wanted. I tried therapy as a client several times at
this stage in my life and profited immensely, but it was really working on
the other side of the relationship in which I made my greatest strides.

Prior to this particular time working as an intern, I had been doing
mostly relationship-oriented, existential therapy (to which I eventually

returned). My supervisor, however, was a passionate cognitive therapist, and he insisted that I follow his lead. It was one thing to read books, and to participate in seminars and supervision devoted to this highly confrontive method; it was quite another to actively see, hear, and feel my clients struggling with their own self-talk. And as I learned to challenge clients' beliefs and language, I noticed a transformation taking place within me as well.

"I just can't take this any longer. Not one more day. I've simply had it."

"You're feeling completely fed up," I responded to my client in the way that I had learned to do traditional active listening and reflect underlying feelings. But I knew my supervisor would skewer me for this "relapse," and so I shifted my approach.

"Yeah," the client responded to the reflection, "I'm so sick of this crap. I can't take any more."

"You're saying that this is absolutely the worst you can imagine," I summarized, but this time focusing on the exaggerated thinking. "It's so bad that you can't stand another moment."

He nodded his head in agreement and then stared down at his hands.

"This is just the worst thing you've ever lived through," I continued. "You don't think you can even survive it."

What I was doing, in a gradual, and I hoped subtle, way was challenging him to examine the ways he was exaggerating and distorting the reality of what was taking place. I followed up by continuing to go after some of his irrational beliefs. These included self-statements such as "This is so terrible, the absolute worst thing anyone could live through." "I won't survive this." "Things will never be different, so there is no sense in even trying."

All the time I was confronting my client with the extent he was exaggerating reality and engaging in self-pity, a part of me soon recognized that I was talking as much to myself as I was to him. I remembered my supervisor saying to me earlier that it was during his most active days of challenging his clients that he felt most stable and centered. (Actually, what he said was that the more he talked to others of their bullshit, the more he had to face his own.) Indeed, I was discovering this was the case: the more I confronted my clients about the ways they were inflicting misery on themselves, the more I had to look at the ways I was doing the same thing.

MY LAST SESSION

Given that I believe so strongly in the kind of reciprocal influence and mutual growth that occurs in therapeutic relationships, I fully expect to be changed by almost all my helping encounters. In one sense, it is always my last session that is the most transformative for me.

Take last night, for instance. I was leading a therapy group in which participants were doing their usual check-in by which we begin each session. This is a time for people to report on progress they've made during the previous week, as well as to declare issues and concerns that they may wish to work on during this week.

This is a fairly diverse group, at least culturally speaking. There are about one-third Latinos, one-third Asians, and the last third split between Middle Easterners and Caucasians. Nevertheless, there is the kind of homogeneity one would expect from a group of counseling students who are attending the sessions as part of a course requirement.

"Things are going pretty well for me this week," one woman said. "Nothing much to report, really. Just the same ol' same ol'." She shrugged, as if apologizing for the stability she was feeling.

"Yeah, I know what you mean," another chimed in. "I'm just worried about my paper due in another class. Once that's done, I'll be fine. But I just can't think about anything else right now."

And so it went for the next half-hour that each person checked in by stating that really there was nothing much to say this week. There were a few exceptions, of course, represented by two individuals who really did have some issues they wanted to work on, but the vast majority were really making clear several messages: (1) "I don't really want to be here"; (2) "I'm bored, but I'll try to stay attentive"; (3) "Even if I did trust you all enough to talk about my stuff (which I don't), I'd rather not stir things up. If you don't mind; I'd prefer to hide."

After a period of time I found it tough to listen any longer. My initial frustration gave way to sadness, then to full-fledged pouting. I was thinking to myself that, to be totally truthful, I didn't want to be there either. It felt like a waste of time to go through the motions, to pretend we were all there to do some work when really most people were just putting in their time.

I found my attention wandering to the point that I stopped listening. I was thinking about an upcoming visit to rural Nepal, where I would be doing some workshops. I pictured the faces of the people I would meet, and especially the children I would see.

". . .so I was thinking that maybe I would schedule myself differently, maybe leave earlier so I'm not always late for group like I was again today. I'm sorry about that, but the traffic on the freeway was terrible. There was an accident or something. . ."

The voice of a group member intruded on my escapist fantasy. More drivel, I thought impatiently. What a waste of time.

I looked around the group to take inventory of what was going on. Some looked bored, but others were doing their best to remain engaged. The woman who was speaking had moved on from her excuses for being late and was now talking about a subject I'd heard before. Should I let this go on? Should I say something about the ways that people were so obviously hiding and avoiding real intimacy with one another? Should I bring up the very real fears that were inhibiting more authentic risk-taking?

Nah, I thought. Too much work. I'll just stay on cruise control. If they don't want to go deeper, who am I to rock the boat?

And so the group proceeded, a carefully prescribed dance in which each person seemed to be following a template on the ground. It reminded me of learning the box step when I was an adolescent, the very first slow dance that they taught us—one step forward, the back foot follows, then to the right with the outside foot, the inside step shuffling next, and so on, carving out precise little boxes on the floor, presumably in time to the music.

The group session proceeded onward, each of us trying hard not to be caught looking at the clock. My pouting that had been related to feeling unappreciated now lapsed into a full-fledged existential twinge. Was I wasting my life working in this middle-class world, helping middle-class therapists work with middle-class clients?

In Nepal, in Latin America, in Africa and Asia, even in so many areas of North America, there is so much poverty and deprivation. But of everywhere I have been, and everything I have seen, some of the Himalayan villages give a whole new dimension to what it means to be deprived. These are places where porters and Sherpas toil endlessly, carrying 70-pound loads on their emaciated frames, tramping (barefoot!) up and down mountains, wearing nothing but rags. I know there are so many other places in the world where poverty is rampant, from the pueblo *jovenes* of Lima to the slums of Calcutta, but the children of Nepal have always haunted me. Sex slavers kidnap eight-year-old girls and take them into northern India, where they are sold to HIV-infected men who believe that having sex with a virgin will cure their disease. It is the only place I've ever been where kids don't beg for money, but for aspirin or vitamins.

I sit in my group, pretending to listen to the obligatory reports, and see the children with their goiters and sores on their bodies. I see the villages I have visited that have among the highest maternal and infant mortality in the world. There is no medical care for hundreds of miles.

And I sit here and live my middle-class life. I'm just wasting my life, I think, as I sit in the group. I'm wasting my time. I'm not doing anything that really matters. I'm not helping people who really need, or even want, my help.

I've got to do something, I think to myself. I must do something, I resolve. This isn't enough.

When the group ends, I literally run to my office to escape. I need some time to think about things, to center myself. I hate the part of me that is so judgmental, so critical of others. I recognize this as a classic conversion reaction—what annoys me about the group members are the same things I want to disown about myself—a superficial focus on the material world of things and achievements and performance.

Partially to distract myself from scary thoughts, I turned to my computer for diversion. Nothing like a little e-mail correspondence to keep me based in reality. I recognized the address of one message as that of a doctoral student with whom I was working in Nepal. Kiran was an obstetrician who had been doing research on cultural beliefs that prevent Nepali women from availing themselves of medical services; many have died in childbirth rather than seek help.

"Jeffrey," Kiran wrote to me in the message, "I have a problem that I want to discuss with you. Maybe you can tell me what to do."

I paused for a moment, still a little off-balance from the group session and the serendipitous way that Kiran's message was waiting for me when I returned to my office. I assumed this would be a routine question about her research methodology or data analysis.

I was surprised to discover that Kiran's request for a consultation was clinically based rather than research based. She told me that one of her patients, an expectant mother, had somehow expelled her uterus and fetus outside her vagina. (I tried hard to block the image from my mind about what this might look like.) Kiran had managed to deliver the baby successfully, but the mother needed two weeks of bed rest before surgery could be attempted to reinsert her uterus.

The mother insisted to her doctor that she absolutely had to leave the hospital as soon as possible; she could not possibly wait even days, much less weeks, for recovery.

"Why must you return to your village so quickly?" Kiran asked her patient. "After all, there is a good chance you will die without proper rest. Certainly you will never have another baby."

The mother nodded her understanding, but there was urgent business that required her to return home immediately. And what was this emergency?

One of the mother's goats was also pregnant and was about to give birth. The mother had to hurry home to help with the delivery, even if it meant she was sacrificing her own life!

I reread the message twice to make sure I got the story right, then continued on to the final paragraph. "So, Jeffrey, what do I tell this woman? Kiran asked me. "How do I make her listen to me? She will surely die unless I can convince her to remain in hospital."

I stared at the computer screen, not sure whether to laugh or cry. Just a few minutes earlier I had been in a group session struggling with reluctant clients who were trying to hide, as best they could, from getting into any real problems. And now this—whatever this was.

I could feel a whirlwind of change going on within me. I had to do something. I decided, in that moment, that I would do something. I immediately fired back a message to Kiran to say that I really couldn't think of anything magical that would make this lady stay in her hospital bed, except to remind Kiran about the power of her own compassion. All she could do was try to understand this woman's world, and work within it. I knew that this would not be nearly as much help as she wanted with this case, but I intended to show up on her doorstep in several months, and I was going to bring help with me in the form of money, resources, and colleagues who might make a difference. By the time the night was over, I had mapped out, planned, and structured a mission to Nepal.

And I swear this happened only last night!

LEADING WITH MY HEART

This is what it is like for me to do therapy, whether in a group or with an individual client. I am constantly touched and impacted by my clients. These are far more than countertransference reactions for me, that is, personal stuff that gets in the way of my supposed objectivity. I've always thought that one of the most precious benefits and side effects of this job is the opportunity we are provided to work on our own growth that parallels what is happening with our clients.

It turned out that I couldn't fully contain myself in the group session, nor pout without visible symptoms, so I did say what I was thinking out loud. "Aren't we all just hiding?" I challenged them at one point. "Aren't we playing it safe by talking about that which is in our control, fearful of venturing outside that safety zone?"

"Yeah?" one group member challenged me. "So what of it? What's the big deal if we—if I—don't want to go very deep. I'm sick of analyzing everything I do. I'm tired of reflecting on every tiny behavior and thought and feeling and figuring out what it really means."

There were a lot of sympathetic heads nodding.

"So there are times when you need to just coast for a while," I reflected, proud that I was responding empathically rather than critically.

"Exactly," she agreed. "But I also know what you are saying. I mean, we're all here, and we paid to be here, and it's like we are not really making full use of the opportunities."

This was the point I was hoping to get across. But by this time, all the while I was helping to facilitate the group process to a deeper, more meaningful level, I was also working hard on myself. I just kept saying to myself, over and over, like a mantra, "I gotta do something. I can't just sit here. Gotta do something."

So now it is 24 hours later, and I'm still processing everything that happened, both within the group and within myself. Even though the work is so fresh and raw, I have already made some decisions about what I intend to do to make a greater difference. Time to put my money, and my time, where my mouth is, I have been repeating to myself over and over again. I'm afraid I might renege on my commitment.

I can't be sure what is happening with the group members right now, how they are working on the issues that were raised in the session. I will know soon enough when I hear their check-in next week, and especially when I read their journals in a few weeks. I have some solid hunches about a few of the members who were touched, some even knocked on their butts, by the last session. Regardless of whatever they got from the experience, I am still reeling from the changes that I am undergoing.

And this is just from last night. What about what happens in my next session later today? And tomorrow? And next week when this group meets again?

Chapter 3

JON CARLSON
Self-Surgery to
Remove the Transponder

Jon Carlson believes that doing therapy is a lot like being in an X-ray room; everyone is affected by the energy circulating in the air. Just as clients are affected by the therapist's compassion, faith, and interventions, so therapists are impacted (for better and for worse) by the client's behavior, feelings, and reactions. That is one reason why there is attention in training to guard against these supposedly negative counter-transference feelings. Therapists are thus taught the importance of maintaining self-control, objectivity, detachment, and psychological (and physical) distance from clients.

This all comes in particularly handy for someone like Carlson, who could easily be described as a workaholic; but if this is true, this is someone who truly loves his addiction. At the time that this present case took place, about five years ago, Jon was not only working as a full-time professor, consultant, video producer, and author, but was also seeing 60 clients per week. Scheduling his sessions every 45 minutes, often without a break, he would devote four 12-hour days to his private practice. He has been working so many years at this kind of pace that he is often puzzled by the question about why he chooses to schedule his time with so many commitments.

"I grew up in a family where everyone worked that much," Carlson said with a shrug. "My father had a business, and he would work all week and I would go to school. Then on the weekends we would go to a summer house, but even there we were always doing projects on the house. So I guess I just learned from my father that some of the greatest enjoyments in life come from working, and working hard."

Having five children to support, and a lot of financial pressure, are also strong drives for Carlson to work so many hours, but that is not the whole story. He just flat out enjoys the diversity of living so many different lives at the same time—as an author, film producer, teacher, clinician, and so on. He seems to thrive on the variety even if he sometimes pays a heavy price for the 90-hour-plus workweeks.

THE TRANSPONDER

At the time that Max came in to see him, Carlson had just gone back to school to get a second doctorate in psychology (after a previous one in counselor education). He had also just written the second edition of a book on psychopathology and diagnosis. Thus, he was particularly focused on disorders that could be treated with specialized treatment plans. This was in marked contrast to his work in the previous decades, when he had been researching health and wellness issues, working at a level to instill hope in people's lives.

There was little doubt that when Carlson first encountered Max, he immediately recognized that this was a seriously disturbed man, certainly more than a little psychotic with full-blown hallucinations. The prognosis could not be very good, Carlson reasoned, since there seemed to be major neurological disruption. This was largely an organically based problem that would most likely respond to medication rather than psychotherapy. Still, he agreed to treat the man as a favor to the former client who referred him.

Ronald, Max's cousin, had consulted with Carlson years earlier and had been quite pleased with the results. He was concerned about his relative, who had been acting so crazy, and had arranged to place him in a group home nearby and to make sure he received good treatment.

When the two of them entered the office together, Carlson was immediately struck by their contrast. Whereas Ronald was rail-thin, Max was one of largest men that Jon had ever seen—easily six and half feet tall and well over 500 pounds. His first thought was wondering whether there was any chair in the room that would not collapse under his huge bulk.

Much to Carlson's relief, Max was able to settle himself with a groan (from both Max and the chair) in a suitable place. He was an unusual-looking guy for sure, physically imposing, even threatening, but also rather timid at times. He would not make eye contact with either Carlson or his cousin Ronald.

"So," Carlson began the interview, a little nervous about being in the room with such a huge man who was actively hallucinating, "what can I do for you gentlemen?" He looked back and forth between the two of them, but only Ronald returned the gaze.

"Well," Ronald began, "this here is my cousin, as I told you on the phone." He pointed to Max, who was staring blankly into space, occasionally nodding his head as if having a conversation with someone else (which perhaps he was).

"Yes," Carlson prompted, "you mentioned something about bringing him here from another city somewhere out West."

"That's right. Max was in rehab for a while. He had some bad-awful problems with drugs and alcohol and all kinds of stuff. The family and me agreed to try to get him some help."

Ronald had originally come to Carlson for his own drug addiction. Once he had gotten clean and stabilized his life, he ended up doing quite well in the stock market. He was now eager to help his cousin make the same kind of recovery.

"He was in rehab, you said?"

"That's right. We put him in a hospital down in Chicago, and now he's doing okay. Aren't you, Max?"

They both turned to look at Max for confirmation, but he was still staring into space, occasionally nodding, and sometimes moving his lips. He sat completely immobile, frozen, as if he realized how precariously the chair was supporting him and he didn't want to subject it to any more strain.

"So, what do you think about all this, Max?" Carlson said directly to his assigned client. It seemed a little bizarre that they were having a conversation about this guy, with him sitting right there, as if he were invisible.

Max nodded again, this time more decisively, and then turned his head toward Carlson. But still he didn't speak.

"Max has got some other issues, too," Ronald added, "but I think he'll need to tell you about those himself. Maybe it would be best if I left you two alone so you could, you know, get to know each other and talk about a few things."

Carlson agreed this would be a good idea, even though he had increasing misgivings about being alone with the big guy. Once they were alone, he asked Max again what his take was on matters.

"Been having trouble with the police," Max said. "They been chasing me and all, going on now about three months or so."

"I see." Carlson was surprised by how softly Max spoke. He seemed so sad, so beaten down.

"I haven't had a place to stay, so I go to this church, where they take care of me. They let me sleep there and give me food."

"You've been living on the street, then?"

"Well, not so much in the street as in the church. Like I told you already."

"Right," Carlson said. "You said the police were after you."

Ignoring that part of the story, Max went on to say that eventually the minister of the church called Max's family and informed them that their son was in serious trouble and they needed to do something quick. That's when Ronald got involved.

"Before your cousin left," Carlson continued, "he mentioned that there were some other things you needed to tell me about."

"It was back in 1986, I think, when I was doing a lot of shit—druggin' and drinkin', and all kinds of other stuff. There were these federal agents who were following me around, and eventually they caught up to me and put this thing in my head."

"This thing?"

"Yeah, they put this device in my head, and now I can't have sex no more."

Seeing his therapist's confused look, Max explained further that he had seen them install the mechanism because the cruel bastards didn't even use any anesthesia. "I watched them do the whole thing. So now I can't even seem to think about a woman."

"You mean have a fantasy, a sexual fantasy?"

Max nodded sadly. "Can't do nothing since they put this thing in my head. Sometimes my whole skull just goes numb."

"Your skull goes numb?" Carlson felt a little silly just repeating what Max was saying but, as yet, he couldn't get a handle on what was going on. The guy was clearly psychotic—that much was for certain—but there was something about his manner, the way he expressed himself, that sounded reasonably coherent.

"They put one of these things in my buddies, too," Max added.

"You mean one of these. . .?"

"They're called transponders. At least that's what I heard them call it."

"And you say your friends had these transponders in their heads as well?"

"Yessir. But they all died."

"They died?"

"That's right. Every one of 'em. You ask me, I think they're trying to kill off every one of us."

Carlson wondered who "us" was, exactly, but was reluctant to press things too far this early in their relationship.

Max went on to tell the story of how he had been living with this thing in his head for many years, until he had managed to remove it himself.

"You took it out of your own head?"

"Well, I couldn't get nobody else to do it. Most of these doctors are all in it with them federal boys. I tried a number of them, but none of them would touch the thing. They been told not to mess with it, so I decided the time had come to take it out myself."

"You did brain surgery on yourself?" Carlson clarified, trying to keep his voice as calm and level as possible.

"Nah, not really," Max answered. "I found me a scalpel and tried to poke around in there a little. I don't think I got it all, but I'm not sure. I just keep digging with a knife—it being kinda hard to see back there and all." As he said this, he pointed to a long, jagged scar that ran along the side of his neck and then disappeared into his hairline.

"That's probably a good idea to not try to do that yourself," Carlson agreed.

"Anyway, I don't think it made much difference. My head is still numb right now. And this morning—I think it was this morning, but sometimes I get my days mixed up—I tried to beat it but couldn't get it up."

"Beat it?"

"Yeah, you know," Max said, gesturing with his fist up and down above his lap in a simulation of masturbation.

Carlson gave a sickly smile of understanding. Truthfully, he couldn't wait to get this guy out of his office—he had to be the craziest man he'd ever seen. Anywhere.

After Max finally left, trailing in his cousin's wake, Jon thought seriously about suggesting that they see somebody else. Not only did he not feel equipped to deal with the severity of Max's symptoms, but he felt genuinely fearful in the man's presence. It was not that he was particularly threatening—on the contrary, Max was rather passive—but his appearance, his manner, his crazy beliefs, when taken together, were one disturbing package. To add to his unease, Carlson had no clue what he could actually do to help the poor guy.

BREAKTHROUGHS

As part of his continued commitment to help his cousin, Ronald gave Max a job in his company. It was a well-meaning gesture, but by the second day of work, and less than a week after their first session, Carlson got a panicked call from his ex-client.

"Jon," Ronald pleaded, "listen, you gotta do something. This is just not a good situation."

"What's the problem, exactly?" Carlson asked reluctantly. Part of him really didn't want to know.

"It's my cousin, man, he's scaring the shit out of everyone at work. He's telling them his stories, you know, about. . ."

"The transponder," Carlson finished.

"Yeah, that and a lot more, shit you haven't even heard yet. My employees want to know if they're safe."

Ronald felt himself in a real bind because he genuinely wanted to help Max, who had nobody else in his life to lean on, but he also couldn't risk disrupting things any further at work.

"Look," Carlson suggested, "you know Max really needs the job. He's got no money, and no means to support himself. He seems to understand this. If he's got one ounce of self-preservation left, he won't do anything that might jeopardize his last chance to stay outside a hospital. You need to be more direct with him. Just tell him that if he tells any more of those stories, he's going to have to go home and he won't be able to work there anymore."

Ronald agreed that this might be a good idea, but he sounded skeptical. He seemed to understand, finally, the magnitude of the challenge he had chosen. Max was a seriously psychotic individual who was spinning out of control.

In spite of their mutual concerns, Max did respond to the feedback and managed to hold himself together to concentrate on his job programming computers. If he heard the machines talking to him, or felt the remnant of the transponder in his head clouding his mind, he chose to keep these thoughts to himself.

During subsequent sessions, Carlson worked with Max to set up structures in his life that could help him to function more effectively. Ronald gave Max a car to drive so he could transport himself to work from a one-room flat. Max worked long hours at his job and seemed to enjoy the work he was doing. Just as important, he agreed to attend 12-step meetings that not only helped him keep his addictions under control but also provided a semblance of social support outside of his relationship with his cousin.

Another breakthrough occurred when Max agreed to begin exercising on a regular basis. In addition to everything else he was trying to deal with, he was still obese, a hulk that drew attention and yet scared people away. Between the structure of work, AA meetings, and regular exercise routines, he not only began to lose weight, but he seemed to be tired enough that the hallucinations diminished in their intensity, if not their frequency.

Although he talked much less about the transponder and its effects on his libido, one day, over a year after they began working together, Max broached the subject more directly. "Can't one of your medical buddies help me out?"

"I thought we talked about this before," Carlson reminded him. Many months earlier, they had agreed they wouldn't talk about the device anymore, since it only seemed to agitate him.

"I know. I know. But I was just thinking that maybe, you know, if one of those psychiatrists or neurosurgeons around here, somebody who can keep a secret. . ."

"Come on, Max. I thought we talked about this."

"Yeah. Yeah. But I was just thinking. Hear me out. If, say, you knew of a doctor who could do a little work on the side. Then it might be possible to take the rest of the thing out before any government people could find out."

Carlson could feel a giggle starting to build up in his throat. He could just picture himself calling up a surgeon he knew and telling him, "I have a patient to refer to you who has this implant in his head and he wants you to remove it. But please don't tell anyone about what you're doing, or the government will find out."

CRAZY OR NOT?

In spite of the occasional setback, Max continued to make steady progress. It turned out that he was a pretty smart guy and had attended university before the drug addictions had addled his brain. He agreed to return to campus and continue his education. Just as important as the self-improvement to build his confidence and social skills was one more structure to get him out of his little flat, where he would remain isolated.

By this time, Max had dropped 150 pounds and was down to a relatively svelte 350. He'd been drug free for over a year. He was advancing at work and doing well at school. He even agreed to join a dating service, though he claimed that he could not sustain any sexual interest for very long. When he met any woman with whom he might have a relationship, he began to feel terrified. The easiest way to scare them off was to tell them about the transponder, so that's what he did. This was one area where progress was both limited and frustrating.

Carlson continued to meet with his unusual client over a period of five years, during which time he never quite got over how strangely Max behaved. They settled into a routine in which each session would begin with Max reporting something good that had happened to him that week. This could mean a new computer he bought, or perhaps a trip he had taken, but sometimes it involved using his increasingly creative powers as an inventor.

One week Max came into the session grinning and carrying a large box, about three feet wide and four feet long.

"What have you got there?" Carlson asked him cheerfully.

Max grinned back. "I got me a portable meth lab."

"A what?"

"You heard me. A meth lab. You know, methamphetamines."

It turned out that Max had accepted the challenge of designing a laboratory for manufacturing drugs that could easily be transported from one place to another. He had ordered various parts from a Web site and then constructed the whole apparatus from plans he had created.

"Isn't that kind of stupid, if not illegal?" Carlson observed, trying to stay calm.

"What do you mean?"

"What do I mean? Now, let me see…. First of all, you're a recovering drug addict. Second, you have a history of going off the deep end when you are under pressure. Then, let's see, unless I'm missing something, I think that manufacturing drugs in this state is a serious crime, punishable by many years in prison. So, unless I'm missing something, this is about the dumbest thing I've ever seen you do." This was saying a lot, given Max's checkered history.

"So, I guess you don't like this idea, huh?" As he said this, he slumped in his chair in shame. This presented a particularly pitiful image, considering that with all his weight loss he now looked like an old man with folds of skin hanging off his neck and arms.

"Look, Max, I don't mean to be angry with you. But it seems to me that you are about the last person in the world who needs to have his own portable factory for making drugs. I thought that was how you got in trouble in the first place." What was left unsaid was that by "trouble," Carlson was referring to the efforts by the government to bug Max's brain with the transponder.

After giving the matter some thought, Max finally agreed. "Okay, maybe you could keep this for me, then?"

"You want me to keep your meth lab?"

"Would you mind?"

Carlson had received an assortment of strange gifts from clients over the years, but his very own portable drug lab had to take the prize. The next challenge he faced was how to dispose of the thing, which turned out to be a donation to the chemistry department at the local high school. The science teachers were grateful for all the equipment the box contained, although this was probably the first time a counselor ever delivered a drug lab to a school.

On another day, after seeing the movie *Men in Black* the previous week, Max came in outfitted all in black, just like Tommy Lee Jones. He'd also dyed his hair jet black and was sporting the same sunglasses Jones wore in the film. His theory was that this might make him a more attractive prospect for future dates, since he still had not managed to keep a woman around for more than a few weeks.

Max made other changes in his appearance as well. He signed up for laser surgery on his eyes. He had surgery to remove the extra folds of skin from around his neck and stomach now that he had dropped another 50 pounds. So far he had held off on plastic surgery for the scars on his neck from the self-surgery because he wasn't yet certain that he might not do self-surgery again once he could figure out a better mirror system for monitoring the incisions that he would be making.

Max also completed his college degree and decided that he might even go on to graduate school in business. He had moved on from his cousin's business and now had a six-figure job as a computer consultant. He finally met a woman at an AA group, and they married. She had two children from a previous marriage, so Max was also learning to be a father.

Although things had now settled down, Carlson was called upon to conduct an emergency session just prior to the wedding. Carla was literally half the size of her future husband, a tiny woman who was somewhat attractive in a rough way.

"This shit has gotta stop," she announced right after the two of them settled into their chairs.

"And what shit would that be?" Carlson asked her.

She gave him a look as if to say, "Give me a break. You've been seeing this guy for five years and you don't know what I'm talking about?"

"Look," she said, getting right to the point, "we are supposed to get married in a few weeks."

"Yeah." Carlson smiled. "Congratulations." He was, in fact, incredibly excited about this prospect that he never thought would happen. Maybe it wouldn't happen after all, but still, this was certainly an interesting development.

Again she gave him the look. "I've got kids. We're talking about spending our lives together. And now he's telling me this crazy shit about this thing in his head. Is he crazy, or what? I want it straight."

Carlson could see them both staring at him, waiting for the verdict. What would he say? He wanted to be helpful, but he also wanted to tell the truth. Was Max crazy? he asked himself. Certainly by any criteria in the Diagnostic Manual, Max definitely qualified as seriously disturbed—active hallucinations, delusions, paranoia, impulsive behavior, erratic decision making.

On the other hand, Max had accomplished so much. He was self-supporting, successful in a career, self-disciplined, and now capable of genuine love. Was this really the behavior of someone who was hopelessly psychotic?

It was true that Max was a strange guy, or certainly spectacularly eccentric. But Carlson was not sure what to say. Finally, he decided to say what he really thought, not only to Carla but for Max's benefit as well. "I don't really know about this transponder thing," he admitted, "but I do know that Max isn't crazy."

"What do you mean?" Carla pressed, confused by the answer.

"Your fiancé graduated from college. With honors. He has been admitted to graduate school. He makes more money than I do." As he said this, they all laughed.

"He's got a great job," Carlson continued, "a great house, a new car, and most of all, he's got a great woman like you. Does this sound like a crazy person?"

The whole time that he said these things, Carlson could see Max visibly straightening in his chair, as if each point seemed to bolster his confidence one step at a time. Carla found the summary helpful as well, because she did decide to marry Max, and they have been doing reasonably well ever since then.

NOT JUST DIFFERENT, BUT BETTER

If pressed, Carlson admits that he is as surprised as anyone that Max made the changes he did; he never would have thought that the man was destined for anything other than a lifetime of Thorazine and a locked ward.

Prior to seeing Max, Jon would never have thought it possible that someone who was so obviously psychotic could ever live a conventional life. Somewhere along their journey together, Carlson stopped believing in the legitimacy of standard psychiatric labels and started focusing a whole lot more on a person's inner resources and strengths. That is what led him to begin every session with Max by talking about what he accomplished, or was most proud of, the previous week.

As for this transponder business, sometimes Carlson wonders if there really was some sort of implant that doctors put inside his patient, perhaps not for the reasons that Max reports but for some other explanation. He has continued to urge him to seek medical consultation about the matter, but so far Max has declined to do so.

"I don't see Max's behavior as crazy anymore," Carlson revealed. "I don't really think that way with anyone, now that I think about it. And that's just one of the things that Max taught me. The effects have affected so many other areas of my life."

"Like what?"

"For one, I have become so much more optimistic about people. I am more trusting of others than I have ever been before, and I think that inspires others to trust me more."

Kottler, who is interviewing Carlson for this chapter, and then writing the narrative, nods his head in agreement. He has long wondered how Jon manages to recruit so many busy, famous theoreticians into our projects, asking them for their time, their best stories, for no compensation except the pleasure of our company and the satisfaction of having good listeners. But now he understands that it is really all a direct result of Jon's work with Max, and the trust that developed in all his relationships as a result.

Carlson's wife, Laura, reports that he has changed as a husband. His children have seen him change as a father. His students have noticed differences in his teaching, just as his clients are now seeing a different therapist. That is not to say that he is not as busy and overscheduled as ever, but that the quality of his interactions has changed.

Was all this the result of Max? Assuredly not. Aging has had an influence on mellowing Carlson. Many of his collaborators on various research and consulting projects have impacted him as well. But perhaps more than anyone else, Max got the ball rolling. He really got his attention, in the most dramatic way possible, that people are capable of doing anything—anything—if they are given the chance.

"I am not only a different person since Max came into my life," Carlson said, "but a better one. I only hope he can say the same about his association with me."

Chapter 4

VIOLET OAKLANDER
The Kitten That Roared

Molly, age 11, had the eyes of an adult who had been through the wringer. She was rather tall for a girl her age, but she was hunched over like an old woman. Her eyes followed her feet as she shuffled arthritically across the room.

While her mother worked the night shift as a waitress, Molly had been left home alone with her stepfather. His idea of playing with his daughter involved undressing and sexually molesting her, then beating her until she promised she wouldn't tell anyone. The stepfather was very careful where he smacked her, so there were few visible signs of abuse. This went on for many years.

When Molly was nine, one of her teachers noticed bruising and reported the case to Child Protective Services, and she was taken out of the home. The social worker had little doubt that the mother had been aware of what was going on but had done nothing to stop the sexual and physical abuse. Molly was placed temporarily in a group home until a determination could be made by the authorities; before a decision was finalized, Molly's mother dropped a letter off at the home, informing her daughter that she was leaving and she was on her own. The stepfather also disappeared and was never apprehended.

After being placed in a series of foster homes, Molly ended up with an older woman who sheltered a number of other children. Seeing how damaged Molly was, displaying almost autistic behavior, the woman brought the girl to therapy.

The first thing that struck Oaklander about this young girl was how docile and meek she appeared, as pliable as a jellyfish. She sat where she was instructed to sit, but otherwise seemed oblivious to her surroundings and uninterested in making any sort of contact.

Sitting with a clipboard and intake form on her lap (which she never actually used, but it looks official and seems less intrusive in the beginning),

Oaklander began to ask a few questions to establish both contact and some sort of relationship.

"Are you sleeping okay?"

Nod.

"How's your appetite?"

Shrug.

"You doing okay in school?"

Nod.

"Do you have friends at school?"

Nod.

This went on for some minutes. After each question, Molly nodded, shrugged, or shook her head, but refused to answer verbally. This continued until, at one point, Oaklander asked if she had any pets.

"I wish I did." Molly said her first words in a whisper. It sounded like her voice was rusty from lack of use.

Realizing that this was the extent of information she was likely to get from this sort of questioning, Oaklander changed directions. "Hey, I've got an idea. Why don't we do some coloring? Someone gave me this coloring book last week, and we could color together."

Molly shrugged again, as if it didn't matter to her one way or the other, but she immediately looked relieved that she wouldn't have to talk.

Oaklander put out an assortment of crayons, pastels, and markers for Molly to try. Usually kids like to use a variety of media, but Molly carefully picked one brown crayon and pretty much stuck with that. Oaklander joined her with another color, and the two of them worked together on the same picture.

"Gee, Molly," Oaklander said at one point, "I just don't know what color to make this dog. What do you think?"

Molly pointed toward a green crayon.

"A green dog?"

The barest glimpse of a smile appeared for a moment.

After some minutes of such consultations, Oaklander continued to engage Molly about their drawing, commenting on the way things were developing, complimenting her on staying within the lines of the tree. Throughout this session and the one that followed, Molly remained compliant and passive, just following directions, seemingly comfortable with staying inside the lines. She was still very much like a jellyfish, without form or initiative. She seemed to float toward the path of least resistance.

SAND PLAY

By the third session Molly used various colors, and each of them had her own picture to color. While they worked on their coloring together,

Oaklander stopped for a moment and Molly looked up. "Hmmm," Violet said, "I just can't decide what color for this bird. What do you think?" She was slowly trying to engage the girl in some way, to get her to take some action on her own.

"And this bird is so cute," Oaklander tried again after Molly had helped her pick a color. "If she could talk, what do you think she would say?"

"I don't know," Molly answered with a shy smile. She seemed amused by the question.

"Would it say something like 'I wish I could be free and fly away'?"

Molly giggled, the first real sign of life in the three hours they'd spent together. "Yeah, and she'd say 'I'm hungry and give me some worms,' and she'd fly all over the place and then she'd go back to the tree at night." She said this all in a rush, as if once she opened her mouth, she wanted to make up for lost time and get in as many ideas as she could before she returned to muteness.

By the next session, their fourth one, Molly enjoyed telling stories with Oaklander about the pictures they were coloring. They took turns describing what the various figures were thinking and feeling and what was happening on the page. These coloring sessions had become so successful that Oaklander found she had difficulty ending them; Molly was very reluctant to leave. Not surprisingly, Molly struggled with boundaries. It seemed to Oaklander that this was one of the few times in her young life that she had fun interacting with an adult. Even though her foster mother was caring and responsible, she worked many hours and didn't have time to play with Molly much, or with the other children.

Molly would have been content to continue the coloring activity indefinitely. Oaklander recalled doing this sort of thing with her own daughter, but when she was 5, not 11. In so many ways, Molly was functioning at the level of a much younger child—in every way except the sadness in her eyes.

"Why don't we try something else instead of coloring today?" As Oaklander suggested this, she noticed Molly looking around the room. Nothing seemed to capture her interest, which was surprising, considering that the office was overflowing with toys, outfits, blocks, dolls, books, props, and a sand tray. Finally, Molly just shrugged, still content to stay with their coloring.

"We could draw pictures instead of coloring them," Oaklander suggested.

Shrug.

"We could work with clay."

Shrug.

"How about the sand tray, then?" Oaklander pointed to a rather large rectangular box full of sand. There were many miniatures lined up on the shelves above it. "Just choose any objects and put them into the sand in some kind of scene—anything you want."

Molly thought for a moment, considering this change reluctantly, then slowly nodded her head.

For the next several sessions Molly worked at the sand tray, fully absorbed, with little conversation. Violet sat quietly next to Molly. Yet the trust between them was building, and Oaklander could feel this girl become more and more comfortable. Occasionally she turned and smiled at Violet. For five sessions in a row Molly built the same thing in the sand tray. After the second time, they began to have a dialogue about the scene. She constructed a hospital, and she reenacted the same scene over and over. "This guy is sick," she explained. "And this ambulance is coming to take him to the hospital."

"Is he going to get better?" Oaklander asked.

"Oh, sure, it's a good hospital and they'll take very good care of him."

"You spent some time in a hospital once, didn't you?" Oaklander said this carefully, knowing that for the first time they were treading on sensitive ground.

Molly shrugged, although Violet couldn't tell if this was because she didn't know, or didn't want to say. Oaklander recalled that after Molly had been removed from her home, she had been taken to a hospital and examined by the staff to determine the extent of her injuries.

"Maybe you weren't feeling well after everything that happened to you."

Shrug.

"But now that you are living with Ginny, who is really nice, and now that you are visiting me, you are feeling much better. It's like how they made you feel better in the hospital."

Molly's whole face lit up in the biggest grin.

THE LADY DOCTOR

Molly began to make some progress, not only in sessions but at home as well. Her foster mother, Ginny, made plans to adopt her. On some occasions, Ginny joined her in the sessions. It was during one such meeting that the most remarkable thing happened: Molly announced that she had a game she wanted all of them to play together and then proceeded to explain the rules. This was a kid who showed almost no initiative in anything she ever did, and now, for the first time, she was in charge. She told Ginny and Violet where she wanted them to stand in the room and what she wanted them to do. She awarded points for certain kinds of scoring whenever a ball was hit a certain way with a foam bat.

She became the director and umpire, the one who decided whose turn it was, and who won the game. Both of the women were stunned by this uncharacteristic behavior, but acted as if it were an everyday occurrence.

In the session that followed with Oaklander alone, Molly again decided what they would do with their time—they were going to play hospital, except this time "for real" rather than in the sand tray. "I'm the doctor," Molly explained, suiting up in an oversized white lab coat, grabbing a felt hat she found on the shelf, and putting a stethoscope from the doctor kit around her neck.

"Okay," Violet agreed happily. "What do you want me to do?"

"You're sick, you see. You're going to call me on the phone."

"Got it." Violet started to reach for the phone when Molly interrupted.

"No. First, before you call me, you don't know I am a lady doctor."

"I don't know you are a lady doctor?" Oaklander repeated, a bit puzzled.

"That's right."

"Okay." Oaklander dialed the number of the hospital and said into the phone: "Doctor! Doctor! Could you please come over right away? I am so sick."

Molly then rushed over to the couch where Violet was reclining, pretending to be sick. "Just a minute," Molly said, as she placed her doctor's bag on the floor, "I have to take off my hat," and her long hair fell down to her shoulders.

"Oh, my gosh!" Violet said dramatically on cue, "A lady doctor! I had no idea!"

Molly collapsed on the floor in giggles. She thought this was so funny—the very idea of a lady doctor apparently was quite novel to her. After recovering, Molly began with her examination and treatment of the patient. She was very gentle, examining Violet's heart with the stethoscope, looking at her tonsils, placing little drops of water (medicine) on her hand with an eyedropper. When she was done with the house call, Molly tucked her hair back into her hat and returned to the hospital.

For the next three sessions, they repeated this exact scenario. The most important part of the game for Molly was the moment when she took off her hat and the patient recognized she was a lady doctor, showing complete surprise. Each time this happened, Molly would laugh joyously.

Oaklander had some idea of what this was about and why Molly became so fixated on the particular interaction around the lady doctor. When Molly had been brought to the hospital after being removed from her home, a lady doctor had examined her. This child, who was not only so beaten and broken, but also severely neglected and sheltered, had no idea that girls could become doctors, and she might very well never have seen a doctor before. Furthermore, this lady doctor was so kind and caring with her, that it stuck in her memory as the first real act of kindness she'd ever felt from a grown-up. She kept wanting to relive those moments over and over.

Eventually, Molly moved on to want to enact other scenes. They played school next; Molly was the teacher, and she directed Violet to be a kid in class. "But you're a bad kid," she said. "You always get in trouble and stuff."

Violet nodded her understanding. They set up a schoolroom and Molly began teaching the class.

"Teacher," Violet interrupted. "I don't like this work! And Jimmy over there keeps pulling my hair. He won't leave me alone."

"Now, Violet," Molly said sternly. "You must behave yourself. How many times have I told you that if you don't do what I say, I'm going to send you to the office?"

Violet continued to act up, and each time Molly intervened decisively and with authority. They resumed this routine for several more sessions; each time the girl who had been a jellyfish was now learning to assert herself.

MOLDING CLAY

The most dramatic change of all occurred one day when they were playing with puppets. Molly had chosen to be a kitten, and Violet strategically picked a wolf puppet with a huge mouth.

"Hello, little kitten," Violet said in a gruff, menacing voice.

"Hello, Mr. Wolf," Molly answered.

"You are really a cute kitten. You look good enough to eat. I think I'm going to eat you, because I'm hungry and you look delicious."

"No! No! Please, Mr. Wolf, don't eat me. Let's just be friends."

The wolf puppet approached closer and closer, saying, "I'm coming to eat you, but YOU'D BETTER NOT HIT ME WITH YOUR PAWS!" And then. . .and then. . .the kitten lashed out at the wolf and started attacking him with her tiny kitten paws, beating the big bad wolf (and the puppeteer) to the floor.

"No, please, no," Violet the wolf pleaded in surrender. "Okay. Okay. You win."

"Let's do that again!" Molly said with the same kind of excitement she'd shown when they played lady doctor. And so they repeated this same game in which Molly would always be the helpless kitten and Violet would threaten her as an alligator or a shark or one of the other "bad" puppets available. Each time, the kitten would prevail, beating the enemy into submission. Then she would pretend to wave a magic wand, bring the puppet back to life again, and they would do it all over again.

Molly's whole demeanor changed after that. She no longer walked around all hunched up. She stopped shuffling her feet when she walked and showed the beginnings of feline grace as she turned 12. She laughed spontaneously at times. And then, for the first time, they actually began to speak about the abuse and the abandonment that she had experienced.

During one of these sessions the two of them were idly playing with clay as they were talking. "Molly, I want you to make a sculpture of your stepfather out of the clay," Oaklander said.

"Do I have to?" Molly looked spooked. Things had been going so well, but now, Oaklander could see real fear in the child's eyes again. She wondered how far she could push her, deciding in the end that she believed their relationship was strong enough to persevere.

"Yes, you have to," Violet said with a smile.

Molly shrugged, in that gesture reminiscent of when she first came in, but then smiled. "Okay." She said this not with dread but with cheerfulness. Then she sculpted a big head out of clay.

"Okay, Molly, this is your stepfather. You can talk to him now. You can say anything you want to him. Since it is only clay, he won't really know what you are saying. He's not really here."

"I don't want to," she said in a small voice.

"It's okay, Molly. I'm right here with you. He can't hurt you. But I want you to talk to him. I think you have some things you want to say to him."

"I can't talk to him," Molly said, shaking her head. "I just can't do this." She was starting to become agitated.

Oaklander didn't want to push the girl. It was obvious that this was beyond what she felt comfortable doing, and thus far, Violet had been very patient and respectful of Molly's pace. The therapy had proceeded so well precisely because the child had been allowed to find her own power, on her own terms, in her own time. But, on the other hand, Oaklander didn't want to waste the head.

"Can I talk to your stepfather, then? There are a few things I'd like to say to him."

Molly looked up from the floor, stared in Violet's eyes, and then, biting her lip, nodded her assent.

"Listen, you," Violet began, talking to the stepfather, "you make me so mad! I don't like you! I don't like what you did to my friend. . ."

Oaklander stopped, because Molly was laughing hysterically, as if this was the funniest thing she'd ever seen. She was rolling on the ground, gasping for breath, laughing and laughing.

Getting even more into the mood, Oaklander continued. "You know what I think you need?" she said to the clay stepfather. "I think you need a good whack." She then picked up a rubber mallet and was about to bop the figure on the head when she said to Molly, "You know what? You do it."

As Molly tentatively reached for the mallet, Violet added, "Remember, though, we are just pretending. This is only clay. We wouldn't really hit someone like this who made us angry."

Molly nodded, grabbed the hammer and then gave the stepfather a good whack on the top of the head. "You'll get more later," she said with real satisfaction.

This was the beginning of the real work. After this moment Molly began to draw pictures about how she felt. She began to talk about her feelings and was led to understand that none of what happened to her was her fault. She had experienced some terrible things at the hands of some bad people. And to complicate things further, she admitted that she liked her stepfather's attention at first, until he started hurting her, and then she didn't know how to make him stop.

Oaklander explained that this was a normal thing. They spent a lot of time talking about this. Molly also began talking about other fears. It was during one of those conversations that Violet invited her to draw a picture of her mother.

"I'd rather draw you instead."

"You can draw me, but then I want you to draw your mother."

After both drawings were completed, Oaklander asked Molly to speak to her mother. "Tell her anything you want."

Molly shook her head.

"Come on. You can say anything you want."

Molly stared at the picture for a long time, then said, "Mama, why did you leave me?" She started to cry. "I don't want to do this anymore."

"That's okay," Violet reassured her. And it was. It was the first time that Molly ever made a direct statement.

Molly continued to grow in the next year they worked with one another, making new friends, and pretty much living the normal life of a young teenager.

This case occurred more than 20 years ago. Looking back, Oaklander still feels thankful to Molly for teaching her patience. Since Violet doesn't really separate how she behaves as a therapist and how she functions in her daily life, this willingness to wait until another person is ready was applied to her personal as well as her professional life. "I've learned how to be more accepting and patient with myself. I remind myself of this every day. Molly also taught me to be more optimistic and hopeful, not only with my clients but with myself. I still think about this kid a lot, even after all this time. Molly went through so many horrible experiences, yet in the end, she came out okay. The relationship we established was so important in helping her heal, and my patience, acceptance, and optimism had a lot to do with maintaining that relationship."

Chapter 5

FRANK PITTMAN
An Affair with an Alien

"Hello. Could I speak with Dr. Pittman?"

"I'm Frank Pittman," the psychiatrist answered cheerfully.

"Dr. Frank Pittman? The Air Force doctor?"

"Well, I'm not exactly in the Air Force, but those folks sometimes refer patients to me. What can I do for you?"

Pittman was working as head of a psychiatric unit at the county hospital. Whenever someone on the nearby Air Force base behaved strangely in some way, they would send over the airman in hopes that whatever was wrong could be fixed. Usually this involved someone who got drunk too often, but it could also involve someone who tried to hijack one of their expensive planes.

"Well, it's my husband," the wife said hesitantly. "The people over at the base said we should call you. So that's what I'm doing."

"I see. So what do they want me to do for y'all?"

"Well, you might have read about my husband," she answered. "He's been in the paper a lot lately." She stopped abruptly, as if this statement would be sufficient for Pittman to figure out what was going on.

"Well, there have been a lot of things in the paper lately."

"Yessir, but I think you'll recall this one. You see, my husband was picked up by a flying saucer of some sort, some kind of UFO, they say."

Of course Pittman remembered the story, not just because it had been in the headlines every day for weeks, everywhere in the country, even at the White House, but also because it was so damn peculiar. Apparently a young man—this woman's husband—had turned up walking down a dirt road, missing his underpants, a bit disoriented but otherwise unharmed. He claimed that he had been picked up by aliens and held captive for three days, during which time they performed painful experiments on him that involved unspecified sexual assaults.

The Air Force had had him under observation and interrogation for the previous week, trying to get to the bottom of this danger to national security. The man's story was so detailed and explicit, and his manner so impassioned, that it was difficult not to believe him. Generals, admirals, and senators were shouting for bigger budgets to fight this threat from outer space. The hullabaloo even got into the upcoming presidential election, with each candidate accusing the other of ignoring a UFO gap.

"Yes," Pittman agreed, "I do remember something about your husband's case."

"I don't understand why they want him to see a psychiatrist. We have never been to a doctor—to someone like you before. We're not that kind of people."

"Well, I am the kind of person who sees people under interesting circumstances, but I have to admit I have had very little experience with flying saucers. I'm really looking forward to this, and I will definitely make the time available. I can see the two of you tomorrow."

MISSING UNDERPANTS

When the young couple showed up, Pittman noticed that the husband, Roger, was particularly cheerful for someone who had been through so much lately. While Ruby was embarrassed by the whole business, Roger was clearly basking in his newfound attention and was eager for any spotlight he could find, even a shrink's office. Pittman also noticed how solicitous Ruby was toward her husband, hovering over him, patting him as if he were a little baby.

Pittman quickly got some basic information. They had been married a little over a year. They had a baby. They were starting a business. He was installing TV antennas, and she was running the office. They were not very well-educated people but were well-fed. As Pittman recalls: "They had teeth and not too many tattoos. Here in Georgia some of the people who come out of the swamps haven't exposed themselves to the light of day, but these people—they were both really very attractive."

"So," Frank finally broached the main subject that brought the couple in, "maybe you could tell me what happened. I heard you had a rather unusual experience."

Roger nodded gravely, and a bit smugly. "I guess it was a little out of the ordinary. But it was just like I told them people at the paper. I saw these flashing lights in the sky. I was looking up at them, watching them get closer and closer. It was like nothing I'd ever seen before. And it was like they were hypnotizing me or something—blinking off and on so fast they looked like pulses of color that just went all the way through me."

"Pulses of light?" Pittman repeated.

"Jut like I told 'em already. I been telling people at the base, the paper. I've been telling Ruby too," he said, nodding toward his wife.

So Roger repeated the story once again, reciting precisely the by now familiar story. First the flashing, pulsating lights. Then, the next thing he knew, he was aboard the ship.

"They did these things to me," Roger said in a whispery, rather conspiratorial voice, confident he was piquing Pittman's curiosity. "They was awful things. Terrible things."

"What sort of things, exactly?" Pittman pressed for details.

Roger shook his head for dramatic effect. Ruby leaned close to him and stroked his arm. "There, there. Don't worry about nothing. I'll take care of you." As she said this, she gave Pittman a warning look to back off.

Once he regained his composure, Roger apologized that things were a little fuzzy. All he could remember was that they'd been doing these crazy experiments on him, trying to impregnate him. He remembered telling them that he was a man, and that men among our species couldn't have children. But they just wouldn't listen. They just kept poking him.

The next thing that Roger could recall was several days later—he didn't know how long, exactly—and he was walking on that road. He seemed unduly upset that he didn't know where his underpants were.

Throughout the narrative, Pittman watched the couple closely, noting again how Ruby constantly hovered over her husband. Finally, after listening to the story for a few minutes without interrupting, he just shook his head and started laughing. He couldn't help himself.

"This is the silliest goddamn thing I have ever heard in all my years of psychiatry," Pittman said. So far his budding career had existed for only about four years, but it still sounded good. Pittman has never been one to mince words or play games with people, and the hallmark of his unique, direct style was already evident. He just couldn't abide colleagues who would sit there listening to their patients describe the craziest things that they do without telling them how irresponsible and hurtful they were being to themselves and others.

Ruby didn't appreciate Pittman's attempt at "reality testing." "How can you treat this poor man like this, after what he's been through?" she complained. What she didn't say, but was quite obvious, was that she thought the psychiatrist was the crazy one in the room.

Pittman was unwilling to apologize or to back down: "Well the whole thing is clearly absolute crap."

Ruby looked pole-axed. She opened her mouth to defend her poor, abused husband (who was sitting stone-still, watching the exchange), then just slumped—collapsed really—in her chair. "Do you really believe that?"

she asked in a stricken voice. "Do you really believe this poor man would make this whole thing up?"

When Pittman just nodded, she added, "But why would he go and do something like that?" At this point she was trying to be polite to this fancy doctor. He looked like an intelligent man, even mostly harmless. She was shocked that he would speak to them like this. He must have some reason, and she wanted to know what that might be.

"Look, I have never encountered anybody who has been carried off by aliens from outer space. Have you?"

"Well, no, but that doesn't mean. . ."

"Doesn't mean what? That it couldn't happen? Was that what you were going to say?"

Throughout this exchange Roger was looking back and forth between them like a spectator at a tennis match. But he could see his champion was faltering.

Ruby started to say something, then stopped and looked toward her husband, as if urging him to jump in any time. It seemed that she had run out of answers.

"So, Roger," Pittman continued the dialogue, "when did all this business with UFOs start, exactly?"

Roger evaded the question. "Well, nothing like this ever happened to me before."

"Okay, then, why do you suppose these alien people. . . Is it okay to call them 'people,' by the way?"

Roger nodded, but his demeanor had changed. He was no longer playing the expert. He seemed to be operating now within the doctor's grid of reality testing rather than Ruby's adoring trust, or the Air Force's eagerness to get a worldwide crisis going.

"Why, out of all the billions of people on this planet, did they pick you to capture?"

Ruby jumped in. "Why, honey, you said it was because you were such an expert on UFOs after that movie you made in Hollywood. What was the name?" She paused for a moment, then broke into a smile of remembrance. "Oh, yeah, wasn't it called something like *They Came from Outer Space?*"

"*It Came from Outer Space*," Roger corrected his wife in a mumbling voice.

"Anyway," she shrugged, "I never saw it. I don't like that kind of movie."

Pittman, an inveterate movie buff, said dryly, "Well, I did see it. It was on TV just a couple of weeks ago. Actually, it was made in 1953. I believe you would have been about 12 at the time, Roger. What was your role in it?"

"Well, Ruby misunderestimated me a little," Roger confessed. "I never said I was actually in it. I said I worked on it, and I did. I made popcorn at the theater where it played, and I saw it lots of times. I know it by heart."

Pittman was calm and supportive as he said, "Thanks, Roger. I understand a lot better now."

As the interrogation continued, Ruby became more and more agitated by the turn of events, eventually interrupting the two men. "Roger," she said finally, "if what you've been telling me all this time is a lie, if you've made a fool of me, I swear. . ."

"Honey," Roger protested, "I told you that. . ."

"I swear," she said again, this time with more force, "if you don't tell me the truth, I'll divorce you faster than you can pack your bags."

Pittman tried to calm things down. He suggested that maybe Ruby, the Air Force, and even the president had "misunderestimated" Roger. Maybe they got a few things wrong, so it was best to straighten it out. Pittman saw that he had stirred up a hornet's nest. Perhaps he had been a little too forceful and confrontive with Roger, humiliating him in front of his wife. Maybe it would have been best to do this in a private session. But upon reflection, Pittman reasoned that his main job was to confront the sort of lies and deception that can so easily poison a relationship. There was obviously something funny going on here, and he sensed it was important to get it out.

"Roger, are you sure it was a UFO that picked you up?" Pittman asked.

There was a period of anxious silence, after which Roger admitted that he could have been a little mistaken. "Well, maybe it wasn't actually a UFO."

Before Ruby could go on the attack, Pittman asked gently if perhaps it was not an interplanetary vehicle at all that had picked him up, but one from our own planet.

Roger mumbled something about a blue Ford pickup.

"Excuse me?"

"I said it must have been a pickup truck," Roger said in a louder voice. "One of them things with an extra-long bed."

"Aliens were driving a Ford pickup?" Pittman asked, now confused.

Roger shook his head. "No, not aliens, exactly."

Before he could explain further, Ruby became absolutely outraged. "I knew it!" she screamed at Roger. "You were with that new girl from work. What's her name? Carin or Kerin. She's always changing the way she spells it, looking for something fancy. She's got a history. Everybody knows about that. And you old fool—you went off with her. And all this time you've been telling people, even them damn reporters, that it was aliens that abducted you, and you've been shacked up with that slut."

Ruby started to cry. When Roger leaned over to comfort her, she pulled away.

"It ain't like that," Roger said. "It's not what you think."

"Don't you dare tell me what to think, you son of a bitch! My mama, she tried so hard all her life to do things right. She warned me not to trust no man, not you, not anyone. You're no better'n your daddy with all his tall tales. Your mama put up with it. My mama may not have taught me much, but she knew how to leave a worthless man."

With some prodding and patience, Ruby explained that her mother had not done very well in the marriage department. She had tried marriage five times, and every one of her husbands ended up betraying her. She had told Ruby over and over again that there was no possibility a marriage could ever work if there were lies—but she never stayed around long enough to find out if men could change. And now Ruby's husband had been caught in the most bald-faced lies imaginable. Captured by aliens, for God's sake! And she had actually believed him! While the whole world laughed at her.

Ruby announced that she would be moving out of the house immediately (or at least immediately after she had fired Caren or Karin or whatever the hell she called herself this week), and she would go and live with her mother. She preferred that Roger not speak to her for a while; she had some things to work out on her own.

With little choice in the matter, Roger had no option but to agree. He looked up at Pittman with complete confusion, begging him for some help, some advice about what he might do. Roger whined, "All I ever did was tell everybody whatever they wanted to hear."

All Pittman could think to do was to shake his head in sympathy. What a mess indeed. "Some of us just want to hear the truth. That's always quite enough to deal with."

MEANINGS OF INFIDELITY

A few days later, Roger returned for a session alone. During this more private conversation he admitted what was obvious: that he had, in fact, spent those mysterious three days right here on earth with Kiran—(careful to point out Kiran with an "i" was not the same as Karin with an "a.") But it wasn't really his fault, Roger assured the doctor. Ruby drove him to it by not trusting him.

Pittman explained patiently that he was mixing cause and effect, putting the cart before the horse. Roger, ever agreeable, agreed that

Ruby had never distrusted him before he took off with Kiran and lost his underpants. So instead of blaming Ruby, he would place part of the blame legitimately in the laps of his parents, who "never taught me no better. And that trashy Kiran came on to me after I started talking about starring in that space movie. Ruby never cared much about my career in the movies. So it's not my fault." Pittman told Roger that they had a lot of work to do, that Roger had a lot to learn about life and relationships—and about reality.

Until this point in Pittman's work and career (more than 40 years ago), the prevailing idea was that infidelity was a conspiracy in which one person goes outside the marriage for sex because the other one secretly wants this to happen. But this case was a turning point for Pittman—the first time he realized that it was actually the lie that was making things so crazy and creating the problem. Infidelity is one thing, but lying about it—consistently and passionately—is quite another.

The second thing that Pittman learned from this couple was that there didn't have to be a problem in the marriage in order for infidelity to take place. Again this went against prevailing wisdom, in which it was believed that adulterers are much too noble to screw around unless it meets some sort of nutty need on the part of their spouse. It was supposed that spouses of adulterers are so mentally disturbed that, while they cause the infidelity, they must never know about it, since they are too unstable to deal with it. And the affair proves there must be something wrong with the relationship in order to drive someone to it in the first place, so it is probably best if the marriage is sacrificed to protect the secrecy.

Yet Ruby was the most adoring, attentive wife imaginable. She even trusted her husband in the face of the most ridiculous deceit and fantastic stories (of an alien abduction!). It was clearly not a defect in the marriage that was leading Roger astray, but holes in his own morality; he was, in fact, behaving like an irresponsible child.

Up until this point, Pittman had followed conventional wisdom with cases such as this. But this marriage did not cause Roger's affair, or the affairs he had in his first marriage (which he had never gotten around to telling Ruby about). Roger had learned from his father that this was the way men were supposed to behave. From his mother he had learned that a husband's tall tales could make a humdrum life seem more exciting. This was just the beginning of an inquiry that would capture Pittman's interest for the rest of his life—the meaning of infidelity.

MORE THAN PROFESSIONAL INTEREST

Pittman became intrigued with Roger's case on multiple levels; for him this was far more than a mere academic pursuit. Pittman came from a family that could most politely be called "eccentric." Among the colorful characters he grew up with was a cousin, Charles, who became the bigger-than-life male role model in an upbringing dominated by powerful women. It is hardly a coincidence that, as a psychiatrist and author, Pittman has specialized in men's issues, especially the role of therapists to provide the sort of fathering that might be missing in some dysfunctional men's lives. In fact, one way that he often describes his therapeutic approach is as a surrogate father figure who is teaching wayward men how to behave.

Charles was a legend in the family, the only member to escape the humiliations of a life of impoverished gentility in the Faulknerian South. First, Charles won the Metropolitan Opera auditions, but his great-aunt, who raised him, would not let him go that far away from home. As if that was not enough, he was also a Rhodes Scholar and ran the decathlon in the 1920 Olympics. A bit later in his distinguished career, he had a radio show in Chicago and then, when his great-aunt died, went out to Hollywood to play Ashley in *Gone with the Wind*, at the invitation of family friend Margaret Mitchell. (Unfortunately, they gave the part to someone else.)

Pittman's mother always thought of her "movie star nephew" as leading a glamorous, exciting life. Every year, around Christmas, Charles would send the family a long letter reporting all the movie stars with whom he was dancing, schmoozing, and working. In turn, Pittman's mother would send her cousin some money to help support him for another year when his career seemed to falter.

The only problem with all this was that eventually the family learned that Charles's stories about his life and work in Hollywood were total fabrications. After his early successes in life and opera and sports, the glory stopped in Hollywood. All the time he was supposedly pursuing stardom in the movies, he was actually working as a lineman for the phone company. When Frank finally met Charles for the first time, he was in his coffin and he looked painfully ordinary.

The object lesson for young Frank, growing up in this environment, was that big lies seem to work better than little ones. If you can make up a story that is fantastic and improbable, off the scale of normal imagina-tion, then people are more likely to believe you. Interestingly, this lesson did not teach Pittman to become a liar himself (though his mother's firm-est advice to her son was: "Always exaggerate; it makes life seem more interesting"). Instead, he learned exactly the opposite: always to tell the truth and rail against deceit, whether directed at oneself or others.

So when Roger came in with this whopper of a lie to cover up his affair by claiming to be abducted by aliens, it reminded Pittman of his growing up in Alabama and Georgia. Just like Cousin Charles, Roger had discovered that he could get by with almost anything as long as his story was outrageous enough.

Over the next few months, Pittman struggled to teach Roger the lessons that had been withheld from his education—notably how to tell the truth. Now that Roger's cover was blown, now that he no longer enjoyed the blind trust of Ruby (who of course took him back), Roger found that he could no longer get away with chronic lying. He had to learn a whole different set of skills.

At the same time, Pittman found himself becoming more and more a student of infidelity and what led people to betray their marital vows. This not only shaped his career but also helped him to remain monogamous to his own wife during a time when it seemed that mobs of people were screwing around as a normal expression of ultimate mental health and emotional freedom.

COMING BACK TO EARTH

Pittman likens the personal effects of this case to *The Wizard of Oz*: it taught him there is no place like home. After listening, for hour after hour, to the crazy adventures of people like Roger, Pittman was struck by the ways that people constructed fantasies to make their lives more complete or more interesting. "It got me out of the grandiosity of my own pipe dreams," Pittman recalls.

There was something quite pitiful about Roger admitting that he had actually been picked up by a blue Ford truck rather than a spaceship. This proud, strutting, arrogant man completely deflated after that. Once the lie was out in the open, Roger lost his celebrity, his wife's trust, and whatever respect he had enjoyed. But he found something better.

It is often interesting how the truth can be so much more compelling than any fabrication. Over time, Ruby came to adore her husband once again, even if she didn't quite fully trust him. Yet the more he told his wife the truth, the more she came to love him, even as she kept him on a short leash. She came to understand the shame Roger felt over his insignificance in the universe, and he came to understand his importance to her.

"I discovered," Pittman said, "that people who have secrets are always imposters. They always carry a load of shame."

Once Roger, and others like him, learn that they can be loved for who they are, instead of who they pretend to be, it allows them to find a degree of comfort with themselves that could not be achieved through dishonesty and deception.

This point has big lessons for Pittman in his own life. Although he would never admit this, he is among the most humble men we have ever met. Still painfully honest, he would confess that it is a false modesty that covers up a secret arrogance. We insist that he is certainly self-deprecating (he always gets a laugh when he describes himself as resembling Elmer Fudd and behaving like an old country boy from Alabama).

Pittman nodded. "It is true that I have never been happier with my life. But I don't feel the need to make my life bigger than it is. Sure, I like it when I get fan mail or a standing ovation. But. . ."

He left the sentence unfinished, thoughtful for a moment during a pause in the conversation.

"What about the temptations of being picked up in a blue Ford truck along the side of the road?"

Pittman chuckled appreciatively. "I think I can protect myself from the woman who says she is from outer space and wants to take me to another planet. I've had enough nutty relatives not to be attracted to craziness. And I don't need bigger-than-life adventures. I have been lucky. I've known a lot of bigger-than-life people, movie stars, sports celebrities, and billionaires, and it doesn't help them. It just keeps them ashamed over not being what everyone thinks they are. And in time it fades. Rita Hayworth plaintively commented that the tragedy of her life was that "men go to bed with Gilda and wake up with just me.""

Pittman's cousin Charles, and his patient Roger, both taught him that striving to be famous didn't help them much. Striving to be a hero like this is about overcoming shame. And it seems to Pittman to be so incredibly sad. "Being human is quite good enough," Frank summarized, realizing that this was the hardest lesson that he, as well as his patient, had learned. Pittman had been raised by his mother to be a star like his cousin Charles.

"So, what changed that for you?"

"Growing bald so early in life."

"Huh?"

"I had to give up the possibility that I was ever going to be so beautiful I could dazzle people just on the face of it. If I were going to go through life as just a guy, just an ordinary guy, I would have to learn to make the best of it."

Just as this realization brought Pittman down to earth, and is perhaps the source of his own humility, so he sees some of his finest hours as a therapist devoted to helping other people come back to earth.

People who are most unhappy are those who are trying to escape their ordinary lives, as if there is shame rather than honor in this ordinariness.

Pittman explained: "It is like the people who are trying to keep some part of themselves out of their marriage. This doesn't work any better than trying to keep a part of oneself outside of a submarine or an airplane. It works only when you get all the way in. It is the same with a marriage."

Chapter 6

ROBERT NEIMEYER
Using Metaphors to Thaw a Frozen Woman

The best way to describe Carol is that she seemed "not there." Her body was present, at least the way an inanimate object might be visible, but she seemed to be empty inside. She stood at the entrance to the office, frozen, immobile, and was led in by the receptionist. Her face was totally blank, and her eyes stared off toward some indeterminate place in the distance.

Neimeyer stood up to greet her, a little in shock at her disheveled, peculiar appearance. As he guided the catatonic woman to a chair, he noted lacerations and bruises on her arms. This evidence of violence puzzled him for a few minutes until he noticed that as soon as she was seated, Carol began rhythmically pounding her arms against the chair, producing more abrasions and bruises. Throughout the first session, this was the only evidence, besides her breathing, that she was alive.

Neimeyer watched Carol helplessly. Since she ignored any of his attempts to engage her, and did not respond to any questions, he had little choice but to sit back and observe her. He noted that she had been communicating with him in a way, letting him know that she was in deep, deep pain. He guessed that the bruises on her arms went far deeper than might be immediately apparent.

"You must be hurting a great deal to be doing this to yourself," he said to her.

Carol's eyes flickered toward Neimeyer for a moment, then returned to a spot on the far wall. He wondered if this represented a slight acknowledgment that he was in the room. So far, he had seen no other overt indication.

They sat quietly for the first hour, and the session after that as well. Carol would continually pound her arms against the chair, but seemingly with less violence. Neimeyer decided to take this as a sign of progress.

When she did say her first words, midway through the third session, Carol whispered, "The pain," and then resumed her frozen position.

"Tell me more about the pain you are feeling," Neimeyer encouraged her.

Nothing. No response whatsoever.

"I see some fresh marks on your arms since last time, so I would guess that your pain is as bad as ever."

Was that a head nod? Neimeyer wondered. And so they struggled together for interminable minutes, eventually settling into an almost comfortable silence. Since Carol had much more practice in remaining mute, it took some time for her therapist to respect her unique style of interaction.

JOURNALING

Eventually, slowly and ever so gradually, Carol began to speak in two- or three-word sentences, all without any elaboration. After some persistent probing, she described the meaning of her self-inflicted cuts: they were intended as messages for her therapists, carved into her flesh.

"I do appreciate the pain you are going through to communicate with me in this way," Neimeyer said sincerely, "but I wonder if you might substitute a pen and paper for those cuts on your arms." And so began Carol's therapeutic journal that served as the primary means by which she would talk about what she was suffering inside.

Neimeyer learned that Carol had recently been released from a hospital after a serious suicide attempt. She had been unceremoniously dumped in the emergency room by her lover, who was angry at being so inconvenienced. The medical staff who resuscitated her were no more compassionate, and seemed (to her) angry that she was keeping them from patients who had "real" problems. Since she was used to abuse throughout much of her life, Carol didn't consider either reaction to be unusual.

From the age of six, Carol had been sexually abused by her father. There was a lot of substance abuse in the family as well, so nobody in the house was particularly stable or consistent. Not far into her childhood, Carol began various forms of self-harm that ranged from self-mutilation to repeated suicide attempts.

Carol tried to escape her family while a teenager and joined a religious cult. It turned out that one of the covenants of this church was that Carol was assigned the job of satisfying the sexual needs of the leaders. She had been trained at an early age for this role, so it took some time before she was able to escape a "family" that turned out to be just as abusive as the one into which she had been born.

Meanwhile, Carol's father was dying of cancer. As much as she despised and resented the man, she felt duty-bound to be with him during his last days. Upon announcing her decision to leave the cult, the leaders warned her that because of this betrayal, God was punishing her by taking her father's life. Sure enough, her father died the next day. She took this as a sign of God's will that she was indeed an outcast. For the next few years, Carol sank even deeper into despair and a lifestyle marked by one abusive relationship after another.

As Neimeyer began to familiarize himself with Carol's history, mostly by reading her journal, he realized just how in over his head he felt. He did not have ready access to supervision. He had just moved to a new city where he had little collegial support. To complicate matters further, he was operating from a cognitive behavioral paradigm at the time, a model that seemed rather limited to deal with the depth and complexity of Carol's situation. He was grateful for the concrete, specific techniques at his disposal but felt ill-prepared to go deeper into the core of Carol's troubles. His client also did not respond favorably to the sort of rational arguments, systematic self-talk, and behavioral assignments to which he had become accustomed. Clearly, he was going to have to go far beyond anything he had tried before.

WALLS

Neimeyer realized that the usual sort of concrete, specific, goal-focused, rational conversations were virtually useless with Carol. Once he began experimenting with a more metaphorical, intuitive kind of communication, he found her responding in kind and making steady improvement. Her hospitalizations became less frequent. She started making friends and extending a support system. She launched a new career in the medical field. All was going reasonably well until she ran into a therapist she had once consulted.

Several years earlier, when she had been especially vulnerable, her therapist had tried repeatedly to seduce her. He enticed her to have oral sex with him in the office. This was during the time when she was manifesting many classic "borderline" symptoms, especially acting out self-destructively. Running into this guy again precipitated a relapse, and she felt herself sliding backward.

Carol returned to a state of sparse verbalizations in the sessions. Through halting language and journaling, she described feeling overwhelmed and disoriented. At times she wondered if she could even separate what was real, indicating that dissociation was emerging once again. At one point Carol even admitted that she was hiding, protecting herself. She talked about walls a lot.

Joining her in the metaphoric language, Neimeyer invited Carol to talk more about the walls. She described a feeling of being a translucent wall that seemed to be placed between her and the rest of the world.

"Including me?" Neimeyer asked.

Carol admitted that some holes had worn through the wall. Some of them had been scratched into, as though someone was trying to get out from behind the wall.

"Carol, can you take me with you to the other side of that panel?"

"I don't know." She paused for a long time after that. "I guess if I had a knife, I could cut myself loose, but I can't do that without leaving a scar."

"That's true. But there are already so many scars on the wall."

"And on me, too." Carol said this in a very little voice. Then she talked about feeling like a little girl.

"What is the little girl doing behind the wall?"

"She's walking back and forth. Like a guard."

"What is she guarding?"

"The world."

"From?"

Carol paused thoughtfully, then looked Neimeyer directly in the eyes. "From you."

"From me? What would I do that the little girl needs to guard against?"

"Well, you could start dissolving the wall, and then she won't have any place to live."

Neimeyer nodded thoughtfully. "Do we have to take the world from her? Can't we allow her to live in it?"

"I don't know."

"Let me ask you something else, then. What relationship does this little girl have to Carol?"

Carol then explained that the little girl represented her dark side. She was everything that was bad and evil.

"I see," Neimeyer said. "If this little girl could talk, what would she tell us?"

Carol laughed, but it was more like a cackle. "She'd tell you to shut up. She's stubborn." As she said these last words, Carol became eerily still and stared at the back wall. After some minutes while her therapist waited, she said: "I think I'm going crazy."

Neimeyer nodded his understanding. "I wonder if I could speak to this little girl, the one who represents your dark side."

Carol nodded.

"Okay, then. Little girl, what is your name?"

"Carol," she answered in a small, high voice.

"You sound quiet, Carol."

"I can be quiet. And I can also be loud." She said this as a warning.

"What would you like to say to me right now?"

Carol smiled. "I want to tell you that I have the right to shut up whenever I want."

"Does Carol, big Carol, listen to you?"

"Yes, she does. She should listen to me more, and she wouldn't get in trouble." Neimeyer recognized that she was talking about the times when she allowed herself to be seduced and abused by people such as the other therapist.

"You wish Carol had heeded your warning that the man was not to be trusted."

Carol nodded. She then went into detail, more than ever before, about the nature of the abuse she suffered. She talked about what the therapist had made her do and how he threatened to kick her out if she didn't obey him.

As he listened, Neimeyer noticed some distinctive body movements that Carol was making. "I see that as you are telling me this, you are scrunching your shoulders down, as if you retreating within yourself, hunkering down for protection."

"Yes, that's true. This is how Carol hides from you, and everyone else."

"And is it still necessary for her to do this?"

Carol shrugged, saying she didn't know. It was obvious that she was quite fearful of where this was going.

HEALING RITUALS

All the while that Neimeyer was interviewing "Little Carol" about the nature of her relationship to "Big Carol," he couldn't stop thinking about what strange territory he was in. "It was a little bit like having an experience many years ago of going to the Cliffs of Moher in the western part of Ireland. It is unlike any other place on earth. It literally looks like a moonscape. It is this broken kind of limestone rock. Nothing is alive. Every now and then some big rocks are discovered that had ritual significance for a bygone race. With Carol, it felt like I was entering that kind of land that was bare and harsh but also absolutely intriguing. I was really directing my attention to what she was saying with a kind of knife-edge acuteness. I felt very intensely connected with her in conversations like these."

Speaking in the language of metaphor, Carol was able to talk about hidden parts of herself behind the wall without having to dissociate.

"I feel like I am a mountain climber who has fallen," she said at one point. "But my wounds have now healed and the scars are fading. I think I'm ready to start climbing again."

Carol taught Neimeyer about the power of nonliteral and meta-phoric language. This was a turning point for him to move away from the linear, overly logical mechanism of cognitive-behavioral theory and to begin trusting his intuition in a number of new ways. He not only began studying philosophy and contructivist thinking, but also delved more deeply into an appreciation of art. Certainly this evolved into a new therapeutic style, but it also changed him in other ways.

Neimeyer and Carol evolved healing rituals in their work together. In one sense, the client became the teacher because she was far more com-fortable devising ways she could put the past behind her. For instance, Carol bought a ceramic pot at a yard sale. She had a party where she carefully recruited friends who could appreciate the symbolic meaning of what she planned to do. She created a ceremony where she buried her past in the form of mementos of her more tortured years and her child-hood. She put them in this ceramic pot, placed it in the ground, and then covered it with earth. All of this in front of trusted witnesses.

As she became stronger, Carol showed even more initiative. She traveled back to her hometown, a place she had fled many years earlier. While there, she sought out and interviewed people who had known her family. She asked questions about her father that she never had the opportunity to ask when she was a little girl. From these conversations she began to construct an autobiography, told through the voices of relatives and family friends with whom she reestablished contact.

Chapter 7

ALAN MARLATT
A New Name

"This is a tough one for you," the psychiatrist said. "I'm not even sure what to do with her."

"What's going on?" Marlatt asked his colleague, a member of the psychiatry department who had called with this referral.

"She's pretty seriously depressed," the psychiatrist said, then paused. "I've been working with her for three months now, and progress has been pretty slow."

"I see," Marlatt responded, waiting patiently for the other shoe to drop.

"So, anyway," the psychiatrist continued, "today she admitted that she's been drinking a little. Actually, way more than a little. Once I realized how seriously out of control she was, I told her that I couldn't do much for her until she gets the alcohol under control."

"So that's where I come in?" Marlatt asked. It wasn't a tough guess, considering that he was known throughout the university, and throughout much of the nation, as one of the pioneer researchers and clinicians in the area of addictive behaviors.

"Exactly. I was wondering if you'd be willing to do an alcohol evaluation on her, and let me know what you think. In the meantime, I also referred her to an alcohol treatment center in the area. The truth is that I don't know much about alcoholism, and I just know that I can't continue to work with her."

In Marlatt's experience, most practitioners knew relatively little about these sorts of problems that often did not respond to usual medical or psychological interventions. He agreed to do the evaluation and promised he'd get back to the psychiatrist after he met with her.

SEARCH FOR A MIDDLE WAY

Tina looked tired more than anything else when she showed up for the evaluation. Marlatt began the session by asking her how things were going.

"You know," she answered thoughtfully, "I'm really kind of confused by this whole thing."

"Confused? How?"

"Well, the other doctor I've been seeing told me that my drinking was motivated by my depression. He said that I'm trying to self-medicate myself."

"And what about that seems confusing?"

"I went to this alcoholism treatment center in town, one of those programs where they expected me to check in for a month. Do you know the place?"

Marlatt nodded. Indeed, he knew the place quite well. It was one of the traditional centers that followed a disease model and demanded total abstinence.

"They told me that I was an alcoholic, and that was what was causing my depression, not the other way around. They said that unless I committed myself to total abstinence and accepted the fact that I'll be an alcoholic all my life, and powerless to control my drinking, I would remain depressed."

"I can see why you're confused," Marlatt observed.

"You got that right. I mean, what's going on with you people? My doctor told me that the depression was causing the drinking. The staff at the center said the drinking was causing the depression, as well as every other problem in my life. I'm not sure what to believe. And now they sent me to you."

"Well, what do you think?"

Tina shrugged. "I don't really know. That's why I came to you. I guess there might be truth in both of these statements, but they seem to contradict one another. The part I don't understand the most is that my psychiatrist won't agree to keep seeing me unless I can stop drinking, but I can't stop drinking if he's right and I'm depressed."

"And are you ready to stop drinking?"

"Truthfully? At this point? No."

Marlatt smiled, appreciative of her honesty. With little prompting, Tina went on to explain that she was dealing with a number of problems at the moment. She was having trouble in her marriage, as well as problems at work. The only thing that seemed to be working for her was the drinking: it dulled the pain and numbed her out. "Why would I stop doing the one thing that seems to help me get through the night?"

Marlatt nodded his understanding; this was a dilemma that he encountered frequently as director of The Addicitive Behaviors Research Center. Whereas in the disease-based model of alcoholism, patients are required to commit themselves to total abstinence, the harm reduction approach focuses instead on allowing people to maintain their coping strategies until more functional, effective alternatives are developed. These are two very different perspectives, one popular within the substance abuse field and 12-step programs, the other representative of public health, and they are at odds with one another.

If there was a "middle way," Tina was certainly a good candidate for it. Marlatt had developed a form of harm reduction therapy for people who manifest co-occurring problems—some form of substance abuse with accompanying depression or anxiety.

CONFLICTING IDEOLOGIES

In conducting an assessment and collecting some background, Marlatt learned that Tina was married, 39 years of age, and the mother of two sons who were 7 and 12. She was a highly educated woman who had been trained as a scientist. Her husband was an academic whom she had met when they were graduate students.

In their early marriage years, Kyle, the husband, had insisted that Tina abandon her career and be a stay-at-home mom. He would support the family, and her role would be restricted to the home. This became an ongoing source of tension between them, and was one of the reasons she felt so depressed. "Here I've got a Ph.D. in molecular biology," she said in exasperation. "I live 30 minutes from several world-class labs where I could get a job in a minute, but Kyle wants me at home with the kids. It doesn't seem to matter what I want."

Tina talked at length about resenting her husband's control over her life, yet she had remained very passive and compliant (except for the drinking, which drove him crazy). Marlatt noted this dynamic but decided to collect more information before proceeding with any sort of intervention.

Tina's father had a pretty serious drinking problem while she was growing up, and there were others in her family who also struggled with alcohol. The staff at the alcohol treatment center had jumped all over that family history as compelling evidence that she had a genetic disease which had been passed on to her. Kyle also liked this conception of the problem, because it seemed to reinforce the idea that Tina was helpless and needed to concentrate on the family rather than her own "selfish" interests. He was the one who insisted she get into Alcoholics Anonymous. He also started going to Al-Anon groups that supported his view that Tina was indeed an alcoholic in denial.

Marlatt didn't think that Tina was in denial at all. She knew she had a problem; it was just bigger and more complex than had originally been conceived. In fact, she had gone to some AA groups, but she just didn't feel the structure suited her. She felt too shy to speak in front of all those people, and she found it difficult to relate to some of the stories she heard. Moreover, she had trouble with the first step in the program—admitting that she was powerless over alcohol. It felt to her like this would represent complete surrender. As far as she was concerned, feeling helpless was the main problem in her life, and like heck she was going to give up even more control!

When Marlatt invited the husband into a session, Kyle was absolutely livid that his own diagnosis of Tina's problem, as well as that of the treatment center, was being ignored. "She won't go into treatment," Kyle raged. "She won't attend meetings. With everything else I am doing for this family, trying to keep us all afloat, she expects me to do this, too."

"So you don't consider what we are doing here to be treatment, then?" Marlatt prompted.

"This?" Kyle said, shaking his head. "What you are doing here is an abomination. If anything, you're making her worse, putting these crazy thoughts in her head. The people in my Al-Anon group say that you are just enabling her. She's an alcoholic. Her daddy was an alcoholic. And until she is willing to acknowledge this, she's always going to be sick."

Kyle crossed his arms, signaling there was little else to say.

SURRENDER

Eventually, Tina did surrender. She agreed to give in to her husband (again) and start attending AA meetings. She tried her best to stop drinking completely, but once she gave up the bottle, she felt more and more depressed.

She felt worse than ever, and seemed to be making little progress. Her psychiatrist still refused to see her until she was totally sober. She was caught between conflicting ideologies and couldn't see a way out.

During this point in his career, Marlatt thought it tragic that there was no way to reconcile the different perspectives offered by the substance abuse and mental health communities. Tina was another example of someone caught in the middle, someone whose depression was both the cause and the effect of her drinking. She clearly needed a more integrative, flexible treatment approach that would respond to her unique needs, but unfortunately, the outcome literature was not encouraging. The dropout rate in the addiction field is huge. The success rate in treating alcohol problems with traditional psychotherapy is even more dismal.

Tina was being told that she had to give up her drinking completely before she could get help with her depression. She couldn't—or wouldn't—do that. Likewise, she felt unable to reduce the helplessness and despair to the point that she could do without her "self-medication."

Marlatt was feeling almost as frustrated as his client. With all the research being done, with all the expensive treatment programs, all the funding for investigations, all the support groups, there really was nothing out there that was well-suited to people like Tina, those who didn't fit into a neat category. He had been trying to fight this battle for some time, advocating for a "middle ground" that recognized the individual and cultural differences in people's life predicaments. Yet the advocates of the disease model were so passionate that they had actually gotten a state law passed saying that all treatments approved for insurance or state funding had to comply with an abstinence-only goal. No exceptions, no matter what evidence was available to support alternative models.

When Kyle was away on a business trip, things came to a head. He had warned his wife repeatedly that she was absolutely not to drink while he was away. After a few days, he called to check on her.

"How are you doing?" he asked suspiciously.

"Fine," Tina answered, weary and resentful that she was being treated like a child.

"You're sure? You sound different."

"I told you I'm fine. I'm just tired and don't feel well."

"You don't feel well? Damn it, I told you to stay away. . ."

"I don't feel well," Tina interrupted, "because I have a sore throat."

"Yeah, sure. And you expect me to believe you? After everything we've been through? I don't know why you insist on ruining everything. I can't leave you alone for even a day. I can't trust you. . ."

Click. Tina hung up the phone. In truth, she had not had a drink since Kyle had left. She did have a cold and a sore throat. Now she was absolutely furious. And she was absolutely dying for relief.

When Kyle returned home two days later, Tina was stone drunk. He felt more convinced than ever that this latest episode confirmed his view that Tina was a hopeless alcoholic.

"And what do you think?" Tina asked Marlatt in the next session.

This was a critical moment, not only in their session, but in Marlatt's career. Tina wanted—and deserved—an honest assessment, but in giving one, he would be going against all the conventional wisdom that was lined up against him. For years he had been under attack by the addictions orthodoxy that insisted he was a heretic for advocating anything less than abstinence in alcohol treatment. But Marlatt had been examining the evidence for years. He had been conducting his own studies and reading the literature that had amassed. He was convinced, more than ever, that there could be alternative models with demonstrated effectiveness. And all these thoughts went through his head during the few seconds that Tina waited anxiously for an answer.

"If you want to know," Marlatt began, "I don't think you are a hopeless alcoholic."

"No?" she said with sad resignation, not really believing him.

"No. I probably don't need to remind you how complex your situation is. There is clearly considerable marital stress. . ."

"You can say that again," she laughed.

". . .that acts as a trigger for your drinking. In one sense, your psychiatrist was right when he observed that you are medicating yourself for depression."

Kyle eventually had his way. He insisted that unless Tina would agree to enter a 28-day treatment center, he would not allow her to remain in the house. He considered her a danger to their children. Finally, she relented and agreed to go, responding to his insistence that she was indeed an alcoholic who was truly powerless to control her disease.

ONE MONTH LATER

Tina returned from the treatment program committed to maintaining her sobriety. About one week after her return, during which time she remained abstinent, she was grocery shopping when she noticed her husband's car outside the market. Curious what he was doing in the area when he was supposed to be at work, she looked outside and saw that he was locked in an embrace with a woman. Later that night, she confronted her husband, who admitted that he had been having an affair. But he excused his behavior as the comfort he deserved during all the time he had felt abandoned by his wife.

"This is when I just gave up," Tina explained to Marlatt. "What's the point? My husband is betraying me. He won't accept any responsibility for our problems. It is all my fault. It is always my fault. Yet even when I do what he wants, and spend a month in a hellhole, a prison, he's out screwing someone else behind my back. What am I supposed to do now?"

Tina was desperate for some kind of relief, something other than medication or alcohol, and begged Marlatt for an alternative. He introduced her to a mild form of meditation, called "Urge Surfing," that could be used for self-management during those times when she would ordinarily be triggered into drinking. He also recommended a book by an influential meditation teacher.

During this time Kyle elected to separate from Tina and move in with his girlfriend. Tina decided that she needed some sort of new environment as well, even if temporary, that could help her rebuild her life without alcohol abuse. She decided to pick a place that was the exact opposite of her last "internment" in the treatment center: a meditation retreat center. Marlatt agreed that this would be an excellent way to begin her new life.

Tina arranged for her parents to care for her children while she was gone and then traveled to the retreat center for a month-long study of meditation. Immediately upon arrival, all participants were expected to take a vow that included avoidance of all intoxicants. Once she got up in front of the whole group, including her meditation teacher, and announced that she would abide by all the precepts, she knew in that moment that she would never have another drink. That was the moment of realization and commitment for her, and she had no doubt whatsoever that her promise would stick.

In explaining later how this program worked for her, while AA groups had not, Tina pointed out that she had not been required to admit she was powerless, as in the first step of 12-step programs. Instead, she did exactly the opposite: she declared that she had the power to make a promise and keep it, no matter what.

CHECKUP

Two years later, Tina returned for a checkup.

"I still feel depressed and upset occasionally," she confessed. "This happens especially when I have to deal with my ex-husband. We had a difficult divorce and custody battle. But I have not had a drink or used any intoxicants since I returned from the retreat center. I am not an alcoholic, nor do I need to go to a group every week to be told I am powerless. It is my meditation that keeps me sane."

Marlatt was sincerely impressed by the progress that Tina had made, work that had mostly been done through her own initiative.

"My mind still says I need a drink," Tina said. "But I realize that it is just a thought inside my head. I no longer have to be dictated to by my thoughts."

After Tina left, Marlatt looked up the word "addiction" in the dictionary, and he noted that it has the same root as "dictator." Indeed, Tina refused to be dictated to by her tempting thoughts, by her ex-husband, or by anything or anyone else in her life. Rather than surrender power, she reclaimed it.

Tina soon got involved in another relationship, and got married. She continued her meditation practice, stayed sober, and started working as a full-time scientist for the first time since she graduated.

PARALLEL JOURNEYS

This case changed Marlatt in a multitude of ways, beginning with the activation of his own anger and sense of helplessness in responding to Tina's needs. "I was angry that people like her, with alcohol and mental health problems, are not getting the kind of integrated response they deserve. I was—and still am—angry at the dominant system for not responding. You have to meet people where they are, not where you prefer them to be."

Marlatt is referring to the "Catch 22" scenario in which someone like Tina is told by her psychiatrist: "I can't meet you where you are because you are drinking, and I can't treat drinking problems." Then she is told at the alcohol treatment center: "We can't meet you where you are because you are not ready to quit."

After this case, Marlatt felt more fortified to stand up to his critics who claimed that his more moderate, flexible approach encouraged people to remain stuck in denial. He was accused of enabling people, of preventing them from "hitting bottom," and of keeping them stuck by providing false hope.

Tina taught him the ways that personal problems and addictive behaviors are linked. There is a circular, recursive pattern.

On a more personal level, Marlatt began a parallel journey with Tina in terms of his own investigations into Buddhist psychology and meditation. He found that Buddhist thought provided alternative ways of looking at addictions in terms that emphasized harm reduction rather than self-labeling. He also discovered that his philosophy provided a solid background for integrating cognitive-behavioral strategies into programs for relapse prevention.

"I had this fear when I first started the study of Buddhism that my colleagues in academia would find this unacceptable. I had been interested in meditation since the 70s, when I first tried it to help cope with a problem of high blood pressure. Instead of resorting to medication, I chose to meditate. I have been doing so ever since."

The turning point in Marlatt's life was sparked, at least partially, by his work with Tina. As she found a certain peace from her meditation practice, so, too, did her therapist turn toward Buddhism as a spiritual pathway.

"It was at that point that I realized I was on the other side. I had come out of the closet, so to speak. Now I do presentations and even panel discussions at the American Psychological Association and other conferences on mindfulness. Now I am not just a psychologist studying Buddhism; I am a Buddhist psychologist."

Looking back on the time he spent with Tina, Marlatt recalls that during this same time he was motivated to apply for a grant to fund a study investigating the effects of Buddhist meditation on prison inmates. He found that this 10 day training course was able to significantly reduce the alcohol and drug problems of inmates who took the meditation retreat, compared with the control group who did not receive this training. This only affirmed empirically what he had been discovering more and more in his own life: that addictive behaviors can be controlled, if not managed, effectively by first adapting a "Middle Way" approach between the dichotomous extremes of a zero-tolerance, abstinence-only requirement, on the one hand, and giving in to harmful indulgences and loss of control, on the other.

"All of this kicked in during my work with Tina," Marlatt recalled. "She deserves significant credit for all the work I have completed since then. In one sense, she was also the impetus for my new name."

"New name?" we asked.

Marlatt explained that when he took "refuge" in the Buddhist tradition from his meditation teacher, she said to him: "If you are ready to take the precepts, to take refuge in the Buddha and the dharma and the sangha, I am going to give you a Buddhist name."

Marlatt explained that when one is given a Buddhist name, it quite often represents something that you are working on, some challenge in your life.

"So, what's your name?" we asked.

"My name is Sopa Gyatso. It means 'ocean of patience.'" Marlatt smiled as he said this, and then added: "I can tell you that I still have a lot of impatience to work on."

Chapter 8

ALBERT ELLIS
Learning from a Difficult Customer

At 90 years of age, Albert Ellis has probably come close to a world record for seeing the most clients in a lifetime. This is not only because he has remained professionally active for over 60 years, but also because he has done group therapy throughout much of his career with audiences numbering in the hundreds, if not the thousands.

Ellis is the founder of rational emotive behavior therapy (REBT), one of the major therapies of the past century. Not only was he among the first to promote an approach to therapy that emphasized cognitive self-talk as a way to change one's perception and experience of reality, but he has always advocated that clinicians should apply the same methods to themselves. In fact, Ellis has commented repeatedly in his writing and lectures that REBT has always formed the model for how he has tried to live his own life—confronting his own irrational beliefs in order to be more accepting of himself and others. He has always been a strong advocate of the idea that just as REBT therapists help their clients to examine their dysfunctional thinking patterns, so, too, are they well equipped to look at their own. It is this context that has led Ellis to remark that by talking clients out of their own crazy beliefs, therapists cannot help but confront their own.

Ellis has written at least one book every year he has been in practice, a total of more than 75 volumes. Some of his best-known works include *Reason and Emotion in Psychotherapy, A Guide to Rational Living, Sex Without Guilt, How to Control Your Anger Before It Controls You, How to Stubbornly Refuse to Make Yourself Miserable About Anything— Yes, Anything,* and *Feeling, Better, Getting Better, Staying Better.*

Ellis is director of the New York institute that bears his name. In between the major commitments involved in taking care of his health, he continues to remain active in his writing, lecturing, and supervision.

A HATEFUL CLIENT

Among the thousands of people whom Ellis has worked with during his distinguished career, including up to 20 individual (half-hour) sessions in a day, people in group therapy, family therapy, audience demonstrations, supervision, and consultations, there is one person who stands out among the rest, one client who helped change him the most. Ellis has done so many therapy sessions over the years, repeating the themes that are his trademark, that the faces of his clients often blend together. There is one client, however, who still stands out vividly in his memory. This was a woman whom he discussed with us for an earlier project about his most unusual case (Kottler & Carlson, 2003), but she merits mentioning again in the context of the client who impacted him the most.

The word that most easily comes to mind for Ellis in describing Natalie is "hateful," and he hardly ever is inclined to use such negative labels. But she was indeed a special case who got underneath Ellis's skin as nobody else had.

Natalie attended a group that Ellis led for many years. She came originally because (not surprisingly, as you will see) she had some difficulty in her relationships with others, beginning with her parents. Her mother, in particular, had been extremely abusive toward her, and this seemed to establish a pattern that Natalie was to follow when dealing with others. In addition, she struggled with severe depression throughout most of her life, a condition that had worsened to the point that as much as she despised therapy and therapists, she didn't believe she could cope without at least some support—even if it came from "quacks and nutcases."

To say that Natalie was hostile would not do justice to that term. Natalie could be so angry, so filled with rage, so mean-spirited and aggressive when going after other people's weak points, that she could reduce almost anyone to tears. As is not unusual for those diagnosed with borderline disorder, she had an uncanny ability to uncover people's vulnerabilities and exploit them as a way to protect herself against perceived attacks. Moreover, she saved her best stuff for her prominent and famous therapist.

"And people actually pay you for this work that you do?" Natalie railed at Ellis during one session when he had attempted to help her look at her self-sabotaging behavior. "I can't believe that you ever helped anyone with this shit you call therapy. Maybe it works when other people do it, or with these sheep in this group." She gestured with her arm toward the others in the group. "But you are just about the worst therapist I've ever seen—or heard of."

It is really something to say that Ellis could be held speechless in the face of Natalie's tirades. This is a man who is known far and wide for his quick wit and fast tongue, who can stand up to anyone and tie him or her in knots. But Natalie was another story.

"I thought we were talking about you," Ellis tried to interject, putting the focus back on Natalie's cognitive distortions and sense of entitlement. "You were talking about that little girl on the subway this morning, the one who was cracking her gum that you said was driving you crazy..."

"See," Natalie interrupted, "there you go again. You must have memory problems or something, because I never said that. And we've got witnesses here, too." Natalie looked menacingly around the room, daring any of the other group members to contradict her. "I never said that little bitch in the subway was cracking her gum. What I said..."

"Okay, okay," Ellis tried to calm her down.

"You just can't stand the heat, can you?" Natalie again took control of the conversation. "You never liked me, and everyone here can see that. They can see how unfair you are, how you play favorites. The only reason you still let me come to this fucking group is because you want as much damn money as you can get." Natalie shook her head in disgust. "And that's another thing—this poor fucking excuse for what you call an institute can't seem to deal with the most simple things without screwing things up. They never get my bill right. They're always overcharging me, or charging for sessions when I wasn't even here."

If they gave awards for the most aggressive and toxic border-line, Natalie would win hands down, Ellis believed. And like seriously disturbed individuals who try to keep others off balance as a means to keep themselves safe, Natalie had an amazing talent for going for the jugular. Even though most of her accusations were false and ridiculous fabrications, occasionally she would hit the mark in a way that made Ellis feel raw. He spent more time thinking about this woman than he cared to admit. He planned alternative ways to get through to her. He consulted with colleagues about possible interventions that might diffuse her hostility. But nothing seemed to work. And worse, even though she claimed she wasn't getting any better and she was such a disruptive force in the group, she insisted on coming back. "You aren't going to get rid of me so easily," Natalie would say scornfully. "You screwed things up royally, and by God, you're going to fix them."

Ellis could only shake his head, try to redirect her anger, and move on to other group members who were still reeling from the latest attack or outburst.

The really strange thing (or perhaps not so unusual after all) was that Natalie actually seemed to be improving her life. Even though she would remain volatile and unmanageable throughout her time in the group, from all reports, she seemed to be making improvements in her relationships with coworkers and family. But Ellis would never see these changes with his own eyes, and Natalie continued to berate him whenever she had the chance.

LEARNING PATIENCE AND ACCEPTANCE

What made things even more challenging for Ellis was that at this particular time in his life his contributions were coming under attack by a number of other psychologists who claimed that REBT had no legitimacy, that there was no solid research to support it, that, by and large, Ellis was a liar and cheat and was just no damn good. Rationally, he knew that these accusations were without merit, but this was still a difficult period for him, and at times he began to question himself. Natalie only poured oil on the flames.

Yet in one sense, this particular client helped to toughen Ellis up in ways that nothing else could have done so well. She helped him not only to stand up more strongly to his critics, but also to refine his methods in such a way that he became even more skilled in dealing with resistant, difficult clients. Furthermore, in order to remain calm in the face of Natalie's attacks and manipulations, Ellis learned to dispute his own judgments of himself, and especially of others, in such a way that he refined his theory to emphasize the unconditional acceptance of people even if some aspects of their behaviors are highly unacceptable. When he was honest with himself, Ellis had to admit that he was not being as effective as he could have been with this client, that her criticisms that he was failing her in some way might have been justified. But be that as it may, he still found that this less than perfect performance did not mean that he was a lousy therapist.

One other aspect of this relationship with Natalie had a strong impact. In being completely frank with himself, Ellis had to admit that there was some truth to at least one of her accusations: that he didn't much care for her as a person, that he treated her unfairly and without sufficient respect. It was hard for him to maintain the requisite empathy and compassion toward a person who worked so hard to be unlovable. But no matter how odious Natalie became, no matter how obnoxious her behavior, she was absolutely right that she deserved to be treated with respect as a person even as her behavior had to be counteracted.

"Even if most, or even all, of what she said about me was true," Ellis realized, "that I was a lousy therapist, that I knew nothing, that I had a poor memory, that I didn't care about her—that still didn't make me a rotten person." Ellis had known this principle all along. After all, it was a cornerstone of his whole theory. Yet Natalie became the absolute test of this belief, and it was hardened under fire. Eventually, Ellis was able to accept her with the requisite respect and caring. This took literally years of work together in a relationship that was among the most difficult he has ever experienced. Even though much of her behavior didn't change as much as could be desired within the group itself, Ellis came to feel differently about his client. Much of this change resulted from his disputing his own irrational beliefs that she needed to be different, that she should be different.

More than most people Ellis has ever known, Natalie taught him to be more patient and to control his frustration tolerance better. "It was largely as a result of working with her," Ellis said, "that I developed the concept of 'unconditional other acceptance,' meaning accepting others no matter what they do or how disturbed they might be. I always had some low frustration tolerance, but this client taught me to work on raising it."

Ellis also learned from Natalie to accept himself more fully. "Because I accept myself, I am able to accept others the way they are, and accept the world the way it is—without needing anything to be different. This is what has allowed me to lead a happier, more productive life."

BEING VULNERABLE

One thing that has given Albert Ellis the biggest thrill in his life is being with people who are working as hard as they can to overcome adversity. This might very well be a testimony to the current struggles he faces with an assortment of health problems that are not unusual for a man who is 90 years old. Yet Ellis has learned from talking to his clients over the years that whining and complaining and self-pity get one nowhere. Instead he treats each day, each moment, as a gift.

In closing, Ellis admitted that he very much liked the types of questions that require him to be as honest with himself as possible. "If therapists would stop being so ashamed of being vulnerable themselves," Ellis remarked, "then they could do themselves, and their clients, a great deal of good."

Chapter 9

BRADFORD KEENEY
A Family of Pirates

It was a time of transition in Brad Keeney's life. He was feeling frustrated with the limitations of psychotherapy, especially when compared with the work of shamans in various cultures. Whereas therapy is primarily a "talking cure," a treatment in which people talk to an expert about their problems, indigenous healers avoid such talk in favor of more active methods that involve dancing, singing, shaking, rituals, and prescriptive ordeals. All of this takes place within the community, in a very public setting, rather than in the private sanctum of a mental health professional. Moreover, Keeney felt an aversion to the usual methods of diagnosis and psychological labeling that take place within the therapeutic community.

After living and working among the Bushmen of the Kalahari, the Zulu, and other cultures around the world, Keeney began to feel an increased aversion to Western ways of conceptualizing helping relationships that he viewed as limited. He was surprised at the ways that helpers in our own culture had all but abandoned the wisdom of traditions that have been practiced for tens of thousands of years. There was something that struck him as so contrived and inauthentic, if not unproductive, in expecting to actually help someone deal with a problem by talking about it in private and gaining some sort of insight into its supposed core roots. By contrast, the shamans whom he had worked with almost never asked people to talk about their problems, much less tried to promote some sort of understanding of their origins. Instead, they would call for a dance, or community intervention, that most often involved music, movement, and ritualized ordeals.

Thus far, Keeney had kept the shaman side of him a secret. He was still being invited to lecture at universities around the world, to conduct workshops, and to teach his trademark "resource focused" therapy that emphasized people's strengths rather than their weaknesses. He was still intrigued with the "aesthetics" of change, that is, the interpersonal patterns that he sought to describe in the tradition of his training as a cybernetic epistemologist. His early mentors, such as Gregory Bateson and Carl Whitaker, had taught him to examine behavior not only in a larger systemic context, but also in a far more playful spirit than was currently in vogue. If truth be told, the field of therapy was far too grim for Keeney's taste, taking itself far too seriously and enforcing a degree of rigidity within the guild that stifled creativity. So, although Keeney was still working as a therapist and trainer of other therapists, he felt himself in the midst of a transformation that was just beginning to impact his clinical work.

THE DEATH OF SANTA CLAUS

The first thing that Keeney noticed was how healthy the family appeared. Jim, the father, looked the part of a record producer, which was what he was. He appeared confident and relaxed in khakis, loafers, and an immaculately pressed white shirt, open at the collar. No tie. His wife, Inga, was a fundraiser for a nonprofit agency. Although she was also thin and fit, she was dressed in marked contrast to her husband—black skirt, black blouse and vest, black boots. The only splash of color were the turquoise bracelets around her slim wrist. They were a strikingly handsome couple.

Keeney's eyes were drawn immediately to the boy standing a little behind his parents. Whereas Inga and Jim were both dark-haired, their son, Sven, was blonde. He seemed unusually polite and sweet for an eight-year-old boy.

The family had been referred to Keeney for a consultation during one of his lecture visits to New York. He had been told that the parents were both therapy-wise, having been in Jungian analysis for some time. Because they were both in creative fields, and active in the New York art and music scene, they had been referred to Keeney, who had been described to them as having a rather unusual approach to therapy.

"So," Keeney began the session after they had settled themselves, "what's brought us together?"

"Well," Jim explained, taking the lead, "Sven worries a lot." As he said this, he placed a reassuring arm around his son's shoulders.

"Worries about what?" Keeney asked, looking over at the boy before returning his gaze to the father.

"Mostly about death. He worries. . . .He thinks. . ."

"He thinks he's going to die," Inga finished the sentence. "He's been constantly worrying—obsessed—that he's going to die before Christmas."

"Before Christmas?" Keeney said, looking directly at Sven, who nodded solemnly. He seemed content to let his parents speak for him initially. Although he was listening intently to the conversation, he was doodling on a pad of paper he had brought with him. Looking at the drawing upside down, Keeney could see he was making some sort of oblong shape.

Jim and Inga explained that Sven had become convinced that he would not live to see Christmas, which was just a few weeks away. The boy believed that he had some sort of heart trouble, even though doctors ruled out any physical problem other than possibly a mild muscle pull in his chest. No matter how he had been reassured to the contrary, the boy remained insistent that his days were numbered.

Sven's parents were paralyzed by his proclamations. Normally he was such a vibrant and happy child, but lately he had become increasingly reserved and sad. This had a devastating effect on their family because they were so close. They often traveled together, even on business trips. They talked to one another in a respectful, loving tone, stopping periodically to let their son speak for himself.

Looking for possible reasons for the problem, Keeney wondered what else might be going on in the family. Jim related that he had been traveling more than usual on business and that none of them liked him being away so much. Whereas a therapist might start looking for the possible sources of conflict in the family, perhaps even explore the marital relationship and its accompanying difficulties, Brad had moved away from a pathological model of behavior. Rather than exploring people's problems, he preferred to move into the realm of their resources and imagination. The one reason why he agreed to work with this family in the first place was that he had been told they were game for something "different."

"I understand you came to me in the first place," Keeney said, "because you've already seen other doctors about this problem. You've tried the usual therapeutic route."

Jim and Inga both nodded. When Brad looked over to Sven, he saw that he was hunched over the drawing, coloring in some of the detail. He could see that the shape had now taken the form of an airplane.

Intrigued by the boy's activity, Brad asked him what he was making.

"It's an airplane. And Daddy is in it."

"It's flying your father on one of his trips?"

"Uh-huh. And this here is the Statue of Liberty. . ."

Keeney nodded, noticing the outline of the New York skyline with tall buildings and the statue in the harbor.

"And the plane is about to go into the statue," Sven said casually, "but at the last minute Superman saves the plane."

Throughout all their time together, Sven would continue to draw pictures with elaborate detail. Some of them would follow the narrative of the conversation; other times, they reflected the boy's own imagination.

"I see you like to draw a lot," Keeney reflected, leaving for a moment his questions about why they came to see him.

"He loves to draw," Inga agreed with a smile. "He's always drawing at home, and at school, and, really, everywhere."

"So you are a very creative family, I see," Keeney observed. "You all work in creative fields and you invest a lot of your energy together in supporting one another's creativity."

They all nodded, pleased that Keeney could recognize one of the most cherished parts of their family.

"And it's that very creativity that brought you to me." As he said these words, framing the work they were going to do together in terms of unleashing imagination, he was reminded of what he had been learning recently about the work of a shaman. He was coming to see that the work of some of his own mentors—Bateson, Whitaker, Salvador Minuchin, and Milton Erickson—was very much like the way indigenous healers work. A key feature of the healing involved large doses of playful interaction, interventions (if that's what they were) that might even seem goofy or nonsensical, but helped people to break old patterns and begin new possibilities.

While other therapists might zero in on the couple's problems, or the child's disturbance, Keeney decided to bypass all the psychological stuff and go immediately to a "beginner's mind" that is so common among the shamans with whom he had been associated. He knew this would also be a challenge for Jim and Inga, who knew quite a lot about therapy and had a lot of experience analyzing issues in Jungian terms. In fact, he was rubbing his hands together (inside his head), thinking that this family had given him a license, carte blanche, to be as creative as he wanted with them. After all, they had already tried conventional solutions without success.

THE LOSS OF IMAGINATION

If he did not intend to address the presenting problem directly, Keeney was already beginning to build a metaphor for death that would make more room for play rather than their grim view of the situation. "All things pass at one time or another," Keeney explained with a warm smile. He then locked eye contact with the boy before continuing: "You can like a toy, for instance, a favorite thing you like to play with. Can you think of such a toy you had when you were much smaller?" Sven had stopped drawing and was now giving the matter serious thought. Finally, he nodded.

"Where is that toy now? Do you still play with it every day, like you once used to?"

"No," Sven answered in his serious way. "I don't know where it is, exactly. It was one of the older Mario Brothers games that went with my Gameboy. I think it broke or something."

"Or maybe you wore it out," his father teased.

"Yeah," Sven smiled. "I did play it a lot, didn't I?"

"But now you draw instead," his father said.

Sven looked down at the pad resting on his lap, the plane drawing forgotten for the moment.

"Exactly," Brad emphasized. "You can like a toy, but after a while, it loses its hold over you. It seems to have lived its life, and then you move on. You give it away or put it in the closet."

Keeney continued to make the point that everything has a natural life, drawing Sven out to talk about whatever connection he felt to death that was associated with Christmas. He seemed definite that his own demise would take place before that day.

"What is it about Christmas," Keeney pressed, "that you associate with loss in some way?"

Jim and Inga were watching the exchange with increased interest. They made an effort always to speak to their son as an adult, rather than to talk down to him the way many parents do. They found it fascinating to watch this interaction between their son and this therapist who seemed to talk to them as if they were colleagues working on a problem together.

Sven confided that he did feel some anger, but not because of a loss; rather, it was because some of his friends were making up lies that he found upsetting.

"What sort of lies?"

Sven crossed his arms and scowled. "It's just. . . these kids, they said something that really made me mad."

"I can see that," Keeney said, then glanced up to see Inga and Jim shrug, as if they had no idea what he was angry about. "What, exactly, did they say?"

"It was about Santa Claus," Sven said shyly, looking embarrassed about how that might sound to grown-ups. He wanted to be taken seriously by adults, yet he was still very much a little boy.

"Santa Claus?"

"Yeah, they said that there really isn't one."

"There isn't a Santa Claus?"

"Yeah, they said he doesn't really do the things that he does, you know, like, bring presents and stuff."

Keeney noticed Sven's parents smiling indulgently. It was apparent that Sven still believed in Santa Claus, and his parents had not dissuaded him from believing this primary myth of childhood. His friends had stopped believing, and now it felt to Sven as if they were trying to kill a part of him as well. He felt as if he were dying. It was more like the death of his own imagination.

Here was a family, Keeney thought, that thrived on imagination. Sven, in particular, lived very much in his own imagination with his drawings and stories. Yet at eight years old, or often much younger, children lose a lot of their ability for fantasy and imaginative play. Some of this demise begins with the death of Santa Claus, when kids realize that this wonderful character is not real. This is in marked contrast to the beliefs of other cultures, where people often speak about their mythological heroes as if they are real. In Iceland, for example, the most literate and technologically advanced people on earth, half the population believes in the existence of fairies. The Icelanders reroute some of their roads to go around suspected "fairy hills." And they talk about the characters from the Icelandic sagas of a thousand years ago as if they are still alive today.

Keeney looked at this family, and rather than seeing a boy who was in trouble with pathological delusions, he saw the members struggling to preserve their own imagination. There were many other factors operating as well, as one would expect in any complex situation, but Brad homed in on this one dimension as a key feature of the situation.

"Sven," Keeney said after a pause in their conversation, "I wonder if you wouldn't mind sitting in the waiting room for a few minutes while I speak to your parents alone."

"Sure," he said, always polite.

"And while you are out there, I would like you to draw us all something special."

"A special drawing?" Sven answered with unrestrained excitement.

"Yes, a surprise of some kind. Just whatever you feel like drawing. And when you come back in, you can show us what you did and tell us a story about it."

A RITUALISTIC LOSS

Once they were resettled in their chairs after Sven left the room, Keeney started to frame an intervention for the parents. "I know of this little game that Sven might enjoy. It would be a way that you can all talk about your concerns in the family without mentioning them directly."

"You don't want us to talk about our problems directly?" Inga responded with confusion. This was a woman who had spent years in analytic therapy and had learned that the whole object of the exercise was to be able to talk about deep material in the most open, direct way possible. And now this guy was telling them not to talk about the very problems that were bothering them. Most peculiar.

"I can see my approach is puzzling you," Keeney reflected, "but remember that you came to me in the first place because you wanted to try something completely different."

Jim and Inga looked at one another for confirmation, then turned their heads toward Brad and nodded.

"Good. What I'm about to ask you to do might not make sense to you, but remember, it doesn't have to make sense." He was taking this introduction right out of the shaman's operating manual, where it was universally agreed that understanding one's problems, their origins and etiologies, did not necessarily do very much to make the symptoms go away. According to the shaman, it is appreciating and honoring mystery, not understanding, that often leads to a cure.

"You've already tried talking to Sven about his death thoughts, and it just scares you all to do so. You make yourselves crazy with fear, and you end up alarming him as well, making him think that he's crazy."

"So you really think this is all related to this Santa Claus business?" Jim interrupted skeptically.

"Let's just put that aside for the moment. It doesn't matter whether that is what is going on or not. What matters is that he is grieving some loss and he doesn't know how to deal with that. So, are you with me or not?"

They nodded their heads.

"Good. What I'd like for you to do is to ask Sven to pick three things in his room that would be okay for him to lose."

"To lose?"

"Yes, to disappear. You are to tell your son that he must select three items from his room and he is to give them to you. Then, he is to guess which of those items is not going to be returned. It is going to disappear. Whichever that item is, the one he thinks is going to be gone, he is to make a drawing of it." Keeney stopped to make sure they were following these precise instructions. With shamanic rituals of this sort, it is very important that the person follow the directions exactly as they are offered.

Again they nodded, although the couple seemed a little unsure about where this was going. They were desperate, however, so they were willing to try almost anything. And there was something about Keeney that they trusted completely. Most of all, he gave them hope.

"So," Keeney continued, "this could be a toy. It could be a sock. Or a book. Or a hat. Or anything at all. But there must be three things that he gives you. Then he is to guess which one will disappear from his life. After he makes a drawing of this one thing that he is going to lose, you are to put it in a box, wrap it up, and put it under the Christmas tree, to open at the appropriate time.

Seeing how hard they were trying to stay with him on this rather unusual therapeutic prescription, Keeney broke down a little and decided to explain his rationale.

"What you will find, if you carry through with this, using all your imagination and passion, is that Sven is going to be so interested in the game about loss that the whole atmosphere of talking about death will become playful rather than grim and heavy. Your goal is not to stop the conversation and thoughts about loss, but rather to lighten them."

Inga and Jim nodded their understanding. They got it. This made perfect sense to them, even though it wasn't really supposed to make sense. After all, the shaman's role is to make mystery rather than sense.

They collaborated on the details of how this might unfold, each of them adding another step or dimension. Jim decided it would be fun if there were some prizes depending on whether Sven guessed correctly which item would be lost. They decided they would bring their son into the negotiations, to let him name what the prize would be, as well as the consolation prize for guessing wrong. But what they decided would be really interesting, and fun, was if the consolation prize was actually the item that Sven would think was lost. That way he would learn that even when you think something is gone forever, it may still reappear.

"What we are doing here together," Keeney said in summary, "is just the beginning of the negotiations and planning. I'm sure when you have discussions at home, Sven sometimes overhears you."

They nodded.

"Okay, then, what I want you to do is to talk about this more at home, but in a way that Sven overhears you. He will hear you talk about how in spite of other children saying that Santa Claus is not real, you are so proud of him for holding on to his own beliefs. He wants to hold on to the parts of the past that he cherishes."

Inga and Jim agreed with the plan, showing both enthusiasm and a playful spirit. This actually sounded like fun to them. And they were especially relieved that they would no longer have to keep pressuring their son to keep talking about a subject that was so terrifying for all of them. Rationally, they knew their son was not going to die, but it was still the most awful thing in the world to think about, much less to dominate their lives.

A SHAMAN'S DREAM

After the family left, Keeney sat quietly in the office, processing all that had transpired. For some reason he felt haunted by a memory of his own past that had been triggered by the session. When he had been an undergraduate student in Boston, there had been a neighbor boy who greatly resembled Sven both in appearance and in manner. Like Sven, the little boy had been precocious, sweet, and creative, beloved by everyone. He had developed leukemia and died soon thereafter, leaving Brad shaken by the loss. Now he was making connections between this relationship from his past and Sven's conviction that he was dying. Although Keeney had done his best to turn the obsession into a more playful metaphor about the loss of imagination, he couldn't help but feel a certain amount of dread. While the family left their interaction with a feeling of real hope, Keeney kept dwelling on the theme of loss.

A few months passed before Keeney returned to New York to conduct his next training session, as well as to see the family again. A couple of nights before they were to meet, Keeney awoke in the middle of the night, thinking about the case and especially about Sven's feeling of impending death. After he went back to sleep, he had a dream that was so powerful he can still recall every detail.

"In the dream," Keeney recalled, "I was with my grandmother, and she was very old and in a wheelchair. I remember listening to her talking to some people in another room, and they were all giggling because my grandmother had this very charming sense of humor. She was a very sophisticated and wise woman who very much acted the role of wise elder. Yet she was also surprisingly playful and childlike. In the dream I heard her cackling and giggling and talking to some people in another room, and so I went to join them. I told her it was about her bedtime, and I wheeled her to another room. When I turned her wheelchair around, she fell over and landed on her head. I thought she was dying.

"I began to weep and hold her, and then my family ran in and they called out her name: 'Doe.' This was a name I had given her when I was little, because she reminded me of a deer. When Doe's eyes opened, I looked at her and wondered if she was okay. At that moment she was transformed into a little white puppy. At the last minute of this puppy's life, fresh milk and foam came out of its mouth."

Keeney stopped for a moment, knowing that the dream might sound strange, or at the very least be fertile ground for a Jungian or Freudian to interpret or deconstruct. But remember that Keeney approaches dreams as a shaman, not as an analyst. He is not interested in making sense of the symbols, or in analyzing the themes and exploring the content, but rather in treating the dream as another extension of reality, the way a medicine man or *curandero* would.

Keeney kept asking himself what the dream was telling him, what it was instructing him to do, rather than merely what it meant. The immediate connection he made was to the case of Sven and how this family had such incredible love for one another. Just as Brad felt such deep love and sadness at the loss of his grandmother, he could only imagine the feelings that were so pervasive in this family. After all, Brad had a son just about the same age as Sven.

What occurred to Keeney was that it seemed so vital, so imperative, that this family, and this boy, not lose their imaginations. He just couldn't shake the dream out of his head the next day, and the day afterward. Even to this day, this moment, the dream still has a powerful hold on Brad that lives within him, as real as anything he has ever experienced.

Keeney shared his dream with the family during the next meeting, just as a shaman would. After all, the shaman does not see him or herself as an expert, but as a participant in the healing process. The influencing process in shamanic healing is always mutual, and so it was in this relationship: when Brad told them about the dream, Jim sat open-mouthed.

"One thing you couldn't know," he told Keeney, "is that Sven's grandfather, my father, died on the day that he was born. When Sven was real little, he used to have these dreams about his grandfather all the time. It was spooky, almost as if a part of my father's spirit passed within him when he was born. Even today everyone in the family remarks about how much Sven looks like his grandfather."

Keeney nodded, pleased at this new connection between them. "So, how is it going? I got your note in the mail."

Soon after their last session, Jim had sent a note to Keeney that read: "I am in rough shape but Sven seems on the upswing. Your advice about metaphor and play, rather than direct reassurance, was helpful. As an analytical type myself, I can over-explain things to him. I told him a story about a boy with a happy and healthy long life who just happened to be like Sven in a number of key ways." Jim went on to talk about his job and his own struggles.

"Yeah," Jim said, looking at his wife, "Sven is doing beautifully and all. He loves the storytelling. But. . ."

Uh-oh, Keeney thought to himself, reverting to his previous role as a therapist. Here we go. They're going to talk about their marital problems. But instead he was pleasantly surprised that they wanted to talk more about rekindling their imagination through storytelling.

"Sven," Keeney directed the next question, "have you ever told your parents a bedtime story?"

Sven smiled shyly, wondering if Brad was serious or not. Seeing that it was a sincere question, he admitted that, no, he had never done so. The very idea of a child telling his parents a bedtime story sounded awfully funny to him, and he started to giggle.

"Okay, then, what I want you to do is continue creating the wonderful stories that you invent, but to pick one special one to tell your parents each night before you go to bed. Can you do that?"

Sven shrugged, as if nothing could be easier. But he looked at his parents to see if this would interest them. Of course they positively glowed. Nothing would give them greater pleasure!

THREE SWORDS AND A SHIP

After this second consultation, Keeney was not able to see the family again for some time. They kept in touch by phone, and it was during one such conversation that he learned that over the next several months the family had begun to be shaped by Sven's imagination. One theme in particular seemed to crop up in a lot of the stories: a pirate theme. Sven absorbed his parents in vivid pirate stories, tales of swashbuckling and adventure which featured himself, his father, and his mother in key roles.

Keeney was delighted with this development. The family had actually joined together in a pirate life through Sven's stories. He is rarely aware of the origins of his interventions, rituals, and therapeutic ordeals, but Keeney suggested to them that they proceed with an intervention he had in mind that would only strengthen their bonds of love and mutual support, as well as foster even greater creativity. "Are you game?" he asked Jim and Inga on the phone.

They giggled, signaling their agreement.

"I want you to designate one corner of your garage as an imaginary world. Find a place that is away from any car or equipment you keep in there. It needs to be an open space. Got that?"

Silence on the other end.

"Are you still there?" Keeney asked.

"Yeah," they both chimed in. "We're here." Then they started to laugh.

"You know I'm serious about this, right?"

"Yeah, Brad," Inga assured him, "we know you are absolutely serious. When are you ever not serious?" she kidded.

"I want you to draw a circle on the floor of the garage in that special space. It has to be exactly two feet in diameter. Got that?"

"Two feet. Check."

"This circle represents your new private universe. Just for your family. I want you to draw an ocean along the bottom of the circle. Then color it blue."

"Like with crayons or something?" Jim asked, ever pragmatic.

"No," Keeney responded, "you have to use paint. Enamel paint that won't easily wear out. After you paint in the ocean, I want you to draw some landmasses in the circle as well, all of you together. Paint those brown and green, as the mood strikes you."

Silence again.

"Are you with me?" Keeney asked.

"Indeed we are!" they both chimed in with enthusiasm. He was glad to hear they were really getting into this task. He loved working with this family because they were so playful and willing to engage him, and one another, on this imaginative level. This was the kind of work he was born to do!

"Good. Next step. You are to take some small toy boats and place them on the sea. I want you to identify one of those ships, your favorite one, as your family pirate ship. Then I want you all to take turns making up stories about your adventures together as a family of pirates. Sven has already gotten you started on this, but now you can all pick up this theme. Over the years, you will accumulate a whole history together."

"But that's not all."

"That's not all?" Jim teased. "There's more? You mean it's not enough that you want us all to stand in a corner of the garage together and pretend we're bloody pirates?"

"Exactly," Brad laughed with them. "I also want you all to create your own pirate flag. And to assign one another special pirate names. These are to be secret names that you use with only one another. Nobody else must ever hear your pirate names spoken aloud."

"Got it," Jim acknowledged. "Anything else?"

"Just that together you will negotiate troubled waters and stormy seas. You make discoveries and celebrate victories in faraway places."

It is a tribute to Keeney's infectious sense of play that the family not only complied with this directive but did so with absolute glee. Over the next months, Keeney received letters and postcards from members of the family, always beginning with "Ahoy, mate!" and ending with "Captain Jack" or their secret pirate name.

Once when Keeney was traveling in Europe with his wife, he came upon a huge pirate flag. Of course he had to buy it and send it to the family. A few weeks later he received a letter from Sven in which he had drawn a pirate flag for Brad in return. The whole background was black, and there was a white ship with two masts in the middle. The ship was literally being held up by three swords as big as the ship. Three of them, just like the family, were holding up the ship.

Over the years, Keeney continued to exchange letters with the family. One card that he received recently from them says: "Bon Voyage, Travelers! The card depicts a shaman awaiting the arrival of his esteemed family." The card has a picture of an old shipyard.

FIGURE 9.1

ENGAGING WITH IMAGINATION

The family has since moved to Europe, where both father and mother have new careers in related and prospering fields. Sven's interests have moved to theater and the arts, not surprisingly.

As for Keeney, he continues to experience more and more effects from his relationship with Sven and his family. This was a turning point in his work, and his life, to trust not only his shamanic instincts, but also the power of dreams. "They helped me to engage with my own fantasy," Keeney related. "When I talked to them, I felt as much like a pirate as they did. I am an honorary member of their family. I have my own pirate flag now."

Keeney stopped for a moment in the telling of the story. It is two days before Christmas, and he is about to leave to visit his family in Kansas City. He is about to visit the home of his grandmother. He is still filled with awe by the power of the dream, as well as the power of imagination to heal.

"It doesn't really matter what I did with this family," Keeney explained. "When you have imaginative people, and you can get their creativity flowing, whatever you do with them is going to end up with something better."

Chapter 10

JOHN GRAY
Little Things Make a Big Difference

When working with couples, it is difficult to avoid personalizing the sorts of conflicts that frequently arise and asking oneself how such struggles apply to one's own primary relationship. During the time when Gray first published his ideas behind "Mars and Venus," he was working with a couple who presented issues that seemed quite familiar to him in his own marriage.

HIRE SOMEONE

Nathan was a very successful and influential businessman who was used to solving problems decisively. Whenever he could not resolve a problem on his own, his first impulse was to rely on one of his able staff or consultants to fix things. Thus, he found himself, and his wife, talking to John Gray about their marriage difficulties.

Nathan and his wife, Marilyn, had each presented their side of things. Marilyn felt neglected in the relationship. Because her husband traveled so much for business, she felt abandoned and isolated, left to manage a complex household on her own. Whenever something went wrong with one of the children, or with the house, she was increasingly feeling panicked to keep things under control.

"I keep telling you to hire someone," Nathan interrupted during his wife's tearful complaints.

Marilyn just looked at him, as if he were indeed an alien from Mars.

"Hire someone?" Gray pressed Nathan.

"Yeah. I keep telling her that she needs more help around the house. She could afford to hire a nanny. Hell, she could hire three nannies if she wanted to!"

"That's not it. . .," Marilyn tried to explain, but then dissolved into tears again.

"What is it, then?" Nathan responded, clearly exasperated by a discussion that they had had many times before. "I've told you before, we can afford to hire anyone you want to help out. You know I've got to be away a lot. How else could we afford to pay all the damn bills?"

"You don't understand," Marilyn said in a voice that could barely be heard.

"Obviously, I don't."

Both of them turned to Gray, expecting him to act as a referee. But at this point John was working very hard to remain with them in the moment. It was very difficult for him to stay focused—for it was the voice of his own wife, Bonnie, that he heard coming out of Marilyn's mouth.

A PARALLEL PROCESS

Once the session ended, Gray easily reflected on his own marriage. Without too much deep thought, he realized that Marilyn and Nathan had been having the same conflict that he and his own wife had been having for years. Like this prominent businessman, Gray had been enjoying professional and financial success beyond his wildest dreams. For the first time in his life he found that he could buy anything he wanted, and especially to hire someone to do anything that he didn't want to do or didn't have time to do.

Whenever Bonnie complained to John about stuff that needed to be done around the house, John's immediate response was to think, "Why not hire someone?" Occasionally he would verbalize this thought, only to meet her resistance.

"I don't want to hire someone," Bonnie would reply. "I want you to do it."

"But why?" John would counter. "This just isn't logical. We can afford to hire someone to fix things around here, to cook and clean, to work in the garden, to do anything you want. If you don't like doing these things, we can afford to get help." Gray had worked so hard to reach this point in his life, where things could become easier and more comfortable. Just like his client Nathan, he couldn't figure out what the big deal was to simply delegate certain responsibilities to others.

Clearly, Gray was identifying strongly with the husband in this relationship. Yet he also recognized that Nathan and Marilyn were not understanding, or even hearing, one another. Every time she would complain to her husband about something going on, Nathan's response was simply to tell her to "hire someone."

What Marilyn wanted most was some meaningful connection with Nathan whereby he understood and acknowledged the stress she was experiencing. In truth, instead of his solutions, what she wanted most was her husband's empathy and compassion. But what she felt instead was his disdain, as if she were a child who needed more and more babysitters.

It was while observing this couple in action that Gray realized there was a parallel process in his own marriage. He had finally achieved one of his life goals, which was to free himself of all the day-to-day activities that would take time away from his work. He recognized in Nathan a familiar pattern of trying to solve any and all problems by hiring someone else to take care of them.

"Could you pick up the kids?" Bonnie might ask Gray, to which he'd respond, "Why not have our limo driver do that?"

"Would you help me clean up the dishes?" Again, Gray's response: "Why don't we hire a housekeeper to do this?"

Gray had grown up in a family of seven kids; each day of the week, one of them was in charge of washing all the dishes and pots. It was an enormous task that would take hours to complete. As a child, Gray vowed to himself that one day he would be able to avoid such chores. And now that he was finally able to afford to pay someone else to do the things he resented doing, Bonnie was giving him grief about that.

Of course, Bonnie, like Marilyn, was just saying to her husband that she wanted him more actively involved in their family life. Recognizing this pattern in Nathan's behavior helped John apply it to his own life. Soon after this session he began speaking to Bonnie in new ways, letting her know that he heard what she was saying—that she wanted more collaboration and sharing in their relationship.

Once she felt heard, Bonnie was able to tell John more about the image of a home that she wanted to create with him. "Yes, you make money, and more than enough to hire people to do things for us. I am very grateful for the freedom it brings us, and I also like creating a home with you."

Gray now heard Bonnie loud and clear. This insight led him to discover and clarify one of the main themes from *Men Are from Mars, Women Are from Venus*: When women are upset and sharing their complaints, they don't necessarily want men to fix their problems. They want a compassionate listener who makes an effort to understand their experience. And the last thing in the world they want is for the man to hire someone else to fix the problem!

LITTLE THINGS

Like Gray's wife, Marilyn wanted Nathan to be a partner in their relationship, not a chief executive officer. It was one thing to see this pattern in his clients' marriage, but a life-changing experience for Gray to see it in his own. And based on this small sample of two, he began to expand his ideas about gender differences in communication and test them out with hundreds of other couples.

"I was able to relax more after this," Gray explained. "I realized the process that we are going through is not necessarily always seeking a solution right away, but creating room for people to express their feelings about issues and work them out to the point that they don't seem as big as they were in the beginning."

This, Gray believed, is what leads to lasting and loving relationships in which partners help one another in small and meaningful ways. Every day.

"As a man I typically thought my job was to help in big ways, which was to achieve great financial affluence and provide for my family. Yet in accomplishing this, I created a greater gulf between my wife and me. My life outside was consuming me. I had filled our lives with other people to do the things we used to do together."

Nathan and Marilyn helped Gray to realize the unfulfilled needs of his wife and his children. They didn't want more money, or more hired help; they wanted more of his active involvement in their daily lives. This included doing the "little" things like driving the children around, helping them with their homework, and doing chores around the house. It was these same small things that helped the Grays to develop a more intimate household, one with a few less things but a lot more love and support.

This became a hallmark of Gray's "Mars and Venus" approach—the little things make a big difference.

LEARNING TO LISTEN

Through talking to Nathan and Marilyn, Gray was able to make huge strides in his own marriage. As so often happens when we allow the insights from our work to penetrate our personal lives, he was also able to help make a breakthrough in this couple's relationship. Gray found that the counseling took on a more engaged energy because he was applying the same lessons to his own life that he was teaching to his clients.

During subsequent sessions Marilyn made the connection between the abandonment she was feeling in her marriage and the same sorts of feelings she felt from her father. In fact, she had felt depressed, lonely, and neglected most of her life. When her father died, and literally left her alone to take care of herself and her mother, Marilyn felt saddled with the responsibility that she would always have to take care of things on her own; she didn't know how to ask for help.

Gray tried to help Nathan to hear what his wife was saying, and to respond with compassion. This was tough going, however, since Nathan had a very different life history that was steeped in self-reliance. He kept insisting, "Look, if you can't do things on your own, or you don't want to, we can afford to hire anyone you want to do it for you."

"You mean, for us," Marilyn said, showing more assertiveness.

"Yes," he said impatiently. "That's what I meant."

"But do you hear the difference?" Gray pointed out. "Marilyn has just made a key point."

Nathan sensed that in Gray he had an ally, someone who understood, if not agreed with, his perspective. So, more often than not, he was willing to listen to his counselor, who was able to hold and honor both of their realities without taking sides.

Over time, Nathan began to understand the nature of his wife's core wounds, and how his own behavior exacerbated her pain. By this time, they had hired a household staff of three, plus a chief of staff just to manage their responsibilities. Yet none of this supposed help was making much difference: they may have had a well-ordered, clean household, but Marilyn was still feeling out of control.

Having just dealt with this same problem within his own family, Gray found that he could be very persuasive in encouraging Nathan to examine some alternative ways of dealing with his family problems other than hiring more staff to fix them. In the counseling as well, Gray altered his approach to stop trying to solve their problem (a reenactment of just what was going on at home), and instead concentrated on more empathic listening. They came to realize that this was not about Marilyn being able to run her household and life, but rather that she needed more reassurance and emotional support.

"These kinds of lessons really stick with you over time," Gray reflected. It is not like this was a problem that was solved once and for all, but rather one that he continues to work with and remind himself about the most important priorities. There are still times when he is inclined to offer a quick fix to his wife or children when they encounter difficulties, but more and more he has learned to take the time to ask more questions and let them discover things for themselves.

"What helps my wife the most," Gray concluded, "is the same thing that helps most anyone—a partner who really listens."

Chapter 11

STEVEN LANKTON
Clients Tune Me Up

In his characteristically diligent manner, Lankton had done considerable reflection and preparation prior to our interview. He had organized his thoughts according to several different kinds of changes he had experienced as a result of memorable therapeutic relationships.

CONTINUAL REMINDERS

First, there are incidents that Lankton calls "continual reminder incidents." These take place when therapists are already working on some area of their lives and a client comes in who reminds them of this unfinished business. During the pep talks that we give to people in these circumstances, we sometimes recognize that we are speaking to ourselves as much as to them. (John Gray's chapter is a clear example of that.)

Lankton has a number of such sessions each month, those times when he realizes that he is giving himself the same motivational speech he is directing to others. This occurs frequently, for example, with clients who have suffered terribly in their lives and find it difficult to retrieve any feelings of joy and success. Under these circumstances, Lankton may try to remind them that it is okay to feel good about some things that have occurred, no matter what else the person has survived. Everyone needs continual reminders to follow through on important things, such as taking constructive risks, or rising above a quarrel with your partner and taking the initiative to apologize first.

DEEPER CLARITY

There are times when a therapist finds some sort of major insight in his or her own life as a result of sitting with a particular client. Lankton recalls working with a nun who had some serious problems growing up. Jane's mother was quite ill when Jane was young, and so she continually received the message that anything she did or wanted for herself was a burden that might kill her mother. When Jane's mother grew worse and worse, eventually dying of a degenerative disease, Jane felt responsible, and ever since had never really allowed herself to give herself much pleasure in anything.

At the time she had consulted Lankton, Jane had accomplished a major success in her life, writing a book that had been a six-year labor. Yet when she came into the session to report the completion of this life's work, she showed no joy.

"How did you celebrate your accomplishment?" Lankton asked.

Jane looked absolutely surprised by the question.

"You haven't planned a celebration?" he asked again.

Jane shook her head in embarrassment.

"Not even cupcakes with your friends?"

Lankton knew that Jane lived in a home with a few other nuns, cloistered and supportive of each other. In fact, they had pooled their funds to pay for Jane's therapy.

"Well, then, that's what we're going to work on today," Lankton announced. "We are going to talk about the feeling of success that comes with accomplishing such a major achievement."

Knowing how difficult this was going to be for a woman who never allowed herself to celebrate anything, Lankton decided to try hypnosis to reduce her inhibition. He asked her to close her eyes and to relax, and then induced a state of peace and relaxation in which she might experience some small joy.

"So, Jane, would you say that you are feeling peace and joy in your whole body?"

Jane nodded.

"Are you feeling them in your heart?"

Nod.

"Are you feeling them in your chest and your limbs?"

"Yes."

"Are you feeling them in your mind?"

"Uh-huh."

"Would you say that the joy comes from the Holy Spirit?" He was capitalizing on her strong religious and spiritual commitment as one source for her joy.

Jane signaled her agreement, nodding her head very decisively. Until this point her affirmatives had been somewhat tentative.

"So, then, right this moment you are feeling the Holy Spirit?"

Again she nodded emphatically.

"So this feeling that you are having some contact with the Holy Spirit isn't just in your head, but it is in your body. And it is not just in your body, but it is in your mind. And most of all, it's in your heart."

Realizing where her therapist was going with this, even in a trance state Jane's head nods slowed a little, becoming cautious again.

"Your entire person is having a personal relationship with the Holy Spirit."

Jane sat still, then moved her chin up and down just a little.

In her frame of reference, everything that Lankton had said was correct. He was slowly securing her consent that it was okay with the Holy Spirit, with her most cherished foundation, to experience joy. It was almost as if he could read her mind, hear her thinking: "Holy cats, that is true. Why have I not been doing this my whole life?"

This experience was not very profound only for Jane; ever since then, Lankton has applied this to his own life. "This whole thing was cocreated," he said. "It wouldn't have come to me if it were not for her being a nun sitting there with those particular circumstances. It forever changed the way I think about my relationship with the universal, all-around-us Holy Spirit."

INTIMACY

Doing therapy requires a level of intimacy between all the participants that involves a certain level of risk. Both therapist and client open themselves up to be impacted and influenced by the other, even if the professional is not doing so for self-indulgent motives.

Lisa was profoundly obese—just a little over five feet tall and weighing more than 300 pounds. During the course of reconstructing her childhood, she admitted that she had been sexually abused by her brother, a family secret that had been maintained to that day.

Lisa described her childhood home, including the configuration of her bedroom, which was an entry point for all the other kids' rooms. They spent time building a re-creation of the house out of cardboard, showing all the entrances and vulnerable points through which others had access to her room at night. Lisa became so absorbed in the activity that she painted and furnished the house just as it had been when she was growing up. Then she made clay figures of each family member and placed them in the house. Lankton noted that all the figures were gray except the brother who abused her—he was made of black clay.

Lisa brought the completed house to a session and placed it on the floor between them. She began to cry as she described all the goings-on in the house at night, especially as she was attacked in the middle of the night.

Lankton sat on the floor across from her, with the house between them. "So, what are you going to do with the house?"

First thing, she reached inside and grabbed the black figure of her brother. All of a sudden, Lisa started screeching. She pulled the clay model of her brother apart and began throwing the pieces around the office. Then she started moaning and jerking to the point that Lankton became a little frightened, mostly because he didn't know what was going on.

Lisa had never expressed a moment of anger in her life, but now she stood up and started stamping on the cardboard house with her sizable bulk, destroying and smashing the structure and everything inside of it that she had so carefully constructed. Lankton watched her cautiously, not really sure if this was therapeutic catharsis or whether she had gone over the edge.

Although he wasn't sure what was happening, Lankton kept calm. He knew there was no sense in interrupting Lisa, or interpreting anything, or explaining anything. This was just pure, raw, emotional energy coming out after a lifetime of keeping it all inside her large frame. She was literally exploding.

After several minutes of watching, Lankton took her hand for support and noticed she was running out of energy. He decided to continue waiting for her to speak.

"I don't know what's happening," Lisa said finally. She looked scared of the power that she had just expressed.

"You look really angry to me," Lankton offered, his heart pounding. "It is your anger. You are just expressing your anger. Finally."

That didn't begin to cover the complexity and depth of what was going on, but truthfully, both of them were confused and at a loss for words. It was as if they were in this together, uncertain and scared, but they would hold hands and come out of it together somehow.

This session was not about smart therapeutic moves or clever interventions; it was about just being with Lisa during a very intimate, risky, scary time. "It was a totally humbling experience," Lankton recalled. "There was no model to follow about what to do. I just stayed with her, and in doing so, I felt like I matured a little bit more as a human being."

Even now, Lankton seems to be at a loss to describe what happened—he says only that as a result of this intimate moment in the relationship, both of them changed.

STAGE FRIGHT

Sometimes the changes we undergo occur as a result of pushing ourselves to take on new challenges. It is not so much that the client changed us, as that we changed ourselves by pushing ourselves in new ways and venturing into the unknown. When these changes last, we are able to apply what we learned about doing therapy to other areas of our lives as well.

Over 20 years ago, Lankton was doing a demonstration of pain control in front of an audience of 1,800 professionals. As if this were not daunting enough, there were three cameras recording every moment. He was assigned the task of putting a volunteer client into a hypnotic trance and helping her get rid of the pain. This was someone who had been experiencing chronic pain for some years.

As they were attaching the microphone, Lankton started to feel a sense of panic. "Oh, man, what am I doing? What if I can't do this? What if she doesn't go into a trance? What if I can't make the pain go away?"

While taking a few moments to calm down, Lankton reminded himself that he doesn't hypnotize people or take away their pain; they do these things to themselves. Furthermore, he reminded himself that he knew how to use language tools, operations of hypnosis, and the pain control protocol that he taught—and that these things were sufficient for the client to accomplish the work. The best he could do was to try and relax (self-hypnotizing himself), and do what he knew to do. After a few moments, and this awareness, he found that he no longer felt anxiety, just a healthy excitement that made him feel more alert and energized. It was an epiphany for him.

Performance anxiety can stop people from doing so many things that they might like to do or want to try. In this case, a turning point in Lankton's life—attempting one of the most anxiety-provoking situations he could imagine (up on stage in front of hundreds)—he found that he could stay in reasonable control.

To this day, he still uses what he learned from that experience to push himself to do things that are difficult for him. The very week that we interviewed him, Lankton's partner, Dr. Donaghy, had a brother visiting for the first time since they had moved to Phoenix. They made plans to meet for pizza quite a way from their home.

"Now," Lankton explained, "there are pizza places that are one mile from me, but this pizza place is more than 45 minutes away. Driving there and back, I could have been in Sedona. I didn't really want to go 45 minutes to have a pizza, but this was the only way to meet him, and that is what my partner wanted to do. It was a good idea, but I wouldn't have done it, just because of the hassle involved in driving there, the anxiety of navigating in another town at night, and meeting a stranger. I know these are silly little excuses that historically were a part of my childhood, and still will creep in and stop me from doing things sometimes. It is easier to say I don't want to do something, but really what is behind it is a little bit of anxiety."

Lankton was reminded of what he would say to a client who used a similar excuse: "Remember why you are with this person. She enriches your life. Sometimes you do things you don't want to do in order to make her happy. And sometimes this leads to new adventures and experiences to which you would not ordinarily be open."

In this case, Lankton and Donaghy had a wonderful evening, got lost on the way back, but found a really remarkable place to explore. Both the experience on stage and the one finding the pizza joint were reminders that good things could happen if he challenged himself to get out of his comfort zone. This message, of course, is exactly what we all try to teach our clients.

STICK A TOE IN

In order to take constructive risks like those previously described, anxiety must be kept within manageable limits. This is another theme that Lankton has learned from several clients that has enabled him to help others, and himself, conquer long-standing fears.

One such strategy involves asking people to dissociate the cognitive from the emotional aspects of some of their earlier difficulties. Often such individuals deny that there is even emotional distress. A few examples come to mind for Lankton.

"There was this one client who, when he was five years old, urinated on the floor in front of company. As a punishment, his mother made him lap up the urine on the floor with his tongue, all in front of the guests. Yet when he tells this story, he sounds like a newscaster reporting someone else's life. No emotion whatsoever.

"There was another client who was 11 years old when he got his first bike, a 10-speed bought for him by his stepfather. He was sort of enchanted by the derailleurs and was looking at them when he bashed into a car in the cul-de-sac in his first hour of having this bike. His stepfather punished him by taking the bike away for an entire year, telling him he was too incompetent to have one."

In both cases it is not surprising that these boys grew up to be men who were rather emotionally restricted. The second guy ended up as a workaholic with huge anxieties related to flying, and no close relationships. Although there seemed to be an obvious connection between the independence associated with having a bike as a child, and flying as an adult, the guy denied it.

Lankton was thinking that he couldn't tell this client to start any communication with his "inner child" in any way, or he'd bolt from the session; the usefulness of having any feelings was too far beyond this client's belief system. Lankton expected the client would strongly protest the inappropriateness of such an endeavor. He imagined he would get a reply from the client like the one in the Eagles song, "Get Over It," that goes something like: "I'd like to find his inner child and kick his little ass." In other words, the client had much disdain for his emotional self.

Instead, Lankton recalled that sometimes the best way to handle scary things is not by jumping headfirst into the water but by a little dissociation that allows one to just stick a toe in. As much as possible, he tries to practice this in his own life.

Lankton may now appear to be the model of competence and self-confidence, but this has been a long battle for him. Throughout much of his early life, Steve was both timid and anxious. "I wouldn't raise my hand in class to ask a question. Basically I didn't think I could do much of anything."

For much of his life Lankton has tried to conquer his fears and overcome his reluctance to take on new things. He wrote his first book just to see if he could do it. He overcame chronic shyness and learned to be more assertive. And, as a therapist, he has learned to trust himself to let go of structure and to work more intuitively, creatively, and improvisationally.

FOREVER TRANSFORMED

Among all those clients whom a therapist sees in a lifetime—thousands, perhaps—there are some who affect us in ways that seem miraculous. The nature of their changes seems so dramatic and profound that it is as if we get sucked into the vortex and go along for the ride. If we think about them, we can easily become moved to tears just remembering some of these relationships. For Lankton, there is one client who comes immediately to mind.

Kyle came to see Lankton because of problems with chronic pain. He owned a pawnshop he had just purchased. One day, a customer came in to buy a handgun, and Kyle began the paperwork necessary for approval. A few days later, the application came back denied, because this customer had a restraining order against him (requested by his mother) because of a propensity toward violence. At this point, however, all Kyle knew was that the application was denied. He had no choice but to pass along the news to his disappointed customer when he returned two days later. The customer left angry.

Later that day, the customer returned to the shop. Kyle was doing some paperwork when the guy walked up to him and stood waiting until he had Kyle's attention. Kyle looked up with some alarm, seeing this man standing so close with a weird expression on his face and one arm behind his back. Before Kyle could react, the man pulled out a Samurai sword that he had been hiding behind his back and proceeded to stick it right through Kyle's chest. Kyle was knocked to the ground by the force just as the man withdrew the sword and prepared to stick him again.

Kyle tried to scuttle away, throwing things at his attacker. All the while the swordsman advanced, and stuck him again and again. Kyle made a mad dash for safety, bleeding from his wounds. He had a handgun stashed in his office, behind a steel door, and tried to get to it before the guy could skewer him again. Finally, he got to the door, slammed it shut, and paused to catch his breath. He was leaning on the door when the sword came through the door! Kyle thought it was like a horror movie now. He ran to the desk. Stumbling, he knocked the computer off of it; he had lost a lot of blood and was in shock. And then, to his dismay, he found the handgun there had been disassembled for cleaning.

Now the attacker was in the room, and Kyle's mind raced to think what he could do next. Too late. The man stabbed him again, this time sticking him all the way through his body at waist level from his left side to his right.

Kyle looked down to see this huge sword protruding from his side. With no other option, he grabbed the sword with his left hand and held on to it, trying to stop the crazy man from withdrawing it. He was pretty sure he was dying, but he wouldn't give up. The attacker maneuvered Kyle around the room, pushing on the sword that Kyle held tightly.

Finally, Kyle hit the wall near the door, When he did, he felt the small handgun in his right pocket. With a last burst of energy, he retrieved a small caliber pistol that was little more than a toy. Knowing that the .22 pistol wouldn't do much damage unless he hit a vulnerable spot, he aimed at the man's head and put four bullets into his left eye. The man fell back, pulling the sword with him, and died.

Kyle managed to call 911 for help before he passed out. He was taken to the hospital and recovered from his multiple wounds. Obviously, he suffered some trauma and considerable pain afterward, but he resumed his previous life running the pawnshop. His only real problem was the constant pain from his wounds and the traumatic memory of the attacker's death. Within six weeks he journeyed to see Lankton.

Lankton used hypnosis and some of his pain control methods, which worked rather quickly to relieve the discomfort. Kyle was absolutely stunned by the fast and dramatic results, and brought up a deeper topic than the sword wounds. He had always felt he could do no more with his life than run a pawnshop. You could say that he felt he was a loser and had very low self-esteem. Lankton related the story of the nun at one point, and helped Kyle retrieve strong feelings of joy in living, some of which Kyle came to attribute to the benevolence of the Holy Spirit, as the nun had done years before.

As the session ended, Kyle felt that he had undergone a profound religious experience that day, one that not only diminished his pain but also gave him a sense of joy and peace. He gained an appreciation for his own life. He decided, then and there, that he wanted to do something more with his life than just own and run a pawnshop. He felt a deeper sense of purpose and committed himself to giving back more to others as a result of his near-death experience.

Kyle was so grateful to Lankton for this spiritual transformation that he began hugging and thanking him profusely. Lankton stood there, totally surprised by what he had witnessed and shared with this man. He knew well the power of therapy to change people in relatively short periods of time, but something amazing had happened during this session—not just for Kyle, but for himself as well.

Chapter 12

DAVID E. SCHARFF
The Patient Who Taught Me to Be a Therapist

It is often the first of anything that sticks in our memories. Our first friend. First love. And for therapists, the first client.

For David Scharff, his very first patient as a psychiatric resident was a 14-year-old girl who looked, in the parlance of the medical profession, much "older than her stated age." Judy was a well-built teenager— voluptuous, in fact—who alternated in her demeanor between being churlish and seductive. If this young doctor didn't respond to her anger, she would try using her feminine charms. Although chronologically young, she was not inexperienced in the sexual arena; she had a history, which she flaunted, of incest with her older brother, and more recently she bragged of having seduced several boys "to see if she had any sexual feeling." On the inpatient unit, she alternated between acting seductively toward staff and enraging them. She was also prone to breaking windows at will, threatening suicide when she didn't get her way, and scratching her wrists with sharp objects. She was diagnosed with what was then a new category: borderline personality disorder.

Scharff learned that Judy had been brought to the hospital soon after she attempted suicide by swallowing a hundred aspirins. This had capped off a chaotic developmental story. Judy's father had died when she was five. Her mother was depressed and apparently neglected the children, at least until she remarried two years later, but even then Judy and her three siblings were pretty much left to take care of themselves. The neglect in the family seemed to have been largely responsible for the onset of an incestuous relationship with her two-year-older brother that began when she was nine years old. Judy grew up depressed and desperate for love and attention. She related to others mostly as objects for manipulation. Soon after admission to the ward on which Scharff was training, she was already wreaking havoc.

FAILURE

Since this was Scharff's first case, he was just learning to do therapy. Like many who have suffered early deprivation and turmoil, Judy had a keen sense of her therapist's vulnerability, and used all her tricks to try and seduce him, just as she had the boys with whom she had had sex. Scharff tried to distance himself as best he could, avoiding any direct engagement with Judy over her sexualized behavior. Finally, one day she blurted out, "Doctor, I want to have your baby!"

"Look, Judy, that's just not going to happen."

"Why not?" she demanded, stamping her foot, used to getting what she wanted.

"Because. . ."

Before Scharff could answer, Judy stormed out of the room. On her way back to the ward, she put her fist through a window. It helped Scharff when a senior child psychiatrist, acting as consultant, was unfazed by the incident and assured him that Judy would give him another chance.

For many weeks on that ward, Judy was Scharff's only case. This was a time, especially within the Harvard medical system, when relatively few patients were admitted into the program because those who were already there stayed for months or even years. Although it seemed like a luxury to work primarily with only one patient, it meant that all of Scharff's investment and learning were unhelpfully tied up in one person. When things were going well in the treatment, Scharff felt on top of the world, that he really would someday become a competent therapist. But at other times, when Judy played games, tested limits, acted out, or regressed, Scharff began to question whether he had made the right career choice. Maybe he would be better off as a surgeon!

Judy continued acting out during the ensuing months, testing Scharff's patience, and his fledgling therapeutic skills and boundary-setting, in almost every way imaginable. At one point, he suggested to the hospital director that perhaps she would be a good candidate for electroconvulsive shock therapy to break up all her fury and depression.

The supervisor laughed. "Sure, you might try that," he said. "But only if you apply the electrodes to her rear end."

Since that didn't seem to be a viable option, Scharff had no choice but to stick with the current plan and hope that Judy's more dramatic symptoms would run their course and she might settle down. But the acting up continued, and the staff eventually had quite enough of her disruptive behavior on the ward. They pressured Scharff to give her an ultimatum: either she abided by the rules and behaved herself, or she would be discharged from the unit. Judy did try to comply, but ultimately she broke another window. She was immediately transferred to another hospital that provided only custodial care rather than any psychotherapy.

While a number of the other staff members felt considerable relief with Judy gone, Scharff felt mostly regret and hopelessness. Although by now he had other patients, Judy had been his first, and he had failed her miserably.

Judy hated her new, restrictive environment, so much that she stopped the borderline behavior that had been so self-destructive and disruptive to others. Her reformed behavior earned a quick discharge. She resumed high school and returned to Scharff for outpatient therapy. It would seem that he was going to have that second chance to redeem himself.

SECOND CHANCE

Scharff recalls, in retrospect, that he had been not only young and inexperienced, but also painfully naïve. He had begun following his interest in psychoanalysis during medical school, and had done considerable reading, most of it theoretical. In his wildest imagination he had never dreamed that there could be someone so disturbed, and so disturbing to others. Yet as challenging as this case was, Scharff was determined that he was going to help this young woman who had suffered so much. He wanted to save her, and the ethic in the hospital in which he was training was that patients stayed with their doctors like glue. There was no getting away from her.

Scharff was married at the time, with two young children. He was just beginning to form a sense of himself as a doctor, as a professional. Many of his friends and colleagues had gone on to residencies in surgery and medicine where, he felt, they were actually curing people through decisive action or providing medications that worked like silver bullets. As much as Scharff enjoyed his work in psychiatry, he still felt helpless and frustrated that there was so little he could do for patients like Judy. Consultation with supervisors wasn't helping much. At this time, there were few medications that were helpful with cases like this—and we now know that the benefits of medication for such patients are limited, helping primarily in the short run with brief psychotic or severe depressive episodes. Yet he stumbled along with Judy, trying everything he could to help stabilize her.

Now an outpatient, Judy's previous volatile unpredictability gave way to a mostly inhibited picture: no boyfriends, no drama. Although she continued to be subtly seductive and tried to sexualize their relationship emotionally, the drama of the hospital period never returned. Her moods from session to session, or sometimes from minute to minute, changed dramatically, but she kept her outside life going smoothly at school and in her family.

PATIENT AS TEACHER

Throughout the three years of his psychiatric residency, Scharff continued to see Judy several times per week. In spite of the supervision he was getting, and periodic consultations with experts, he felt clueless much of the time about where things were going. But Judy was getting better. The alliance between them improved, and gradually they seemed to be on the same wavelength about her growth and development.

A patient like Judy can be humbling at any stage of one's career, but at the very beginning, this case had driven Scharff (and the hospital staff) to distraction. He had felt confused, frustrated, helpless, and humiliated. Throughout, he continued to like Judy enormously and to want to protect her from the world, and especially from his colleagues, who often responded to her acting out with something less than the compassion he felt for her (in what he later felt was an overidentification). Now the work of psychotherapy had settled down to a calmer mode, and in this two-year phase of examination of her past story and consideration of her progress as a teen, things went pretty smoothly. Scharff became aware of how much gratitude he felt to Judy. "Everything that I learned about doing therapy, I learned from her," Scharff admitted. "In the course of our first year together, I learned more than I could ever read in books about the nature of transference and countertransference. I learned about how to set and enforce boundaries, how to sit with, and hold, volatile energy and turmoil. More than anyone else I have ever seen before—or since—Judy taught me what it is like to live inside someone else's skin. Then as things calmed down and we continued to work together, I learned about the nature of growth in therapy, about how the give-and-take over time can intertwine with development outside the therapy office. Working with her was as transformative for me professionally as it was for her personally."

FAMILY THERAPY

Ever since Scharff was in medical school, he had been interested in family therapy and had been doing a lot of reading about this new approach to therapy. It seemed to him that Judy's case might be perfect to try out this untested modality. Initially the plan was that he would see Judy with her parents, but eventually her younger brothers were included as well, because the family brought one of her brothers, Bob, aged 12, for help with depression and failing school performance. So for the last year of therapy, Scharff teamed up with the parents' therapist, the ward social worker, to conduct family therapy.

At first Judy had been reluctant to allow her family into the therapeutic space, fearing it would mean less attention for her. It quickly developed, however, that Judy became a kind of cotherapist in their sessions. Because she was already so experienced in therapy, as well as quite sensitive interpersonally, Judy was often able to offer thoughtful interpretations during sessions and to act as a helpful ally in the process.

The family drove over an hour each week for sessions. One session was devoted to Judy and a second included the whole family. Throughout this, Judy (and now the family) continued to teach Scharff valuable lessons that have stuck with him until this day. During one meeting with Judy, for instance, Scharff had kept the phone turned on, rationalizing that he was waiting for an important call. Judy became furious that he would dare interrupt her session by answering the phone when it rang. While his hand was poised over the receiver, Judy piercingly told him how rude and disrespectful he was being. He decided to let the call go. And ever since then he has not permitted such interruptions. This lesson, which should be taught to all therapists by supervisors, was especially powerful to Scharff because he learned it from a patient.

THE FLOWER

Judy's stepfather was somewhat older than her mother, a dry and serious sort of fellow. With the mother prone to bouts of depression, this was not exactly a couple that was easy to engage. Fortunately, Judy and her siblings were playful with one another during sessions, teasing in a good-natured way. Judy's 13-year-old sister Deb, and the younger brother, Bob, aged 12, who had been depressed, were spending a lot of time together. In one session they discussed feeling good about their closer relationship. Judy worried that the feelings they had for one another might develop into an incestuous relationship that could be a reenactment of what happened between her and the older brother who had molested her. She led the family in examining the difference between the situation then and the improvements that pertained now.

While she was talking, her six-year-old brother Sam was drawing a picture. When Scharff looked down, he noticed that it was a picture of a tulip with a dragonfly and a butterfly apparently circling around it. There were smaller flowers next to the larger flower that dominated the picture. The sun beamed overhead. The drawing was skillfully rendered, foreshadowing Sam's eventual career as an artist.

FIGURE 12.1

"Tell me about the picture, Sam," Scharff said.

"Can't you see?" said Sam. "The tulip is Deb, my sister."

"You're right," Scharff answered with a smile. "Now I see it. What about the rest?"

"Well, the butterfly is me. And the other thing. . ."

"It looks like a dragonfly," Judy said.

"Yeah. I guess," Sam answered with a shrug. "That's Bob."

"What about the rest of the picture?" Scharff probed.

"The tulip might also be Mommy, and the other flowers are the rest of us," Sam explained patiently. "And the sun is Dad." (Sam was the only child of the second marriage.)

The boy's image then led the family to talk about the feelings of the boys for their mother and for Deb, the kinds of feelings that had been out of control when Judy was younger, but now could be understood as natural and much less threatening. Now they could have such feelings and still protect one another. Sam and Bob could fly around the way the insects were circling the flowers, but there was Dad as the sun to keep an eye on things from overhead. At this, the children began to sing the Beatles' song "Hey Jude," coming together in harmony on the lines about taking a sad song and making it better. They noticed that this was exactly what they were doing in family therapy, and then they proceeded to have an open conversation with one another about the past, about the inappropriate things that occurred as a result of so little adult supervision, and about the difference in the family now.

Scharff watched the interactions with awe. He was amazed at the healing power of family support harnessed in this way. Before this session he had not thought it possible that they could talk so honestly, and even more, so creatively, about family secrets. In a way, Scharff felt envious that the family could do therapeutic work that he had been unable to initiate on his own. He felt it wasn't absolutely clear that he was needed. Later he would learn to value such times when a patient or family does the work on their own, held by the attitude of the therapist and the structure of the therapy.

At this time, Scharff was undergoing his own psychoanalysis, both as a patient and as a prelude to becoming an analytic trainee. His own analyst was almost completely silent in their sessions, but now Scharff could see the value of becoming more active. He was beginning to realize that even within the analytic orthodoxy, many different styles were possible. Judy was helping him begin to go beyond his own experience of analysis.

ENDING

Three years after their relationship began, the sessions with Judy and her family ended because Scharff was moving from Boston. By this time, Judy had graduated from high school and had been admitted to college. Although not finished with therapy, she was doing quite well.

Scharff recalls a moving experience from one of their last individual sessions.

"You know the show *Carousel*, about a no-account carnival barker who gets his girlfriend pregnant? They are going to get married, and then the guy realizes he is going to have a child, so he sings the song, "My Boy Bill." It turns out he has a daughter. He dies before she is born, but in the show he gets to come back and see her as an adolescent. I was sitting with Judy when "My Boy Bill" came unbidden through my head. Suddenly a wave of nostalgia came over me, as I realized the enormous investment I had in the relationship with Judy, a kind of daughter—and at that point I had two daughters myself. I felt an unexpected regret that I would not be around to see her grow up. I didn't say anything about it to her, but I felt this tremendous loss. It let me feel the mutual quality of the loss, something that provided one of my early experiences of enormously useful countertransference."

By the time Scharff left Boston, he felt a dawning sense of competence and confidence in himself as a professional, and much of it was the result of his work with Judy and her family, who also were experiencing a new competence. He continued to think about Judy over the years, wondering how she was doing. Then, while he was writing his book on family therapy 15 years later, he received a letter from her that filled him in on what she had been doing. She reported a difficult young adulthood that seemed like a reenactment of her earliest childhood. Perhaps it was not surprising, given the way her development had been sexualized by her brother, that she got involved with a cult figure who abused her. Eventually, she extricated herself from the relationship and was now doing much better. Judy's story became the closing chapter of the book.

Almost ten years later, Judy contacted Scharff again. She was now married and had a seven-year-old child who had recently been diagnosed with attention deficit disorder and learning difficulty. Judy felt devastated, because she was convinced her past had doomed her daughter. She thought it would be helpful if she could talk to Scharff again. He said he would be near Boston in a few weeks, and would be glad to see her.

Scharff was shocked at the 40-year-old woman who walked into the room. Whereas once she had been a little Lolita, that seductive adolescent was now a grown woman, no longer seductive, still intelligent, and still with an impressive capacity for insight.

"There's a lot of stuff I never told you before," she began the session. "There's stuff I've never told anyone." She obviously felt deeply ashamed.

"I know I told you that I had sex with my brother. But in a way, that was the least of it. What really made me feel so deeply ashamed was that I did things for him with other boys. He said to me that he needed friends, and I could help him by doing things to other boys so they would like him. He was the only person I felt I had, so I did it—even in elementary school. I've never told anyone this, not even my husband, and none of the other therapists I saw. And I keep feeling that this is what has damaged my daughter, although I know it's not really true."

Scharff said to her, "Your daughter is the same age that you were when this began to happen. Maybe you're afraid something awful will happen to her, much worse than what people know about her, and you feel it will happen because you're a bad person and a bad mother, just as you felt your mother was."

As Scharff sat with this woman whom he had known from the beginning of his professional life, he realized what tremendous influence each had had on the other. Here they were again, continuing their work together, but so different than they had been decades earlier. Each had matured and changed in ways that made them familiar, yet also unrecognizable. Scharff was now an established analyst, a leader in the field of psychoanalytic family therapy, a supposed expert on the effects of trauma, knowing things he had not known when he worked with Judy.

And here she was, his first patient, sitting in front of him again. And she still had things to teach him, things he was even then working to understand about the effects of sexual trauma on survivors, things her words would help him with in the investigations on trauma he was doing.

Scharff said to Judy, "I understand that you're here because you have more work to do, work your daughter's difficulty makes possible in a way. I'll help you get to someone who can do it with you. But meanwhile, it might help you to know how much I learned from you when we worked together. You had a capacity to look at yourself and to be honest that will help you now, too. And it should help your daughter pull through her own difficulty. One of the things I learned from you is the power of that ability and that honesty to help people grow, and I think it will help you over these next few years as it did 25 years ago."

At that moment, Scharff felt that, more than any of his supervisors, any of the books he'd read, any of the colleagues he consulted, any of the training seminars he attended, in some ways more than his own analysis, Judy had taught him what it meant to be a therapist.

Chapter 13

PAT LOVE
The Broken Heart

As she walked into the therapy room, Loretta looked like a classic Austinite: bright; attractive; casually dressed—someone who fit in well with the diversity of the Texas capital.

Yet in contrast to her comfortable appearance, Loretta was in obvious misery. More than merely miserable—she seemed to be in complete anguish.

Pat Love was drawn to her in ways that she couldn't understand or describe.

She felt a foreboding as well as a resonance within her, some close connection to this woman who was in such pain. It was like meeting a kindred spirit.

This was a time in Love's life when she was just beginning to experiment with a way of working, a way of being, that involved as much authenticity as possible. With increased wisdom and experience, she was giving herself permission to be more spontaneous, more intuitive, and more vulnerable.

As the woman seated herself, Love took a deep breath to center herself. She nodded with a smile, encouraging her new client to begin.

"You're my fourth therapist," Loretta began the interview. "Or maybe the fifth. I can't remember."

Love nodded, prompting her to continue.

"I lost my son." That's all Loretta could get out before the tears started falling. She cried quietly for a few moments, then calmed herself enough to continue. "I just don't know if I can go through all this again."

Love could feel her heart pounding in her chest. "Take your time," she said, hoping to center herself and provide support for her client.

"My son was killed a year ago." Loretta was biting her lip, willing herself not to cry again.

Love became aware of the intense attunement she was feeling toward Loretta. She didn't feel the need to say much. She just concentrated, with all her being, on remaining open, available, and totally engaged.

"I just can't seem to let go of the guilt and pain I feel," Loretta continued. "I'm just totally immobilized. I can't work. I can't sleep. My mind always wanders."

Love nodded, finding it easy to understand how a son's death could easily immobilize one's life.

"Yeah, that's about it. I'm a teacher. I used to love my work. I'm good at it, too. But lately, sometimes in the middle of a class, or even a conversation, I forget where I am."

Noting the symptoms that were being reported, Love decided to return to Loretta's opening statement. "Loretta, when you first sat down, you said you had been to four or five therapists…"

"Yes," Loretta replied, "Two were ministers from my church."

She looked down at her hands and went on, expressing the guilt she was feeling.

"I know I'm supposed to have moved on from this. But some days it is as if it happened yesterday. I don't know if what I am feeling is normal or if I'm just making matters worse. I seem to have lost my way and any form of sound judgment."

As Love sat listening to the story, she became very aware of the excruciating pain that her client was in. She felt this not only because of what she was witnessing, but also because of what she, herself, was feeling on the inside. As soon as Loretta mentioned that her son had been killed, Love couldn't help but think about her own son. She felt immediate empathy for this woman who had lived through any mother's worst nightmare.

Loretta filled in some of the details of the past year or two. She had been going through a divorce that had become final the previous year. It was a difficult time for all of them. Loretta felt especially guilty because her son, Shane, had become very angry at her because she had been the one to initiate the proceedings. She had been unwilling to tell him, or anyone, that she was doing so because of her husband's repeated infidelity.

Shane had no choice but to live with his mother because his father moved out of state with his latest girlfriend. The boy began acting out in a number of ways that included drinking, skipping school, and, most of all, expressing his anger toward his mother. His behavior became increasingly impulsive and erratic until, one night, he stormed out of the house in a rage. They had been having a bitter argument, and the boy told his mother that she had ruined his life.

"You don't love me," he screamed. "You don't give a shit about anyone but yourself. That's what drove Dad away. And now you're doing the same thing to me. I hate you!" And with that he ran out the door.

Later that night Shane was involved in a car accident and was hurled through the windshield. During his flight through the broken glass, his chest cavity was cracked open and his heart was ripped out of his chest. He literally died of a broken heart.

ATTUNEMENT

This was absolutely the saddest story Love had ever heard. She couldn't imagine anything more devastating, more crushing; and again she thought about her own son. In fact, in this moment, as Loretta was telling the story, Love began crying anew.

Love said, "This case raises an important issue. When you know you have made a mistake, what do you do about it? In my own case I have gone to each of my children more than once, and owned my part in our struggles. I let them know how I felt and promised to do better in the future. I have done better as a result, and I think I am a really good parent. I have learned to forgive myself for my mistakes. But the pain and the regret are still there."

Love paused for a moment to gather her thoughts. "I don't understand people who say they don't have regrets. I don't relate to that. There are some things I wish I had done differently. I don't have a problem telling my children that."

When Loretta described what happened with her own son, and the excruciating remorse she felt, this hit a tender spot in her therapist. Love took another deep breath to compose herself. It was very important that she remain focused on her client and not stuck in her own stuff. Love could never recall feeling more attuned to a client in her life.

Instead of doing the usual routine of reflecting Loretta's grief, her guilt and sorrow, Love abandoned the traditional role of therapist altogether: she gave in to her deep feeling of compassion that brought tears to her eyes. "But this was not countertransference," Love was quick to point out. "I was not getting in touch with my own issues. Rather, I was feeling absolute compassion for this woman. We both sat there together, grieving for her son. I could see Loretta watching me the whole time, as if to make sure I was still there. With her. And I was."

Pat remembers not having to do anything or say anything. It was just a pure sort of human attunement. They sat together, moved to tears—for minutes that could have been hours.

"This is. . .," Loretta said, between sobs, "the first time. . . the . . . only time . . . that . . . I felt like . . . anyone . . .really understood."

Love leaned closer.

"The other therapists I've seen—they told me things or gave me reasons why I was feeling the way I was. They said I was still feeling guilt and responsibility. They said I was punishing myself. But, really, they were all telling me that I should just get over this; that what is done, is done; and I should get on with my life as best I can."

"This is something that you don't get over. You manage it, you learn from it."

Loretta nodded, grateful that she had been understood. "It's hard to let go of the pain, the guilt. I feel. . .I am. . . just immobilized. I can't work. I can't sleep."

Love didn't feel the need to say a thing, just to close her eyes and nod her head, encouraging Loretta to keep talking.

When Loretta paused, Love said, "As I listen to you, I have this feeling of heaviness, almost like trying to push a truck up a hill. No matter how hard I push, I feel myself slipping backward."

Loretta nodded, and then took her first deep breath.

Just relax," Love urged. "Take your time."

What Love was really saying was that she was perfectly fine with holding on to where they were. She didn't need to escape, or move away from the core.

"I know I am supposed to move on from this," Loretta said. "That's what all the other therapists told me. That's what my minister told me, too. I have to get on with things. But. . ."

"When you lose a child like this, especially under the circumstances that you described, it takes time. I am not saying that you should wallow in your suffering, but sometimes this pain can be a source of transformation. In that sense, you do kind of move on, but not by leaving your son behind; you take him with you in a different way."

Loretta nodded. "I appreciate that," she said. "I know this is the way it is, but nobody understood that. They all kept telling me to get over it."

"You will move in your own way, in your own time."

Loretta just nodded again and sat crying silently. For the rest of the session, that was about the only interaction between them. The rest was silence, unless one considers the language of tears.

TRANSCENDENT EMPATHY

This client, and this session, opened up a new reality for Pat Love in ways she could never have anticipated. She had discovered a more genuine way to respond to pain and suffering. "I didn't think," she said. "I just tuned in to this person and concentrated on being with her as fully as I could."

To grasp the meaning of this statement for Pat Love, it is necessary to understand something about her life. She grew up the only child of a single mother who was an alcoholic. Out of necessity, she learned that if any of her needs were ever going to be met, it wasn't going to be done by her parent. Becoming upset about something was never useful, since her mother would rarely respond to any emotional expression; she simply was not available, in terms of either physical presence or psychological comfort. Love's favorite expression through most of her childhood and adolescence was "I don't care." This indifference became her protection.

In spite of her studied apathy, Love cared deeply about the people around her. She was secretly sentimental, though she would not permit herself to show it. It was as important to hide her feelings as to hide her needs. Instead, she devoted herself to entertaining and helping others; that way she could at least feel useful. She denied her feelings for years, until they started to spill over and take on a life of their own.

BACKGROUND

About eight years before the session with Loretta took place, Love had divorced and moved to Texas for a university job. She and her ex-husband had agreed that their daughter would go with her, and their son would stay with his father. During her first semester as a new professor, a senior colleague invited Love to cosupervise a group of male doctoral interns. This was a very accomplished group of young therapists.

During a particular supervision session, one of the interns presented the case of a mother who knew she was dying and would be survived by two sons. The intern was working with the mother to make a plan for preparing her sons for her death.

Love was still grieving the loss of leaving her son, and as she was listening to the case presentations, her grief was so strong, she could not hold back the tears: not just a few stray tears but deep, wracking sobs that startled everyone in the room. She was aware of the startled responses from the students and the other faculty member, but she could do nothing to stop herself. She felt both helpless and totally humiliated at falling apart in front of her colleague and students.

While the others waited with some embarrassment, Love finally gulped down a few breaths and regained a semblance of control. "This. . .reminds me. . .of my son," she said in between gasps of air. "He's back in West Virginia. And I miss him so very much."

The other faculty member offered an empathetic response and the students quietly left as soon as the session ended. Love was able to finally pull herself together.

A few days later, Dan, one of the interns, came into her office and sat down.

"Your tears the other day in supervision really touched me," he said. "My mother and dad left me and my brother on the doorstep of an orphanage when I was a little boy, and I always wondered if they missed us."

Pat was surprised and deeply touched by Dan's words. It had never dawned on her that her tears could have provided anything but embarrassment to others, let alone comfort. This experience forged a bond between the two of them, and Dan later became Love's first doctoral student advisee. She remembered this incident after recalling her first session with Loretta because that supervision session was the first time she had ever had the courage to be truly authentic with her feelings in front of strangers. At the time, though, it didn't feel much like a choice that she made.

There is another example of Love's tears making a public appearance. After about two years on faculty at the university, Pat was asked to be the luncheon speaker at a Texas state professional conference. She selected as her topic "Why I Love Texas." Using her trademark wit, she began the talk in the company of many of her colleagues, including her supervisor.

"So there I am, talking about funny things related to Texas, like good ol' boys and country western dancing, and then I shift to the many things I love about Texas, like bluebonnets, barbecue, and the big sky. And then I go on to talk about some of the people I love in Texas, including the man who hired me and made all this possible. And as I say this, I start to feel tears welling up in my eyes. I press on, but the more gratitude I feel, the more the tears start to take over. Finally, I'm standing before this crowd with my corsage already pinned, plaque pending, and I am crying so hard I can no longer talk.

"I look out at the audience, and they are wide-eyed, waiting for me to continue. I look down at my speech, but the words make me cry even harder. Finally, I give up and decide to just hand the damn thing to someone else to read. So I turn to my right to give it to my colleague, and she is crying, too, so I turn to my left, and that fellow quickly looks down at the table, as if to say 'don't hand it to me.' So there I am, three-quarters of the way through the speech, when I just have to sit down. I am crying, and I just can't stop. That was always my worst fear: that if I really let myself go, if I really allowed myself to feel the depth of my emotions, I would just totally lose control. And that's exactly what happened!"

During the following weeks, as Pat processed this incident, she came to the realization that anytime she felt a strong feeling, tears accompanied it. It didn't matter if the feeling was positive or negative, strong feelings made her cry. When she became angry, or happy, or fearful, or frustrated, each of these feelings would bring tears. For a long time she avoided feeling because her tears embarrassed her. But finally she realized that if she was going to reclaim her emotions, she would have to accept the tears.

This was how she taught herself to reclaim the emotions that had been buried throughout much of her early life. She just felt the feelings and let the tears come—and trusted other people to deal with it.

So in the session with Loretta, when Love began to feel strong feelings and felt tears coming to her eyes, she had to check first to see "Is this about me, or is it about her?" There is a distinct difference. When the awareness came back as "This is not about me and my history, this is about compassion and empathy," it felt appropriate to let the feelings come and the tears flow. The therapeutic effect of this authenticity seemed miraculous, not only for Loretta but also for Pat.

"This was my first conscious awareness of having appropriate feelings, empathy and sadness, for another person, but I didn't lapse into my own issues. It gave me a whole new way to relate to clients. I have never been the same since then. When I work with people, I just do my best to show up authentically, and that is about it."

REMEMBRANCES

Since that episode in the supervision program, which had occurred eight years before her work with Loretta, Love had learned a measure of control, so she didn't have to reveal herself authentically unless she wanted to, or unless the situation seemed appropriate. In this present case, it did not seem right that she should focus on herself in any way, so the tears she was expressing mirrored those of her client; they were what brought them together.

The other therapists whom Loretta had consulted put distance between themselves and their clients, beyond what would be expected as professional boundaries. It was as if the pain was so scalding that the only way that others could deal with it, and Loretta, was by offering advice and rational explanations. But Love felt it was important that she remain fully present.

It has taken Love years of hard work to be able to stay attuned to someone in so much pain. This means having empathy without either lapsing into sympathy or getting into one's own personal stuff. This is what she considers to be the main difference between countertransference and the healing of compassion. Love is very clear that she considers this compassion to be truly healing—for both participants.

Loretta stands out for Love when she thinks about the clients who changed her, because the sessions taught her to trust the healing power of her own caring. She could be vulnerable, transparent, and authentic, and yet do so without being self-indulgent.

"I do believe," Love said in summary, "that it is more blessed to give than to receive, because giving really is receiving. And that is what I experienced with Loretta. I can't say for sure what she got out of our relationship, although I have some hunches. We saw each other for a brief period of time. But I have told you for sure what I got out of it. It was one of those times when what we learned from one another was equal."

Chapter 14

LAURA BROWN
A Spiritual Awakening

Many of the theorists we interviewed had little difficulty identifying how clients changed them professionally. You have already seen how one's model of practice is strongly impacted by those seminal clients who push clinicians to grow in new ways in order to accommodate them. It has been far more challenging, however, to elicit examples of personal transformation—those times when therapists have been irrevocably changed beyond professional boundaries.

Laura Brown had little problem talking about the impact of her clients on her personal life. "There is something real that goes on in therapy," Brown admitted. "Anyone who meets us, changes us. Every encounter we have transforms us. How could we be therapists and not be transformed profoundly in all kinds of ways?"

BECOMING REAL

Among the hundreds of clients who have changed Brown, the one who stands out the most had gone through a series of devastating experiences. Ellen had been a nun, and even though she had left the order, she was still quite observant as a Catholic. This presented some challenges for her because she was also a lesbian. Nonetheless, she had a clear sense of connection to what was important to her in her faith, and was a deeply spiritual individual.

Ellen made it clear in the first session that it was important to her to have an authentic relationship with her therapist in which both persons were transparent as humans. Brown was used to having an egalitarian relationship as part of her feminist model, but if "authentic" meant she was supposed to open herself up to her client, there was no way she was going to make herself emotionally vulnerable.

"Ellen," she explained, "even if I was open to what you suggest—and I'm not sure that is appropriate—I'm just not capable of what you want from me. You are a spiritual person who lives her authenticity. I'm not spiritual; I'm too much of an empiricist. This is a real limitation of mine, and it is also something that I am not open to changing right now."

"But you are a spiritual person," Ellen insisted. "You may not know that about yourself, or identify yourself that way, but I can see it inside you."

"Even if that were true—and I'm not saying I agree with you—I still don't think that being emotionally open with you—or, as you say, "being authentic"—is part of my job. In some ways, what you want is against the rules. It is important that we maintain some boundaries. Otherwise, the therapy could end up being more about me than about you."

"I understand about boundaries," Ellen insisted. "Remember, I have a master's degree in counseling, and I know the rules you practice by. I'm not trying to argue with you. I don't want to have sex with you; I'm not asking you to be my friend. I just want you to be real with me. There are some wounds that I need to heal, but in order to do that, I need to do it within an authentic relationship where I know that I can trust what's happening between us." Brown was not really sure what Ellen was asking for. She didn't appear seductive or exhibit the kind of behavior that might set off warning bells of some underlying (so-called) personality disorder. She didn't see evidence of manipulation. This just seemed like a woman who knew exactly what she wanted and what she needed most to heal herself. Given what was being asked, Brown thought seriously about referring her to someone else. She didn't want to hurt Ellen or give her an experience of chronic withholding.

"You're not getting off that easy," Ellen laughed. "I sense that you have the capacity to help me, and I really want to work with you."

Finally, Brown agreed to give it a try, although they didn't come to any definitive agreement. Whenever Ellen did press her therapist to be more disclosing or, in her words, to be "more real," Brown would firmly but gently set limits. "I know that you are frustrated with me," Brown reflected. "I'm not responding to you the way you want."

"Will you cut out all that psycho-crap already! I can't work with someone who hides behind all these lines you've memorized in therapy school." There was no rage in what Brown heard. If anything, Ellen just sounded sad and disappointed. Laura was actually feeling that way as well. During the months that they had been seeing one another, Brown had been undergoing a change in her own spiritual beliefs. After many years of feeling estranged from conventional religious practices, she started attending a synagogue once again. Was this simply a coincidence?

Not long before she began working with Ellen, Brown had been severely ill, the result of toxic reaction to environmental allergens. The nerves to her vocal cords stopped working, and Brown had been told by her doctors that she might not ever speak again. For someone who makes a living with speech, this was absolutely devastating: it would mean she could no longer do the work that gave her life meaning.

Although she did begin to recover, Brown lived continuously with the possibility of a relapse. Needless to say, this sparked quite a lot of existential issues for her that paralleled those of her client. For these reasons, or perhaps because the battles became too stressful for both of them, they agreed to stop their work together and Ellen was referred elsewhere.

A SECOND CHANCE

Over a year later, Brown received a message on her voice mail: "Hi. This is Ellen. I have decided to give you another chance. I need to work with you, and I think you need to work with me, too. Please call me back."

They spent the next year struggling to reach a healthier relationship, and in so doing, Brown realized that she was a different person than the one who had worked with Ellen a year earlier. Brown respected Ellen's willingness to return and, in turn, found herself much more willing to open herself up. This was a huge step for Brown, who considers herself to be fairly rigid at times, if not a bit obsessive-compulsive.

In being honest with herself, Brown admitted that her previous reluctance to be more authentic with Ellen was not just about concerns with maintaining appropriate professional boundaries. In truth, Ellen scared the hell out of her because of what Brown perceived as Ellen's far greater and better-developed capacity for intimacy and genuineness. This applied to not only their therapeutic relationship; Brown was realizing that throughout her entire life, including her primary relationships, her behavior was built around cautiousness and formality. "I was not willing to have genuine relationships anywhere in my life; all of my passion went into my politics and my writing."

With Ellen, Brown found that the greater authenticity was not only therapeutic for the client, but also transformative for herself. Brown realized she wanted more of this not only in her work, but also in her personal life, an awareness that had what Brown refers to humorously as "interesting and revolutionary consequences." Of course, not every client needs this, or wants this, or would respond favorably to such transparency from a therapist, but this was a turning point in the way that Brown did therapy and conducted her life.

Since the time that Brown became more spiritual, and more active in her congregation, she has been involved in a relationship with a partner who is neither Jewish nor religious in the least.

"My partner can't understand why educated people are willing to participate in the rituals of an organized religion or would need to subscribe to the notion of some kind of God. She's very much a secular humanist. For me, although I'm not particularly tied to a construct of a divine being, my spirituality has come to mean having access to experiences that are transcendent and very essential to what I do in my work, which is largely with trauma survivors. You can keep things intellectual for a long time, but ultimately, most people want to go deeper than that. Most people have some sense of a divine and of something bigger than themselves. Ellen opened this up for me by requiring me to meet her where she was, at the center of what grounds her, which is her spirituality."

MIDDLE GROUND

Brown paused for a few moments after telling the story. Although she now prides herself on being self-revealing and authentic, she has sometimes gotten in trouble for being too honest. She readily agrees that there is a point at which one can go too far, become too transparent (or inappropriately so). In the process of embracing this way of being as a therapist, she's stumbled a few times. "It's one thing to intellectually subscribe to the notion that one size doesn't fit all; it's another to put into practice the strategy of being authentic in a manner that's reflective of the particular client who's in the room with you in that moment. What might have been good for Ellen would not be ideal for others." She has learned to find a middle ground.

Brown mentioned a client she is seeing right now who is struggling with issues similar to those that Brown had resolved earlier in life. It would seem to be a perfect opportunity to use self-disclosure or otherwise be more transparent, yet Brown has made a decision not to do so in this case, and is even quite emotionally careful with this person because of her particular needs and personality. She recognizes that this client is so vulnerable that she would most likely not respond well to the same sort of authenticity that empowered Ellen.

In concluding the conversation, Brown observed that most therapists seem to feel ashamed that they get something out of their work as therapists. "Yet we are healed by it. We are made bigger by it. It is not all altruistic. I think we are ashamed of this because it reeks of exploitation. How can we take something and not be exploitive?"

The answer that Brown offers is that it depends on how we acknowledge our humanness when we are with our clients. She is skeptical of any professional who claims that he or she gets nothing from the experience. She wonders how that is possible if you are truly present for your clients. "If we show up as fully human for our work, if we are open to the experiences that our clients offer to us, then we have no choice but to grow."

Chapter 15

KEN HARDY
Mister Black Doctor

"Mama, I don't want to go in there," the boy whispered to his mother. "I ain't goin' in there."

Hardy stood in the doorway to the waiting room and observed a young, blondish boy who looked to be about nine years old. He was leaning over his chair and speaking frantically into his mother's ear. She put a comforting arm on his shoulder but kept nodding her head.

"Hello," Hardy greeted the family cheerfully. "Would you like to come in?"

The family sat frozen in their chairs, eyeing one another. Eventually the father and mother stood up, but the boy remained resolutely in his chair. "Mama," he said, abandoning his attempts to be discreet, "That there's a nigger. I ain't seein' no nigger doctor."

"Shush now," she said to him, but without much force. "You come on, now."

"I tole you, I ain't goin' to see no nigger doctor." The boy crossed his arms and locked his knees together, daring anyone to move him.

Hardy stood in the doorway as frozen as the rest of them. He felt embarrassed, not so much for himself as for this family. He knew that on the other side of the one-way mirror, several colleagues were watching this exchange as well, on call to provide supervision and feedback as needed. Well, the interview hadn't even started yet, and already he wanted to call for help.

Hardy took a deep breath and resolutely approached the boy. "Joey, isn't it?" he said as he held out his hand for Joey to shake.

Joey remained statuelike in his chair, staring down, his lip curled. He ignored the outstretched hand.

"Okay, then," Hardy responded with more forced cheerfulness, "why don't you follow me?"

After Hardy and Joey's parents started to walk into the office, Joey realized he had no choice but to follow. Hardy could hear him muttering to himself as he shuffled in, although the only distinct words that he could hear were "damn nigger doctor."

Hardy had been working in Florida for some time, and although he had been concerned about overt signs of racism in the Deep South, this was a university town. Throughout much of his life he had been largely shielded from such aggressive racism; Hardy was more used to the subtle kind: being ignored altogether.

After the family seated themselves, Joey taking the chair as far away from his therapist as possible, Hardy asked what he could do to help them.

"Well," the mother began, "Joey here, he's been having some troubles in school."

"I see," Hardy answered. Then, looking across the room at the boy, he addressed him directly. "What sort of problems, Joey?"

The boy pressed his lips together and shook his head back and forth. He was whispering again, in the direction of his parents.

"I'm sorry, Joey," Hardy said. "I didn't hear your answer."

For the first time the boy made eye contact with Hardy. It was a defiant look, aggressive and hostile. "I said. . . that I don't. . . talk. . . to no nigger doctors!"

"I see," Hardy said, not seeing at all. He looked helplessly in the direction of the one-way mirror where his colleagues were watching. He was hoping for some telepathic message that might guide what he should do next. Before he could figure out how to respond, he had to determine exactly what was going on here. Surely this kid wasn't so surprised that he had been assigned to see an African American therapist; the community was fairly well integrated.

Hardy soon learned from the parents that Joey had failed the second grade two times already, was repeating it for the third time, and still was not doing well. They were concerned about their son and felt at a complete loss as to what to do. Hardy knew just how they felt.

"So, Joey," Hardy asked him, "what is it that you would like?"

"I want a white doctor."

"You want a white doctor?"

"Thas all I'm sayin'." And then to prove it, Joey crossed his arms again and turned away.

Hardy watched all of this with increasing concern. He was feeling less taken aback by the child's behavior than by that of his parents. It was as if they were covertly approving of their son's behavior, or at least doing little to keep him in check. Each time Joey said something rude or inappropriate, the parents just shrugged and halfheartedly told him to mind his behavior. Even Joey could tell they didn't mean it.

This went on for some time, Hardy trying unsuccessfully to engage Joey and the boy only insisting that he wanted a white doctor, that he wouldn't talk to a "nigger doctor."

Okay, then, Hardy reasoned, if the kid wouldn't talk to him, they'd have to do something else. "Let's play a game, then," he said, and took down the box of Candyland and started setting up the pieces on the floor.

Joey's father nudged him. The boy rolled his eyes, as if to say, "Hey, if this is what it takes to get ya'll off my back, then so be it." He settled on the floor and methodically began rolling the dice and moving his pieces around the board. Hardy thought it interesting that although this game was more suitable for younger children, Joey seemed to find some comfort in the simple, orderly sequence of moves.

Throughout the game, taking turns throwing the dice, Hardy continued to try and engage Joey in some conversation. This could not exactly have been thrilling drama to the parents and spectators watching, but it seemed to be all that Joey was willing to do.

After several attempts to ask him questions about school, Joey became annoyed by the interruptions. "I already tol' you I won't talk to no nigger doctor. I want a white doctor."

"Yeah, Joey, I heard you say that several times."

Joey smirked and then covered his mouth with his hand. At least that was some progress, Hardy reasoned. The kid seemed to restrain himself a little.

"So, then, why you askin' me again?"

"I'm just curious why you won't talk to me."

"'Cause white doctors is smarter." Joey flashed a grin for a moment and then went back down to the board, methodically counting out spaces.

"Well," Hardy answered, "I think I'm pretty smart."

"Oh, yeah?"

Hardy nodded with a smile.

"Okay, Mister Black Doctor, then how much is one and one?" Hardy hesitated for a moment, wondering what this test was all about. It did not escape him that Joey had dropped the "nigger" when addressing him. He seemed to realize that it wasn't getting the sort of rise out of Hardy that he had hoped.

"Two," Hardy said.

"Yeah? Well, how 'bout two plus two?"

"Four."

"Three plus. . ." Joey stopped for a moment, his tongue slipping above his upper lip as he concentrated. "How about. . .five plus five?" That was as far as the boy could go and be sure of his answers.

"That's ten, Joey. See, I am pretty smart, aren't I?"

"I still want a white doctor."

"Look, Joey, I just passed your test. Why don't you give me a chance to work with you?"

"Because. . .I already tole you. . .that. . . I don't want. . . a nigger doctor."

So much for the progress Hardy thought they'd made. And so it went for this session. Hardy was totally mystified about what to do. He couldn't seem to make contact with the boy in any way or penetrate his defiance. And the parents were doing absolutely nothing to help matters. They just sat passively on the couch, watching the interaction unfold as if it were a television show that had nothing to do with their own lives.

THE CONSULTATION

Hardy decided it was long past the time when they needed to take a break so he could consult with the observation team. As soon as he joined them behind the one-way mirror, he asked for help: "How do I work with this kid? He won't talk to me. He refuses to work with me."

"Look, Ken," one colleague said, "you've done a good job not letting yourself get distracted by the loaded content. He's obviously trying to get underneath your skin."

"It's working," Hardy said softly.

Another colleague chimed in. "I agree with what's been said. You've got to stick with the underlying process of what's going on. You can't allow this racialized interaction to distract you from the real issues operating here."

"I should just pretend like this kid isn't calling me a nigger every minute or so? I should ignore that his parents are doing nothing to stop him?" Hardy was surprised how calm he was, considering the situation. First, he left the room with this racist white family and he went behind the mirror for some help, and now his white colleagues were telling him to pretend he was not black and pretend he was not being deliberately provoked.

"You just gotta hang in there," a third colleague said, attempting to be reassuring.

Hardy nodded, but he felt more angry at his coworkers than he did toward Joey and his family. He expected more from them—at the very least, some understanding of what this must be like for him. Later in his career Hardy would do research on the legacy of slavery and its impact on the lives of contemporary African Americans. This would result in a film he produced about the psychological residuals of slavery, a situation that was very much being enacted during this session. He had worked long and hard to attain his education and professional status, and now he was being told by this kid that he was nothing but a house nigger who escaped from the fields— how dare he think he was an equal to a white person? He could understand why Joey might be acting this way—a failure in almost every aspect of his life, heading downward with no hope. He lashed out because it was all he knew how to do. But he had expected more from his peers—if not some understanding, at least some compassion.

Somehow, Hardy managed to get through that first, awkward session, although Joey remained belligerent throughout. In a subsequent consultation with the parents alone, they claimed they were absolutely shocked by their son's behavior. "We got no idea where he gets that sort of thing," Joey's mother said. "Probably at that school of his. I swear, I don't know what they teach them kids there."

Hardy recruited the parents' assistance as allies, but decided that it might be better to work with Joey alone. Indeed, without his parents present, the boy did seem less obstructive. He even remembered (most of the time) to call his therapist "Mr. Black Doctor," instead of "Doctor Nigger." Hardy took this as some effort at compromise on the boy's part.

They limped along for another session until Hardy's supervisor at the clinic finally concluded that Joey's racism was so entrenched that it might be best to refer the boy elsewhere. Hardy felt defeated, but also somewhat relieved.

KNOWING WHERE THINGS STAND

Looking back on this case, Hardy still feels haunted by Joey. "The whole thing was like a roller coaster ride. I had a kind of optimistic myopia. I really believed I could get through to that kid and help move him to a different place. I was determined to get through to him, but. . ."

Hardy trailed off at the end, remembering some of the hurt and pain he felt, and feelings of betrayal by his colleagues. At the time this was going on, it was hard to make sense of it all, to process it constructively. This was the first time in his life that he had been forced to confront someone who felt such raw, unbridled hate toward him because of the color of his skin. It didn't matter that he was educated, cultured, worldly, intelligent—he would always be just a "nigger doctor."

To make matters more complicated, because Hardy was in a position of power and responsibility with Joey, he didn't feel he had the right to defend or protect himself. If anything, his colleagues told him it was no big deal. He was just being oversensitive, and should ignore the taunts. After hearing such comments, Hardy wondered how things would have been different if the supervision team had included any people of color. His confidence was shattered, however, so he kept such thoughts to himself.

Until this experience, Hardy had believed the messages he received during his training—that therapy was color-blind and that race was inconsequential in the process. After Joey, Hardy not only began to acknowledge racial (and gender) issues in therapeutic relationships but he also addressed them as soon as they surfaced. "Diversity dialogue keeps people connected to the process but at the same time honors everyone's individual integrity around these issues. I think that with Joey I was over-whelmed with his directness and his view toward race; frankly I felt like I didn't do a good job of participating in the conversation. I didn't move it to a greater level of depth, which I thought was needed. I'm able to do that now, and I think this is due to Joey because he really pushed me to think more critically about these issues and the skills needed to move this conversation along in a way that I hadn't done before."

Hardy's different view of therapy has been extended to the role he plays as a helper. "I shun the notion that there is one self I carry inside the therapy room and another self I carry on the outside. I believe there is one self that is portable, that I carry around with me wherever I go. I think the case with Joey highlighted and magnified that for me."

Hardy realizes now that one reason why he struggled so much, both during the sessions and making sense of the interactions afterward, was that he distinguished between the way he was "supposed" to be as a thera-pist versus the way he would be as a human being. He knew well how to respond to racism out in the world; he had not known how to do so in his therapeutic role. "Here was this nine-year-old child, repeating second grade for the third time, and yet he still felt unquestionably superior to me. There is a long historical legacy for this type of behavior that went unchallenged for a long time."

Hardy had had little guidance, either from his peers or from his supervisors, about when it was appropriate to challenge issues related to race or oppression. He understood that, ethically and professionally, his job was to make it safe for his client, but what happens when the client becomes abusive and disrespectful?

"In one sense I felt grateful to Joey for what he taught me. He saw me as a nigger and he treated me like one. In some ways that is easier than dealing with people when they say one thing verbally and everything about them is suggesting something different. At least he was honest. I understood clearly where he stood. I was not so certain about colleagues behind the mirror."

Chapter 16

MICHAEL YAPKO
Caught in a Controversy

"You're younger than I thought you'd be," were the first words out of Bob's mouth as he sat down.

"You expected someone older?" Yapko said with a smile.

"Sure. I mean, your book and all. I thought you'd be, you know. . ."

"Older."

"Right."

Yapko examined his new client, a fairly nondescript man in his forties. Bob seemed distracted, yet eager to make a good impression. This was a time, in the early 90s, when the second edition of Yapko's popular textbook on hypnosis had just been published. One of the sections in this revised text provided a brief discussion of the growing preoccupation in the field with the phenomenon of repressed memories. In that section, Yapko described how the techniques used to recover such memories could contaminate retrieved memories and even create entirely false but seemingly real recollections. Among clinicians using hypnosis, it was already fairly well known that memory was quite unstable and, under certain conditions, could be manipulated through suggestion. But most clinicians didn't have such specialized training, so it was a frightening trend when, after using suggestive techniques of memory recovery, they began to report a large increase in the number of women who were suddenly recalling previously unknown episodes of early childhood sexual abuse. Historically, since the time of Freud, such reports had typically been dismissed as fantasies, delusions, or distortions; now, in light of the growing evidence that the sexual abuse of children was more common than previously realized, they were being taken far more seriously. Unfortunately, clinicians now overcompensated for their dismissive attitude, and thus were likely to believe any such report, regardless of the circumstances in which previously buried memories might surface.

In his text, Yapko made a rather neutral observation that sometimes such reports of recovered memories could be true, yet they could also be the result of therapists (and others in positions of influence) unintentionally leading people to believe they had been abused when, in fact, they never had been. This was not a major area of interest for Yapko at first—it was merely one of hundreds of observations he made throughout the book to illustrate certain key concepts related to the practice of clinical hypnosis.

Most surprising to Yapko, the book generated tremendous response from clinicians and laypeople alike. He was contacted by many individuals who sought him out for help with the very issues he described in the book. Bob was one such person; he made an appointment to talk about how repressed memories had ruined his life.

"So anyway," Bob launched into his story, "what brought me here to see you was some research I was doing about false memories, and I came across your book."

Yapko nodded.

"You described so perfectly what was going on in my own life. It's like you understood what I was going through. I knew then I needed to see you, to talk to you. If anyone can help me, I just know that you can. I've tried to understand what has happened to my daughter, but..." Bob stopped to compose himself.

Yapko waited patiently and then gestured for him to continue.

"So, that's why I flew all the way out here to see you."

"I can see this is very difficult for you," Yapko said. "Why don't you tell me what happened?"

"It was about two years ago that my daughter, Angela, was seeing this therapist. I use that term loosely, because I think she was more of an antitherapist. Angela was seeing this woman for therapy because of her difficulties in dating. Angela wanted to know why her boyfriend dumped her and why guys she dated since didn't seem interested in her. The therapist told her that her difficulties with men indicated she'd been sexually abused as a child. When Angela dismissed that viewpoint as a load of crap, the therapist said her defensiveness, as well as her lack of early childhood memories, further supported that interpretation. The therapist told her in no uncertain terms that unless she recovered and came to terms with the memories of what had happened to her, she'd never have a good relationship with a man."

Yapko could no nothing but shake his head in amazement. He'd heard a lot of such stories, but this one was beyond comprehension.

"So," Bob continued, "Angela and this therapist did hypnosis to try to take her back to her birth or some such crap."

"You mean age regression?"

"I don't know what it's called, but it sounds pretty crazy to me. I didn't think you were even supposed to remember anything before age three. Supposedly, during these hypnosis sessions she went back to being an infant, a few months old. She said she remembered me changing her diapers. She says that now, with the help of her therapist, she remembers that while I was diapering her, I began molesting her and touching her inappropriately." Bob looked at Yapko and just shook his head disgustedly, as if this was too absurd to comment on.

"And then what happened?" Yapko asked, knowing full well what was likely to follow, having heard variations of this story many times before from equally perplexed and indignant parents.

"I just can't believe it," Bob muttered. "So then Angela accused me of molesting her and being a pervert who is attracted to infants. I told her that her accusation was utterly insane and that her memory was flat-out wrong. Of course I didn't abuse her. Why would I do such a thing? Naturally there were times when I changed her diaper and I had to wipe her bottom or something, but what does that have to do with sexual abuse? The whole thing was just preposterous. I wish her mom were alive to tell her she's way out of line, but her mother died years ago. She would have been as devastated as I am by this craziness."

Again Yapko just waited and nodded encouragement for Bob to continue.

"So then Angela began asking me all kinds of questions, interrogating me as if I'm a criminal. She asked me what business it was of mine to change her diapers. She claimed that was always her mother's job for as long as she could remember, and that it seemed suspicious to her therapist that I would be involved in such a chore."

"So what did you say to her?"

"What could I say? The accusations just got wilder and wilder with every therapy session. After the diaper accusation, she went on to accuse me of being the leader of some crazy satanic cult. She said we were sacrificing babies and cannibalizing them, and that we were engaging in all kinds of terrible and disgusting things. How she could even dream this stuff is way beyond me. Somehow her nutty therapist thought these fantasies were credible and believable, and even coaxed weirder and weirder ones out of Angela. Is that what they teach you people in school, to believe every cockamamie story that anyone tells you?"

Yapko didn't want to let the conversation stray, so he ignored the question, gesturing for Bob to continue with his narrative.

"So the whole thing just kept getting worse and worse. Every week she'd accuse me of something else, some other ridiculous fantasy. Finally, she gave me an ultimatum—at the instigation of her therapist—that unless I confessed my crimes and validated her memories, she would never speak to me again." At this point, all the effort Bob had been expending to keep himself together dissolved. He bowed his head and watched tears fall against the backs of his hands.

"Our relationship was ruined. I felt totally destroyed. If I confess to her crazy accusations, I'm saying I'm a pedophile and a satanist, and if I don't, I lose my daughter. What was I supposed to do? There was nothing I could do but tell the truth and tell her she's very, very wrong about me. Now she's telling everyone who will listen—our neighbors, our family, the whole community—that I am some kind of a satanic child molester. I've heard from people that she's told them that I steal babies for the cult, that I'm a deranged sexual predator and they should watch out for me. People don't believe her, of course, but they really don't know what to think about this soap opera. Even I don't know what to think anymore. I get so emotional about it, and I don't understand why it's happening or what I'm supposed to do about it. I just want my daughter back. She's all the family I have."

"It's a nightmare that just won't end for you," Yapko observed. He wished he could reassure Bob that everything would be okay, but he'd seen enough of such situations in the previous year to know that in this current climate of hypersensitivity, all an accuser had to do was point a finger and the parent was automatically presumed to be guilty.

"There isn't a day that goes by," Bob continued, "that I don't cry until my eyes hurt. I was a good father. Please believe me, Doctor, I am a good father."

Yapko nodded that he understood.

"Angela won't take my phone calls. She won't see me or talk to me. She has told people to warn me to stay away from her. She even tried to get a restraining order against me, but the court threw out the request because there was no evidence whatsoever to support her wild claims that I was a danger to her. But that didn't stop her from trying to keep me away, either. There just doesn't seem to be anything I can do, and it's killing me. I was about to give up, try and pretend she died or something, and then, then I came across your book." Bob looked at Yapko with a piercing gaze so intense that it was difficult to stare back without blinking.

"You gave me hope, Doctor. That's why I am here." And with that last statement Bob seemed to collapse into himself. He had exhausted himself, and now he needed a break from saying anything more about the enormous burden he was carrying.

BOB HELPS SPARK A MOVEMENT

During the rest of that first session, Yapko learned that Angela had been deteriorating significantly since she had been seeing the "anti-therapist." The therapy was hurting, not helping. She was unable to hold a job. She couldn't keep up with school. And throughout the deterioration she had been told by the therapist that she "had to get worse in order to get better." Meanwhile, Bob could do nothing but watch helplessly as his daughter progressively worsened, all the while blaming him for the damage.

As Bob began to empty the box of tissues, drying his tears and blowing his nose, Yapko waited for him to regain some focus. Once he seemed ready, Michael nodded. "One thing you should know, Bob, is that you are not alone. I have heard this type of story too many times over the last few years. It's true that child abuse does happen, and there are very few molesters who will admit to their actions. Almost everyone, whether guilty or not, says what you say—that they didn't do it."

Although Yapko wanted to show sympathy to this man in obvious pain and humiliation, he also wanted to earn his respect and trust by being completely honest and not mincing words. He told Bob that he didn't know what actually happened with his daughter, and he would never know. He also told him that memory is an unreliable process that can be influenced by many different factors. Then he briefly described some of the mechanisms underlying false memories.

The truth was that Yapko did believe his client, almost immediately. From what was well established about memory from cognitive and neuroscientific studies, the chances of someone accurately recalling a memory from the age of less than a year were exceedingly small. To have a detailed memory, involving actions and dialogue remembered along with contextual variables, was a virtual impossibility for a one-year-old. But historical accuracy is different from personal belief, and Angela came to believe in the authenticity of her memory. It was her personal truth, even if it had nothing to do with objective truth. As a result, she made some of the worst accusations one person can level at another.

Yapko could clearly see the extent of Bob's devastation. Although the things Bob had been accused of did seem highly improbable, it was not Yapko's job to believe his client or disbelieve him. Instead, he spent those first hours with Bob helping him gain some understanding of what might be going on with his daughter; how the therapist was wrong to suggest a history of abuse in response to the presentation of symptoms that could have been explained just as readily in other, far less damaging ways; how such beliefs could become entrenched; and how he could best handle this delicate situation skillfully. Bob listened attentively, took careful notes, asked lots of questions, and vowed to carefully consider Yapko's recommendations.

By the time Bob left, Yapko was feeling not only drained but furious. He was just amazed at how these crazy stories could get going, and how therapists were oblivious to the ways that they might be creating problems for their clients that they didn't come in with in the first place. Too many therapists didn't seem to understand the most basic aspects of

the relationship between memory and suggestibility, apparently errone-
ously believing that they could help people recover presumably repressed
memories without influencing the types and qualities of memories that
emerged. For Yapko this was the last straw. Something just snapped
inside him. He'd had enough of people's lives being devastated by poor
therapeutic practice.

Yapko realized that he was in a unique position, having established
some credibility as an expert within the fields of hypnosis, human suggestibility, and the practice of psychotherapy. He recognized that there were
not many people who could sensibly bring the recovered memory issue
to the foreground for the public, as well as the mental health profession.
There weren't many people who could write a credible book exposing the
current, misguided therapeutic practices based on fallacies about memory.
Bob was the last straw, the final push he needed to drop his current writing
project and instead devote himself to collecting data and writing what
would likely be an explosive book about repressed memories arising in
response to therapists' misinformed interventions.

Yapko knew he couldn't just write a book about his opinions. He
knew he needed data to demonstrate to all concerned how too many
therapists were terribly misinformed, and influencing their clients on the
basis of their misinformation. Yapko surveyed more than a thousand
practicing therapists about the ways they understood and worked with
memories, and their beliefs about their validity under varying conditions
and their vulnerability to suggestive influences. Though many professionals
were surprised by the results, Yapko was not. He'd already been exposed
to some of the more preposterous beliefs and their harmful clinical
consequences. Although the sample he surveyed was mostly composed
of well-educated and highly experienced clinicians with an average of
well beyond a master's degree and 11 years of practice in the field, the
vast majority of them had huge misconceptions about the workings of
memories. Their misconceptions generally overstated the reliability of
memory and understated the vulnerability to suggestive influences such
as therapy. Simply put, therapists didn't realize they could create the very
problems that they would then have to treat.

Yapko tried to take a balanced position in the book, reporting on
what he found. Basically, his conclusion was that the evidence indicated
that repressed memories can be true. And they can be false. But without
corroborating evidence, there is really no way to know for sure. Even
memories that are rich in detail and highly emotional in the telling aren't
any more accurate. This led Yapko to suggest in his book therapeutic
guidelines for minimizing the likelihood of therapist contamination that
might help prevent tragedies similar to the one that occurred with Bob
and his daughter.

After the book was published, it became a lightning rod for anyone with an opinion on the subject, and there was tremendous media coverage worldwide. Here a respected psychologist was coming forth, with substantial evidence, and saying that some of those who reported sexual abuse and other traumas may, in fact, have unintentionally fabricated the stories in response to therapists' misguided suggestive practices. Letters poured in from professionals and the public alike, many of them very supportive and appreciative that someone was finally taking therapists to task for shoddy practices, but much of it was hate mail saying such vicious things as "The fact that you question the memories of people about being abused as children means that you are defending the perpetrators. You are probably a pedophile yourself. You should be castrated. How can you possibly question these painful memories that come up that people don't want? People work so hard to try to get their lives back to normal after being abused, and there you are leading them to doubt themselves and thereby contributing to them becoming more mentally disturbed. You are not a psychologist who tries to help people. You shouldn't be allowed to practice. You should be locked away. You are a danger to the community."

At first, Yapko thought there were just a few crackpots out there who refused to look at the issue in a balanced, objective way. They spoke in mantras—"Believe the memories" and "Believe the children"—but they did not question whether memories or children could be always be believed or whether, under some conditions, memories and children could deceive. As more and more criticism was leveled at him, Yapko realized that he was fighting against entrenched prejudice that traumatized one group of people at the expense of another.

In his book, Yapko cited some of the research on hypnosis and memory that had been done over many years. The law enforcement community had been routinely recruiting the help of hypnotists to refresh eyewitness testimony. As a result, the research question that had been tested empirically was whether hypnosis increases the amount of recall and the accuracy of people's memories. The clear answer is that it does not. The research unequivocally shows that hypnosis does not increase accurate recall, and hypnotically obtained testimony is no more likely to be accurate than that obtained in some other way. The research also showed that people can be very sure about what they recall and still be very, very wrong.

There was one study Yapko cited in our interview with him that he found particularly compelling in this regard, clear evidence of how easy it is for children to say something happened when it did not. Children were videotaped while being examined by a physician, a brief physical in which the doctor looked inside the mouth with a tongue depressor, looked in the ears, and then tied a little string around the

kid's wrist. One week later the children were interviewed about what
they remembered about the exam, and most gave a fairly accurate
description that matched what was on the video. But as the children
were repeatedly interviewed over the course of ten additional weeks,
being asked the same questions over and over, the answers began to
change, often dramatically. Eventually many of the children reported
that the doctor had stuck sticks up their behinds and tied them up with
rope. The repetitive questioning led the children to make up outrageous
stories that would have all but crucified the physician had the actual
exams not been videotaped. Such repetitive questioning is what typically
occurs when children are grilled by social workers, attorneys, and their
parents after a suspected incident. The evidence is irrefutable that the
mantra "Children don't lie" isn't entirely true.

THE THERAPIST FEELS THE CLIENT'S PAIN

Just when the attacks against Yapko seemed to become more and more
aggressive, the American Medical Association published a widely dissem-
inated position about repressed memory that was virtually identical to
what Yapko had been advocating. What he had recommended 10 years
earlier about how to work ethically and knowledgeably with such sensitive material is now considered to be standard professional practice. But
that does not take away the decade of attacks and abuse that he suffered.
Yapko, and others like him who squarely took on the biggest controversy
in the mental health profession in the last half-century, paid a price in
friendships lost and reputations assaulted.

"All this changed me personally, as well as professionally," Yapko
revealed. "Until all this happened, I was never aware of how absolutely
poisonous people can be when you contradict one of their sacred beliefs,
even when it can be shown to be a misguided belief. I am somebody who
likes to get along with people. I'm not big on confrontation. This was a
very painful time for me. I was ostracized by many of my colleagues. I was
disinvited to conferences by organizers who didn't want to be associated
with the controversy. At one point my reputation felt as battered and
misunderstood as many of the victims I was helping to defend."

Just to be clear on this point, Yapko was not defending perpetrators of sexual abuse. Rather, he was trying to help therapists, trusted
authorities charged with helping, not hurting, their vulnerable clients,
stop engaging in therapeutic practices that could devastate individuals
and their families. He was also trying to help those who had already been
falsely accused, without a shred of evidence beyond memories uncovered
with techniques known to foster confabulations—those people whose

lives and reputations were ruined by accusations that, subsequently, were found to be fantasies stoked by therapists who had their own misinformed agendas.

On a personal level, Yapko became far more appreciative of the ways that "reality" is a very flexible construct. Anyone is vulnerable to the influence of trusted and credible authorities who have no apparent motive to deceive, who present misinformation as fact in the name of benevolent help. This led him to be more introspective in his thinking, more challenging of his own (and others') beliefs, yet also more tolerant of different worldviews. Instead of asking himself, or his clients, if a particular belief was right or wrong in absolute terms, he began asking: Is it effective? Does it enhance the quality of life? In Angela's case, the answer was clearly no. She became a victim in every sense of the word.

Bob was the turning point in helping thrust Yapko onto a much more visible, emotionally charged stage. He didn't seek to become an advocate for social justice. This was not a career goal that he aspired to. But there came a point where he could no longer sit on the sidelines and watch people's lives and reputations be destroyed by therapists who through ignorance used their expertise and influence to hurt the people they were supposed to help.

FOLLOW-UP

It is now 13 years later. Recently, Bob scheduled a follow-up appointment with Yapko to fill him in on what had happened since their brief consultation more than a decade earlier. Yapko recalled from his own memory (backed up by case notes) that he'd advised Bob to keep a distance from his daughter, Angela, and not to push her to recant her accusations. He urged him to try to keep the lines of communication open, but doing any more than that would likely polarize her more. He advised Bob to send a birthday card every year or an occasional brief, upbeat note, but not to try to defend himself. Don't explain himself. Don't contradict her. Although Yapko had only the faintest glimmerings of the role that he would someday play in the controversy, he urged Bob to let the debate play out in the public arena. The issue would grow and eventually explode, Yapko was sure. Yapko felt certain that someday people would come to their senses and look at these issues in a more balanced way. Until then, telling Angela she was wrong would only convince her Bob was lying and incapable of taking responsibility for what he'd done. Once a person's mind is made up, it's very difficult to change it when you're the alleged perpetrator. As difficult as it was for Bob to accept this advice—to surrender, in a sense—he realized that he had no other choice.

As soon as Bob entered the office with a huge grin on his face and an outstretched hand, Yapko knew immediately that his client had been one of the lucky ones. It turned out that Bob had done well to control his impatience. He'd worked long and hard to keep his distance from his daughter, to follow the simple advice of sending brief, supportive messages.

After five agonizing years, things between father and daughter began to thaw. Angela called her father on occasion to ask him an inane question about something. Then after another year went by, she invited him to lunch. He was smart enough not to question any of these overtures; he just enjoyed the opportunities to again be the father of his daughter, whom he so adored and who had been taken from him.

"We have a great time together now," Bob said. "There's this unwritten rule between us that we don't talk about what happened before."

"There's no closure, though," Yapko observed.

"That's true. She's never said to me that she knows I didn't do what she accused me of. And I've never asked her if she believes me to be innocent now. We just pretend that none of that happened."

"You put it behind you and moved forward."

"Yes. Part of me desperately wants to hear her say, "I'm sorry, Daddy, for ever thinking you were a satanic pedophile. Can you ever forgive me?" Maybe that will happen one day, but I'm not going to hold my breath waiting for it. But we have a great time together now. We laugh, we go places and do things together, and she even has a new boyfriend who seems to genuinely care for her. We see one another all the time. Now we. . ." Bob stopped for a minute, reaching for the box of tissues just as he had so many years earlier. But this time they were tears of joy rather than of despair.

"You were saying?" Yapko prompted.

Bob nodded. "Now. . .now we have the kind of relationship that I'd always hoped for."

Chapter 17

JOHN MURPHY
A Language of Shrugs

Michael had a number of challenges in his life. At 10 years old, he was already an abject failure as a student. He had been diagnosed with moderate mental retardation, an IQ estimated in the high 60s. As if that was not enough for him to deal with, Michael lived in the "projects," the euphemism for federally funded community housing. He was poor, black, and classified as mentally handicapped.

John Murphy, out of graduate school only two years, was assigned as a psychologist to Michael's inner-city school. It was in a district characterized by pervasive poverty, transient residents, and violent crime.

Michael was referred to Murphy because his special education teacher was concerned about some of his behavior problems. He was verbally, and sometimes physically, aggressive toward other students. "The good news," the teacher told Murphy, "is that I haven't yet seen him use any weapons. But I won't be surprised if that comes next." What was left unsaid was that given the environment Michael went home to, it might be only a matter of time before his behavior escalated to the use of knives and guns.

"So," Murphy probed the teacher a little more to buy some time, "what do you think is going on?"

The teacher shrugged. "Who knows? He's just been acting up more and more. Sometimes he seems really quiet, almost depressed. Other times he just snaps at me or other students. I just don't know what to do with him."

Was she asking for an instant cure? Murphy started to panic. Sometimes it felt as if teachers thought he was some kind of magician who could just wave a magic wand or offer an incantation that would make everything better. Although he was a fan of brief therapy, there was no way he could formulate a plan without more information.

"What more can you tell me?" Murphy asked, hoping there was more to come.

"The kid scares me, if you want to know the truth. I just thought you might talk to him," the teacher said. "I know you can't give me any suggestions right away, but I was hoping that after you see him, you might get some idea of what is going on."

"Sure," Murphy agreed. "Do you know anything about the family?"

"One older brother. He's in some kind of a residential facility. Also with behavioral problems. There are other kids as well, most of whom have problems of their own. I know for sure that there's no father around. The mother is doing the best she can, but she has her hands full."

Murphy nodded. It was a familiar story. "And so you were hoping. . ."

"Exactly. You're a guy and all. And I was hoping he might connect with you because he's got no decent men in his life at all. He might talk to you. He sure won't open up to me."

Murphy spent a few more minutes with the teacher, gathering information about her interactions with Michael, what had worked in the past, and what had not. He got the distinct impression that there was something going on at home that was a source of challenge and difficulty for Michael. They agreed that Murphy would schedule a time to meet with the boy in the coming week.

THE (MOSTLY) SILENT WALK

Michael shuffled out of the classroom, his eyes following the tips of his shoes. He was quite tall and well-built for his age, and strikingly handsome. His clothes were dirty and tattered, holes showing through at the knees of his pants. It was as if he had worn the same clothes every day for a week, which he probably had.

Murphy's first impression of the boy was that he seemed rather shy and quiet, not at all like the aggressive kid he had been led to expect. When Murphy asked him how he was doing, Michael just shrugged his shoulders. They walked silently down the hallway to the office, where they might have some privacy.

They passed a window, cracked open, through which the sounds of children playing outside could be heard. "So, Michael, were you out there during recess?" Murphy pointed toward the window, forcing the boy to look up from his shoes for the first time.

Michael made a sound that Murphy took as affirmative.

"You were out there this morning, were you?"

Nod.

"Just got back, then?"

Another nod.

"What do you like to do during recess?"

Shrug.

This was pretty awkward, Murphy had to admit. He was trying to make some contact with the boy, but it was as if he were empty inside. Michael's body was walking alongside him in the hallway, but his spirit was somewhere else. Murphy hesitated for a moment while they stood looking out the window, then tried again: "Do you have a choice what you do out there doing recess, or does the teacher tell you what to do?"

Michael gave the same shrug, then said in small voice, almost a whisper: "We can do what we want."

Murphy had to lean down to hear, not at all sure what the boy said. He thought about asking him to speak up, but he wanted to avoid pushing him in any way. Throughout the rest of their walk to the office, Murphy remained hunched way down so he could hear the boy's whisper.

"What's your favorite sport?" he asked, trying another means of engaging Michael in conversation.

"Basketball."

"Oh, yeah? That used to be my sport as well."

Michael glanced up for a second, then back to his shoes.

"You're pretty tall for kids your age. You play close to the basket?"

Nod.

"I thought so. You look like someone I'd want to get the ball to. Tall and strong. That's who you want to get the ball to."

For the first time, Michael actually turned his head and momentarily looked Murphy in the eye. They sat down at a table and continued to talk about basketball—or, rather, Murphy continued to ask questions and Michael gave one-word, whispery answers. It wasn't as if this was a planned line of inquiry or anything; it was the only thing that Murphy could think to do, the only way to engage this boy. He was just trying to make a connection and to establish some sort of relationship. In spite of his training and expertise in developing behavioral interventions, he realized with increasing clarity that the power of change rested partly, maybe even largely, on the quality of his relationships with students—especially with a young, lost boy without a father.

TALKING WITHOUT MANY WORDS

The basketball talk went on for some time, perhaps 15 minutes or so, before Murphy changed the discussion. "You know, Michael, your teacher said you might want to have the chance to talk to somebody. She thought it might be a good idea if we visited for a while. Did she mention this to you?

Michael shook his head. "Not really."

"Well, she is concerned about you. She wants you to do good in school. And she wants you to pay attention in class so you learn stuff. She said that's been hard for you."

Michael raised his shoulders in a shrug, but a different one than the others. Murphy was beginning to read the various kinds of shrugs that Michael used to communicate, each one a little different from the others. It was as if he were speaking in a language of shrugs.

"She said that sometimes you get distracted by the other kids, and sometimes you bother them."

Shrug.

"And that these. . .these problems with other kids are making it harder for you to do your work."

So it went for the rest of their half-hour together (that seemed much longer to both of them). Murphy would attempt to engage Michael in some way and the boy would just shrug—sometimes indifferently, sometimes indicating confusion or agreement or disagreement or even interest.

"Well," Murphy said to wrap things up, "I'm glad we got this chance to talk. I'm wondering if you might be willing to come back sometime. We can continue the conversation, if you like."

This time, when Michael shrugged, he seemed to be saying that this would be okay with him.

"So you'd like to talk again, maybe next week?"

Shrug, then a small nod of the head.

"I'm sorry. Does that mean yes?"

"Yeah," Michael said in his whisper.

Murphy could tell that Michael was a little taken aback and intrigued by this whole encounter that had not gone at all the way he expected. He thought he'd get the usual scolding, perhaps a punishment, but not a conversation about basketball. And this guy seemed to be comfortable with the silences. The truth is that Michael just didn't like to talk much. He had so much inside of him that he couldn't begin to find the words to describe what it felt like.

SITTING IN THE HALLWAY

A few days later, Murphy was shuffling along the hallway to get to a meeting on the second floor. He made the turn to the stairwell, burst through the double doors, and was about to start up the stairs two at a time when something caught his eye. There, outside of a classroom, was a desk positioned by the door. Sitting in the chair, slouched with his feet crossed on the floor, was Michael. He was just sitting there, staring out into space. He didn't notice Murphy watching him, didn't seem to see much of anything around him. He had a book with him, but it was tucked underneath the seat.

"Hey," Murphy called out to him. "Michael."

The boy slowly turned his head in the direction of the stairwell but didn't say anything. He just looked blank. Murphy could tell there was something going on here. This was a tough, street kid, used to hiding his emotions, but Murphy sensed a very lost and hopeless expression in Michael's eyes.

Murphy abruptly reversed direction and walked back to where Michael was sitting. Without saying a word, he simply sat on the floor next to the desk with his back propped against the wall. They just sat there in silence.

One thing you should understand is that sitting quietly did not come easily or naturally to a young Irishman from a family of seven. Murphy not only liked to talk, but he was pretty good at it. Despite his preparation and experience formulating interventions and applying process skills, everything just stopped at that moment. He sat there, perfectly still, just like Michael.

A minute went by. Then another. And another. They could hear the sounds from within the classroom—voices, shuffling feet, muffled laughter. They could hear the sounds of footsteps down the hallway, up and down the stairs. But still they sat together, quietly, neither speaking or even looking at the other.

Murphy could hear this voice inside his head screaming at him: "Do something already! Don't just sit there like an idiot. The kid is dying inside. Help him. Fix him." But he ignored the voice and continued to wait, mostly because he couldn't think of anything useful to say. He felt as if he were in some sort of trance, almost as if he couldn't move or speak even if he had wanted to.

Five, ten, fifteen minutes went by, all without a word. At one point, Murphy reached over and placed a reassuring hand on Michael's arm, just a light touch, but that was all. He looked up and saw tears coming down Michael's face. He wasn't making a sound, just crying in a whisper, just the way he spoke.

After a few more minutes, Murphy brought his hand down and started to rise from the floor. He looked at Michael, who continued to stare at his own feet. He felt so close to the boy during the time they'd just spent together. He couldn't begin to describe what he felt, other than to say that he was sure there had been some sort of close connection that went beyond words. He'd never had an experience quite like this, and it had a powerful effect. It was as if he had been totally present with the boy.

"Well, then," Murphy said softly, "I'll see you Thursday." And with that he started to head back to the stairs, hurrying to the meeting that he had almost forgotten.

Murphy's head was spinning as he walked away. He felt totally drained and exhausted. To an observer it might have looked as if he was just relaxing on the floor, but he felt that he'd never worked so hard. His mind had been swirling with choices much of the time—things he could say, things he should say, things he might do—all of them rejected in favor of just being with Michael. On one hand, he felt the heavy burden of Michael's pain and sadness. At the same time, there was an unexpected sense of contentment and gratitude—a genuinely positive feeling of being helpful to another person and being part of a meaningful and intimate interaction. "Imagine that," thought Murphy, "a counseling intervention with no words!"

He stopped at the top of the second landing to gather his thoughts. "Okay, what do I do with him next time?" Murphy wondered. "I don't even know what happened this time. I've got to talk to his teacher and find out more about what's going on with Michael in the classroom."

Murphy soon learned that Michael had been kicked out of class for mouthing off to the teacher. When she tried to get him to calm down, things escalated to the point that she had to ask him to leave. That's how he had ended up sitting in the hallway.

On Thursday, Murphy found an envelope on the floor under his office door. Probably another referral or two, he thought. Once settled, he opened the envelope and found a ripped-in-half piece of lined, yellow paper, just the sort that kids use for their schoolwork. That was weird, he thought. When he unfolded the sheet, he found written in large, block letters:

THNKS!!!!
MICHAEL

Murphy turned the paper over to see if there was something else written, but that was it. So their encounter had meant something to Michael after all.

THE LIMITS OF SOLUTIONS

During the ensuing weeks, Murphy met with Michael a few more times to work on improving classroom behavior and dealing with anger. He doesn't recall a lot of the details, mostly because they seemed relatively unimportant compared with what happened between them in the hallway.

"Everything we did after that," Murphy recalls, "was contextualized in a respectful relationship that was strongly influenced by that experience. Michael felt safe enough to be vulnerable in my presence. I allowed myself to be vulnerable in his presence as well."

This experience had a huge impact on Murphy. He realized that being with people, really being with them in the sense that Carl Rogers described, could be immensely powerful in itself. He had known this was possible, intellectually at least, but now he really knew it in his head and his heart. He had also known this in his personal relationships. But Michael taught him, more than he ever realized, how much intimacy and connection could mean in healing relationships.

In graduate school Murphy believed that the pathway to effective therapy was to find the "best" or "right" intervention model, master it, and implement it with clients. He was led to believe that, over time, he would just get better and better in using his chosen model and techniques, and that outcomes would improve accordingly. Yet this experience taught him that he could be useful to people without telling them what to do. Here was a boy who was black, dirt poor, and mentally challenged, a kid who desperately needed direction—who needed to be told what to do—and yet Murphy had avoided that almost completely. What had meant so much, to both of them, was their mutual connection. In this case, there were no rabbits pulled out of a magical hat of interventions, or even many words.

Murphy learned, more than ever, how gratifying and useful it feels to truly be with someone. This experience was instrumental in changing his approach to therapy and other forms of helping in a manner that honors a respectful relationship as the cornerstone of effective helping. It also changed the way he viewed other key relationships in his life, most notably the relationship with his wife and children. "Although I knew this intellectually, I realized on a deeper level that simply listening and being present can be the most helpful and loving thing I can do for my wife and kids when they tell me about a problem or decision they are facing.

"I had been a behaviorally oriented solution-focused therapist—and I still might describe myself this way—but Michael taught me not to fall in love with my solutions or try to impose them on others, because to do so carries the risk of running roughshod over the more important task of establishing and maintaining a respectful relationship with clients. In the case of Michael, this required me to shut up, listen, and be present. As has been the case with most of the powerful lessons I have learned throughout my career, this one came from the greatest of all teachers—the client."

Chapter 18

JOHN KRUMBOLTZ
The Story of the Sun and the Wind

"So," Martha said to start the session, "the reason we're here is because of George and me—our marriage is not working very well."

Krumboltz nodded and surveyed the couple. They seemed composed enough, at least for now. He could feel some tension between them, but at the moment they looked like an ordinary couple in their forties.

"George, here," Martha continued, as she pointed with her thumb toward her husband, "he just doesn't seem to be interested in having a good marriage—at least with me."

Krumboltz looked at George, as if to confirm this assessment, but George just sat silently while his wife continued to speak at some length about his failings as a husband.

"And besides all that," she drew to a close, "he does so many things to annoy me."

"What kinds of things?" Krumboltz asked.

"Well...," Martha hesitated, as if taking time to compose a very long list, "his table manners are atrocious, for one thing. He eats with his mouth open, and he knows how much this bothers me. Sometimes I think he deliberately uses the wrong fork—you know, the smaller, salad one?—for his main course. I go to a lot of trouble to prepare his meals just the way he likes them, and this is the way he repays the favor. It's just. . . it's just. . . aggravating."

"George?" Krumboltz prompted him.

George shrugged, as if to say: "What can I do?" He seemed unwilling to defend himself.

"See?" Martha said. "Sometimes he just sits there and won't say anything, just like what he's doing with you right now."

"You don't talk much, George?" Krumboltz clarified.

Before he could answer, Martha added, "And when he does speak, his grammar is atrocious. He should know better. He's been educated.

But sometimes, I don't know. . .." She trailed off, utterly baffled by why her husband would behave in these ways she found so upsetting. It felt as if he were doing those things to her.

"George," Krumboltz intervened, this time more decisively, "how do you see the situation?"

Again George shrugged, uncertain how to begin. "I don't know. I don't really have a problem with things the way she does." He looked over at his wife for a minute, then back to the therapist. "I kind of do what I want. I'm pretty content, more or less."

"What is it that you like to do, exactly?"

"Well, you know, like antiques and all."

Before Krumboltz could ask him what he meant, Martha jumped in. "See, that's what I mean. He's always in the garage—he converted the whole garage into a wood shop or some damn thing. He's always in there, at all hours, working on his projects. That lathe in there makes such a mess, too. Wood chips everywhere. There's sawdust that gets in the house. I try. . ."

"George," Krumboltz interrupted her, "you were saying you like antiques."

"Yeah, I love to find old pieces of furniture, hidden gems, that just need some restoration." For the first time, George's face lit up. "I try to find some pieces, real cheap, and then I strip them down and refinish them. I know Martha thinks I spend too much time doing this, but it relaxes me. It makes me feel like I'm accomplishing something."

"George," his wife responded, "sometimes it seems like those damn pieces in the garage matter more to you than I do. It just seems like such a waste of time to spend all your time hiding out in there."

Krumboltz had heard enough at this point to get a sense of what was going on between them. "Would you say that you love one another?" he asked each of them.

To his surprise, George answered first this time. "I would say that I love Martha, but I'm not in love with her, if you know what I mean."

"That's a terrible thing to say," Martha responded right away. "How can you say you love me when you say things like that?"

THE SUN AND THE WIND

The conflict and accusations went on for some time until Krumboltz felt that he was learning nothing new, except how entrenched their destructive patterns were. "Excuse me," he said at one point, "but I'd like to tell you a story that I first heard as a child. Maybe you've already heard it."

Martha leaned back in her seat and crossed her arms. George seemed to steel himself for more criticism that would now come from the therapist.

"I'm wondering if you've ever heard the story of the battle between the wind and the sun."

Both looked puzzled and shook their heads.

"I think it might be pertinent to what is going on here. Let me tell you the story, and then let's see what you make of it."

They signaled that they were ready to listen.

"The wind and the sun were having this big argument about who was more powerful. The wind claimed that he was obviously more powerful because he could destroy things: 'I can blow people around. I can knock anything down. I am clearly more powerful than you are.'

"The sun said, 'Oh, really? Why don't you show me what you can do?'

"The wind said, 'Okay. See that man down there, wearing an overcoat?'

"The sun nodded.

"'Okay, good. Watch me blow that overcoat right off his back.'

"'Fine,' the sun answered. 'Let's see what you can do.'

"The wind started to blow. He blew harder. The harder he blew, the tighter the man wrapped the coat around himself.

"Temporarily frustrated, the wind said, 'No big deal. I'll just make it colder.' The wind became freezing cold and blew with maximum ferocity. The harder and colder the wind blew, the tighter the man held on to his coat. Finally the wind said to the sun, 'Well, I'll bet you can't do it either.'

"The sun replied, 'Let me try a different approach.' Then the sun came out from behind the clouds and smiled warmly on the man. As the man became warmer, he started to unbutton his coat. As the warmth increased, the man removed his coat completely."

Krumboltz paused for a moment and waited for the couple to react.

Martha nodded her head up and down several times. "That was very meaningful," she said. "Very meaningful!"

A STEP FURTHER

After George and Martha left, Krumboltz was feeling quite pleased with himself for the clever way he had used the parable to initiate a breakthrough in the ways this couple interacted. Obviously, Martha had achieved insight into the reason why George stayed away from her. Obviously, she would now change from using cold criticism to using positive warmth. Although he was inclined to work behaviorally, Krumboltz had also been trained in the usual insight-promotion methods of the time.

The prevailing theory instructed that insights like those experienced by this couple would make a difference in changing their behavior. That was the theory.

The next week George and Martha were back, bickering as much as ever. It was as if the previous session had never occurred and they were starting over again. In some ways, things were worse because now, rather than just Martha launching attacks toward her husband, he was fighting back more vigorously. It was as if they really were the sun and the wind battling to the bitter end.

Although these sessions ultimately had little positive effect on his clients, they taught Krumboltz an important lesson: insight alone is insufficient to promote changes in behavior. From that point on, he became more convinced than ever that giving people insights was largely a waste of time, unless it was accompanied by some instruction and rehearsal of more constructive behavior.

This insight—that insight itself is useless without action—not only changed the way Krumboltz did therapy but also altered his teaching style.

"I don't give lectures anymore," he confessed. "I don't think the lecture method is a very good way to teach. Students could just as easily read a lecture or watch a video. I see it as a waste of class time to give lectures. Class time provides a unique opportunity for a teacher and students to interact, to solve problems, to practice new techniques, and to share experiences. This is what produces learning. It helps people to put insights to actual use."

In looking back on the case, Krumboltz wished he had gone a step further. He should have asked Martha how the story was meaningful to her. He could have said, "How was this story meaningful to you? How do you see it affecting what you do in your marriage?"

George wasn't spending time with Martha because she was making it so unpleasant for him to be around her, but Martha found it hard to be pleasant when George ignored her so much. According to Krumboltz: "Neither one ever quite got it that in order to have a better marriage, each was going to have to change behavior." Krumboltz has found that he can learn from his mistakes as well as from his successes.

TAKING ACTION

This couple's case reminded Krumboltz of another very similar one, although much earlier in his career, when he was a school counselor. He had just obtained a master's degree during a time when Carl Rogers was advocating nondirective therapy and E. G. Williamson was pushing for a far more directive approach. Krumboltz had been indoctrinated quite passionately that the only way to help people was through the relationship-oriented, Rogerian approach that emphasized reflecting feelings with warmth and genuineness. Since he was young, naïve, and impressionable, Krumboltz followed the "party line" into his first high school counseling job.

One student, Jim, came in to see him one day to talk over a few things. "I'm taking this course in geometry," Jim said, practically gushing with enthusiasm.

"I can see you're excited," Krumboltz reflected as he had been trained to do.

"Yeah, I'm learning to do proofs and stuff."

"So you're really enjoying the feeling of solving problems."

"Oh, yes," Jim continued. "And I'm also taking this history class and we're learning all about the American Revolution and the French Revolution. They took place at about the same time, but they were really different."

"You're getting some understanding of how these two events in history are affecting the way we are today. Is that what you're saying?"

"Ah," Jim hesitated. "No, not exactly. I'm just interested in how people used to live in those days."

"I see." Throughout this conversation, Krumboltz was doing his best to be as empathic and warm and understanding as possible. He was concentrating with all his might on using his reflective listening skills, which turned out to be pretty easy because Jim was a fluent talker with a lot to say.

Krumboltz continued to see Jim for about a half dozen sessions, each one following the template that he had learned in graduate school. They were developing a solid relationship. Jim was covering many different aspects of his life. And his counselor was feeling damn proud that things were going so well. . .that is. . .until they reached the end of their sixth session.

"I was thinking of trying out for the baseball team," Jim was saying. "But. . ."

". . .but you're not sure you're good enough," Krumboltz finished for him.

"Well, no, actually what I was really wondering was whether we were ever going to do anything in here."

"What do you mean?" Krumboltz asked, genuinely puzzled. They had been making excellent progress during their sessions.

"It's just, you know, I come in here and I tell you stuff and all. You listen to me real good—and I appreciate that, I do. But we don't ever actually do anything."

What Jim had been trying to tell Krumboltz is that he appreciated their conversations and found them interesting, but they had not yet gotten around to what he was having trouble with. And even when they did talk about it, or try to develop some understanding, this was not nearly enough to change his behavior.

At first, Krumboltz thought his lack of progress with Jim, as well as with several other kids in the school, was the result of his own inadequacies as a nondirective counselor. But later, the first inklings of his dissatisfaction with insight-oriented, nondirective therapy, which had begun with Jim, came into full blossom with George and Martha.

Whether in his therapy, his classrooms, or his personal life, Krumboltz is most interested in the question: What are you going to do about that? The bottom line, for both of the stories he shared, and for the guiding principle of his life, is that making changes is all about taking constructive action. As a result of mistakes made with counseling cases like these, he now believes that constructive action needs to start right in the counseling office.

Chapter 19

PAUL PEDERSEN
A Lesson in Humility

In the mid-1970s, a private foundation funded a project to bring together experts from around the world who could collaborate on cross-cultural communication. In one such gathering of scholars, 37 experts from the United States, and another 37 from Japan, were brought together at a small ski resort in the town of Nihonmatsu in a province north of Tokyo.

The plan was that participants would meet in small groups of about eight people, from early in the morning to late in the evening, every day for a week. This was just the work schedule; members awakened earlier for exercise or walks, then ended the day socializing until 3 a.m.

Pedersen had spent the past four years working in Indonesia, Malaysia, and Taiwan, establishing his credentials as an expert on Asian cultural practices. He was, therefore, selected as one of the two directors of research for the project. This was a pretty exciting opportunity for him—to work with such distinguished experts in the field, all brought together under one roof, for the express purpose of testing their theories in wide-ranging, open conversations. After all, now they would have the chance to really practice what they taught to others.

All interactions between them would be videotaped so they could be scrutinized later for research purposes. A control room was set up with monitors of all seven groups operating simultaneously. This would enable participants to view what was going on in the other groups as a basis for comparison with their own experiences.

BE CAREFUL WHAT YOU ASK FOR

During the first meeting, everyone was polite and respectful, and showed appreciation for one another. "It is a great honor to be part of this group," Pedersen began his session. "This work that we are doing

153

together could have great importance for the future of intercultural communication throughout the world." Although he kept these thoughts to himself, Pedersen also had grandiose fantasies that they might actually make steps toward achieving world peace or developing breakthroughs in intercultural conflicts.

Members of the Japanese delegation returned the compliments, each sharing a feeling of privilege in working with such esteemed colleagues from America. They had many formal ceremonies and greetings in highly ritualized interactions.

During the second day, things started to loosen up a bit. Maybe it was a result of their all having gone out the evening before to take hot baths and drink sake into the wee hours of the morning. Perhaps, after so many hours together at one stretch, they had exhausted the usual customs and could now relate to each other in less guarded ways. Or it could just have been that members from both countries saw this as a real opportunity to be honest with each other in ways they had never done previously.

At one point, a representative from Japan to the United Nations completed the customary ritualized preliminaries and then asked permission for them to go deeper with each other, maybe even into unknown territory. After all, this was their goal, was it not?

The Americans readily agreed, with relish. "So, Ito," Pedersen encouraged his Japanese colleague, "what is it that you'd like to say to us that you have been holding back?"

"Yeah," another of the Americans jumped in, "tell us what you really don't like about us. Surely, with all your time spent working in New York at the U.N., you've had lots of experience with Americans. Tells us what you really think of us."

Ito nodded solemnly and looked around the group for permission to continue. All of the participants, from both the Japanese and the American sides, nodded, acknowledging that they should indeed pull back the curtain on their usual polite, careful rules of communication. In a sense, they agreed they would talk to each other about some of the things they said only to their own kind, when nobody else was around.

Ito was obviously uncomfortable with this new territory they were about to explore. After all, he was a diplomat and was used to saying things couched in carefully managed language. Finally, he took a deep breath and, encouraged by his colleagues around the group, started saying out loud some of the things that he had observed for a long time. "There are three things we don't like about Americans. One, they slam car doors when they get out. Two, they start every sentence with the first-person singular. Everything is I, me, I, me. Third, they don't see the world from anyone else's cultural perspective. They have only one way of looking at things, and that is their own way."

Pedersen was stunned by the honesty. He had noticed the way that Ito had talked about "they" when referring to Americans, as if (at least temporarily) excluding the Americans in the group from this criticism. In all his years working with Japanese colleagues, he had never heard such a breach of their etiquette. After all, the Americans were guests in their country. Yet this was exactly what the group was supposed to be doing together. If this research was to mean anything, then they had to take risks with each other. They had to be honest in ways they had never been before. Since they were all experts in intercultural communication, there was nobody else on the planet better prepared for this task.

Several others Japanese group members chimed in with their own observations about Americans and their arrogance. They mentioned how loudly they talked, and how arrogant they appeared. They talked about the derision and disrespect they felt from Americans who ridiculed some of their most cherished practices. They commented on the gluttony in America, the rudeness, the crime. They went on at some length, listing many other things that Pedersen had never heard before. It was as if a great dam had broken open and there was now a great force of honesty rushing forward.

As Pedersen listened to this list of complaints and criticisms about his people, his initial feelings of gratitude gave way to more than a little defensiveness. Sure, this was an amazing opportunity to break down the usual cultural barriers, but he couldn't help feeling under attack.

During the rest of that day, and the ones that followed, the Americans returned the favor and told the Japanese about the reactions they felt along a similar line: that Japanese were the ones who were arrogant, who thought that they were the center of the universe. All their rituals and traditions were designed to prevent the real expression of honest feelings. And then there was all that repressed aggression that comes out in the form of warmongering every few decades.

"You talk to us about war?" another of the Japanese members said with indignation. "Do you have any idea what you did to our country, to our people, when you killed all those innocent people with your bombs? And afterward, you have tried to take away our dignity and our honor. What do you expect us to do?"

It did not escape Pedersen and the others that now the attacks were becoming far more personal. Instead of talking about Americans in general, they were using "you," no longer exempting the group members from the criticism. And then they began to get far more specific.

"Look at the way you behave in this group," a Japanese business consultant pointed out. "You interrupt us when we speak. You only see things from your own perspective, as if you cannot comprehend how others might view situations differently."

This was a particularly low blow, Pedersen thought, considering they were all experts on doing exactly the opposite. They had all spent many years living and working abroad, and took great pride in their cultural sensitivity. And yet now they were all accusing each other of being frauds, of being no different from their unenlightened countrymen and countrywomen back home.

"It seems," one member said at one point, in a soft voice that stood out amid all the anger, "that right now we are doing exactly the same things that we have accused each other of doing. We are breaking all of our own rules by insulting each other and failing to show understanding."

This was an excellent point, one intended to diffuse the growing conflict, but by this time there was too much emotion. The dam had completely broken, and it seemed, at least for now, that there was no way to rebuild the barriers that had kept things safe and polite. And so the criticisms continued throughout the day, at one point leading to raised voices and members storming out of the room in indignation. Pedersen was glad there were no weapons around, or things might have escalated even further out of control. He now understood, firsthand, how easily wars could begin. He also felt like an incredible hypocrite that with all his experience and training, all his research and writing about intercultural communication, he now felt powerless to practice what he preached to others.

BREAKING THEIR OWN RULES

The strangest thing about this whole encounter was that, at the end of the day, at 6 p.m., they all bowed to each other and headed off to the bathhouse and then the sake bar, where they drank and caroused together until the early morning. Whatever had happened during the day was soon forgotten. Then they grabbed a few hours of sleep and began again the next day. In all his years teaching and doing research about intercultural communication, Pedersen had never seen such a peculiar compartmentalization of behavior: during the days the participants broke every one of their rules about respectful communication; then, at night, they became fast friends again while under the influence of hot baths and sake.

"We were so concerned about coming off as professional," Pedersen recalled. "We were so concerned about being respected by the others that we broke the rules to do it. I learned more during this long week than from any other such experience I ever had. In some ways, it was my biggest success, but also my biggest failure. Under that kind of pressure, I was absolutely unable, or perhaps unwilling, to take seriously the principles of good intercultural communication. I learned how stress kills the best of intentions. When you are under attack for a prolonged period of time, and in this case for more than two days, you respond to the attack irrationally, with anger, and you try to hurt the other person rather than hear the other person. I would be thinking, as they were talking, how impolite and how terrible these people were. I am sure they were thinking the very same thing about me. Only afterward, when we had a chance to reflect a little bit on what happened, could we see clearly how badly we had stumbled in terms of looking at what was going on."

INTERPRETATIONS OF CULTURAL CONTEXT

Pedersen was profoundly changed by this group experience. Even after 30 years he continues to learn from everything he experienced during that week in Japan. Prior to this gathering, Pedersen had considered himself one of the world's true experts on intercultural communication (the way he is still viewed in the field), but after that experience he could no longer think of himself that way. "I learned that I will never be an expert. I will always be a student. I'm now much more comfortable in the role of being a learner."

Second, Pedersen learned how important it is to listen. He knew this, of course, from all his training and research, but he didn't really know this. "I learned how important it is not to respond, especially during conflict situations, until you are absolutely certain of what the other person has said. This can be done either through clarification or through restating what you think was said and checking it out. The problem I had was reacting too impulsively."

Third, Pedersen learned the power of emotions, especially under stress.

"I became very aware of how shallow, how superficial, how thin that skin of rational thinking is, and how quickly we can cut through that membrane to reach a much more volatile, emotional, destructive self underneath."

The whole time that things were spinning out of control, Pedersen had been watching himself behaving inappropriately, yet he felt powerless to stop himself. "It was like I was up on the ceiling, or in the control room, watching myself and the whole group, thinking, "This is ridiculous. Look at what I am doing. I am insulting these people and that is making it necessary for them to insult me. And I am the guest. I know what guest–host relationships are supposed to be like, yet I am doing the very thing I teach my students not to do. What is going on?"

During the brief "truces" in the evenings, when they drank sake and went to the hot tubs, everything was fine. Then they could talk in calm, rational, respectful ways. They were exhausted at that point, their defenses worn down. By this time they didn't feel like fighting anymore.

They would laugh instead, and avoid any topic that might lead to a disagreement. They would compose haiku together. They would take turns performing their creations and then applaud each other. Then, the next morning, the war would begin anew in the workshop.

Pedersen's old friend and the codirector of the Nihonmatsu experience, Clifford Clarke, gave Pedersen his interpretation of this behavior:

> Their atmosphere (*funiki*) had changed because the location (*basho*) had changed from one where they had been asked by the guests to violate their norms of communication. In the bath they felt released from that request and free to return to norms appropriate with guests. The bath is certainly no place to argue!
>
> Both forms of communication were genuine from the Japanese point of view. There was no inconsistency therein for such high-context people. One of their favorite sayings is *basho ni otte, toki ni otte, hito ni otte*, which means "according to place, according to time, according to person." In other words, in English, there is appropriate behavior for every place, time, and person, especially in a high-context culture. Not responding to a guest's request would certainly convey an unacceptable arrogance unbecoming to one in the role of the host.
>
> From the U.S. perspective, such swings of behavior might readily be judged as inconsistent and irrational, but the rational guidelines of behavior in one culture are often hidden to members of other cultures, as we all know. The ways we balance our rational and emotional thoughts and feelings are more integrated in high-context cultures and more separated in low-context cultures. Hence, we find the integration of role and person in one and the separation of role and person in the other, which often leads to the mutual judgments of childishness across these two cultures for very different reasons. To one it is childish to behave as though one's role and person are separable, and to the other it is childish to behave as though they are not. Such judgments are expressed on one hand as "they are so insensitive," and on the other hand as "they are so thin-skinned." Both of these judgments usually result in building distrust in the binational workplace, which happened in spades at Nihonmatsu.

WHEN LEARNING BEGINS

After this experience, Pedersen no longer believed that people are guided by reason. "I think we decide what we want to do, and then we just go ahead and do it, and then come up with some explanation afterward."

This led Pedersen to develop more profound respect for the emotional, nonrational parts of ourselves during interactions with others. He believes now that such feelings are the foundation of who we are and what we do.

"Another thing: prior to this experience I used to have the irritating habit of interrupting people—the Japanese pointed this out to me several times—and since that time I have learned to listen." It is this listening, finally and eventually, that made it possible for long-held secrets to emerge.

During this week's group, Pedersen and the other Americans learned the depth of anger and resentment felt about Hiroshima and Nagasaki. "Everyone pretends as if this is all behind us, but in Japan it is still very much a part of their consciousness. There is never an opportunity to deal with it, and we don't have to deal with it. That sort of becomes a metaphor for a lot of other areas in our life where anger may control what we think and feel more than we realize, or more than I am willing to admit. That emotionality is profoundly powerful energy deciding where we go and what we do."

Pedersen now seems quite at ease talking about how he was changed personally and professionally by this group experience, and others that he has had as a therapist and teacher. He prepares himself for his work by opening himself up as much as he can to what his clients and students might offer. He can't imagine working any other way.

Based on his studies of other cultural practices, Pedersen has trouble with the ways that therapy is structured and controlled by professional organizations. He has identified 13 aspects of the Ethical Code that are profoundly culturally biased and privilege Western beliefs over those of other parts of the world. With regard to the main premise of this book—that therapists are indeed regularly changed by their clients—the Ethical Code makes great efforts to prevent or deny that this phenomenon occurs. It is deemed as exploitative, unprofessional, and self-indulgent to have one's own needs met during sessions. And indeed it certainly can be, if a therapist engages in behavior to deliberately meet his or her own needs at the expense of a client.

"Ethical codes presume that all the learning is one-directional," Pedersen pointed out. "We know that is not true. There are times when the therapist, or the teacher, learns even more than the client or student. Throughout Asia, this is fully acknowledged—the expert is also a student. Whereas in our culture we do everything we can to prevent dual relationships, there are other parts of the world where it would be unethical not to be engaged in such a reciprocal relationship."

Pedersen also pointed out that the reluctance on the part of therapists to admit they have been changed by clients stems from the hierarchical nature of the relationship. Whether we admit it or not, clients are clearly in a one-down position. And the assumption is that we are not supposed to learn from people who are beneath us.

So what Pedersen learned most from his group experience in Japan was humility. His real learning began when his learning ended. He became suspicious of so-called experts thereafter, and he encourages others to follow this lead. It is one thing to "know" things, and quite another thing to be able to practice them during those times when it matters the most.

POSTSCRIPT

Pedersen was not unique in the feelings of shame he experienced after the gathering. Most of the participants, from both Japan and the United States, felt that they had behaved in a hypocritical fashion. A few of the Japanese group members felt such acute embarrassment that they seriously threatened to commit *seppuku*, ritual suicide, if the results of the conference were ever published. This is why the Japanese copy of the tape recordings is forever locked in the basement archives of the International House of Japan.

Chapter 20

LENORE WALKER
Finding Justice with a Sledgehammer

Mercedes seemed to have walked out of *Women's Wear Daily*, dressed immaculately, consistent with her profession as elite interior designer. The way she presented herself—groomed and polished—made it clear that appearances seemed very important to her. Clearly, she was quite successful in her work.

With little preamble, Mercedes said that the reason she had come for help was that she was being battered by her husband, a notable political figure in town. They had been together for about 10 years. "Nobody believes me when I say the son of a bitch can be so vicious." She said this as if she expected Walker to doubt her as well.

"Why wouldn't I believe you?" Walker asked.

Mercedes ignored the question, instead focusing on her main concern at this point. "Look, whether you believe me or not, there's one thing we have to be clear about. Under no conditions must you ever contact my husband. If he ever found out that I was talking to you. . ." She left the rest unsaid.

Walker nodded her understanding. They spent the next few minutes devising a signal system so that if Mercedes needed to be reached, Walker could leave a coded message for her. This was common practice among the battered women who came for sessions.

So composed and in control when she had first walked in the office, Mercedes soon began crying as she talked about her terror living with a man who could be so violent and unpredictable.

"Who else have you talked to about this?" Walker asked.

"Do you mean the police? They'd never believe me. To even suggest that means you have no idea just how powerful and well connected my husband is in this city. Besides, if he ever found out that I contacted the authorities, he'd make things worse than I could ever imagine." Mercedes' sobs communicated the depth of her despair.

"You must have confided in someone about this," Walker pressed. "A friend, for instance."

Mercedes shook her head. Between sniffling and blowing her nose, she indicated that she had seen a psychiatrist once before, but the man had ignored the complaints and just offered her medication.

"What sort of things does your husband do to you?"

"He chokes me," Mercedes answered in a small voice, embarrassed to admit the extent of her daily terror. "He usually does it when he wants an excuse to leave the house, but it can come any time. I try to stay out of the bedroom as much as I can, because sometimes he uses a pillow to smother me—just to the point where I pass out." She laughed bitterly, then said, "He is really quite skilled at knowing just when to stop."

"Does he ever punch you or hit you?"

"You mean leave marks? Are you kidding? I told you, he's very powerful, and he would do nothing to risk his reputation in this community. Otherwise, he'd probably have killed me long ago."

"So, then, what brought you to see me now?"

"My doctor. He was doing a breast exam and saw bruises on my throat. Usually, my husband is careful not to leave any marks, but I guess that time he must have gotten out of control. Anyway, my doctor, he said I should come to talk to someone. So here I am." She said this as if now that she had appeared, her therapist would have some kind of magic wand to make everything all better.

The first priority, of course, was to get Mercedes out of immediate danger. She had to get out of the house. But the situation proved to be more complex than initially presented. Like many battered women, Mercedes had a love–hate relationship with her husband. There had been times when he was on the verge of moving out and she had begged him to stay. These conflicts provoked the worst outbursts of rage, as if the price of his staying with her was a particularly brutal smothering or choking.

"So," Walker clarified, "sometimes you end up escalating things and making things worse."

Mercedes nodded miserably.

"And what is it, exactly, that seems to set him off the most?"

"When I grab him," Mercedes said. "Whenever I try to hold on to him, it just drives him crazy."

"You seem to know that," Walker said, "but you do it anyway." This was a common pattern she had seen in other battered women: they were afraid of the beatings, but even more terrified of being abandoned or of being hurt worse when he returned.

"Yes," Mercedes agreed. "It's gotten worse since the kids left. Now that we're alone, he seems to feel more anger toward me." She was referring to her children from a former marriage who were now away at school. As long as they had been home, the violent episodes had been more controlled.

FAMILY SECRETS

During the ensuing months, Walker offered her client as much support as possible. They discussed, and then practiced, alternative ways she might respond that would reduce her vulnerability, or how she could have handled things any differently.

As the therapy progressed, Mercedes disclosed that she had recently learned that her husband had secretly rented his own apartment. She was not sure if that was because he was soon planning to move out or whether he needed a place to take a girlfriend. She couldn't decide which was worse.

The trust in the therapeutic relationship improved over a period of several months. Mercedes continued to gain confidence and build her strength, eventually to the point where she told her husband she had been seeking help. His reaction was predictable.

"Who the hell do you think you are?" he said to Walker in a menacing tone. (He had called her on the phone as soon as he was able to find out whom his wife was seeing.)

"Excuse me?" Walker responded, trying to figure out what was going on.

"I said, who the hell do you think you are, screwing with my marriage?"

"I'm not. . ."

"I'm not interested in your excuses, Doctor." He said this with the kind of scorn that indicated he didn't quite recognize a therapist as a real professional. "You seem to be trying to break up my marriage. And I will not stand for that."

"First of all," Walker protested, "I'm not trying to break up your marriage. What I've been trying to do is stop some rather violent, dangerous patterns from getting worse. And that's been pretty difficult to do as long as your wife has had to keep it a secret that she is trying to get help. For both of you, I might add."

"If you are threatening me, I'll have you know. . ."

"I am not threatening you, Mr. Frederick. But I am warning you that unless you both get some help, your wife is likely to end up permanently injured, or worse, and that's not going to be very good for either of you."

"I don't know what she's been telling you, but I've never laid a hand on my wife. So help me, God. That woman is crazy. That's why she's seeing a shrink like you in the first place. And this isn't the first time either. I bet she didn't tell you about the other doctors she's seen as well."

Walker could see what was happening, and she wasn't happy about having this conversation on the phone. But this might be her one and only shot to get the husband involved in the treatment. It was difficult, if not impossible, to work on this marriage with only one partner present.

"Yes, Mr. Frederick," Walker said as calmly as possible, trying not to respond to his attacks. After all, he was trying to "smother" her just as he did routinely with his wife, and probably other women in his life. "Mercedes did mention she had seen a psychiatrist before."

"Oh, yeah? And did you speak with this doctor? A real doctor, by the way, not a—what are you? A psychologist?" He said this as if it were just this side of being a witch doctor.

"Let me ask you something, Mr. Frederick." Walker changed the subject, still refusing to rise to his provocations. "What do you really want from this relationship with your wife?"

"It's none of your business what I want."

"I see."

"Do you? You should stop meddling where you don't belong."

"Mr. Frederick, as long as your wife chooses to seek my help, I will continue to become involved in things." Walker paused for a moment, then added, "Especially if there are criminal acts going on."

Walker held her breath, waiting for an explosion or, at the very least, for the sound of him banging down the phone. She could feel her heart pounding even though she was trying hard to appear calm. As her client had repeatedly pointed out, this guy was a very powerful, very vindictive, very violent man. During the moments she could hear him breathing heavily on the other end of the line, she felt a barrage of images—of being sued or harassed by state officials, or perhaps of being attacked during the long, dark walk to her car at night.

Finally, the man's anger seemed to cool. "What, exactly, are you talking about with my wife, anyway?"

"I'm sorry, but I'm not allowed to discuss that without her permission. In fact, I shouldn't even be speaking to you on the phone right now." What was left unsaid was that Walker was telling him she had a certain amount of power and influence as well, so perhaps it might be better if they tried to work cooperatively.

"We will see about that," he said, then abruptly hung up the phone.

Walker just sat there for a while, staring at the phone, unsure of exactly what happened.

"What did you say to him?" Mercedes asked, before she took her accustomed seat. She appeared pretty agitated. (This was the day after the phone call.)

Walker summarized the conversation, as well as her impression of it. She had taken detailed notes so she could make a full report.

Mercedes was downright relieved that the secret was out. Not only did her husband know that she was seeing a therapist, but now he was also aware that there was a "witness" who knew what was going on behind their closed doors.

"I think it's time I consulted an attorney," Mercedes announced. Walker had never seen her look more confident. "I wonder if you could give me a referral." Walker was both proud and excited about Mercedes' new proactive stance. Finally she was going to do something to protect herself, to get on with her life instead of living in constant terror. She had hoped that once Mercedes saw an attorney, she'd be able to reassemble the pieces of her life. This was not to be.

During this time, Mercedes' business began to crumble. This was partly the result of the economy but mostly due to her inattentiveness and stress levels; she was just unable to focus on anything for very long. The prolonged abuse had taken its toll, and now was affecting her behavior in other areas. She became increasingly obsessed with all the bad things that could happen to her after the marriage ended. She made impulsive decisions, including one to go back to graduate school even though she had no specific plan for the future.

Mercedes' attorney found it difficult to keep her on track. He could not get the information he needed to proceed with the divorce. At times, he couldn't even get her to comply with the simplest instructions. Walker had to intervene at points, working closely with the attorney to help Mercedes manage her life.

The husband called again to inform Walker that he wanted out of the marriage just as fast as possible. "I know Mercedes has started the legal papers, but this is taking forever. If she doesn't follow through, then I'm going to take over."

"Look, Mr. Frederick," Walker tried to calm him down, "this is taking your wife some time to get it all together. She's trying. . ."

"Tell someone who gives a shit," he interrupted. "I'm telling you I want out. And I want out now. I am calling you as a courtesy, so you can—I don't know—do whatever it is that you do."

"I understand. And I appreciate your calling, I really do. But I want you to know that Mercedes is very vulnerable right now. She is doing the best she can, but she has been beaten down pretty good and she's trying her hardest to pick herself back up."

"I told you, I don't care. It's your job to keep this woman sane."

Walker indicated she understood. And she did. First this man did everything he could to drive his wife to the brink of insanity, and now he was feeling a little guilty about it. He wanted her to fix his mess so he could get out of there. His wife's setback was a mighty inconvenience for him, and he was blaming Walker for it.

True to his threat, he moved out of the house soon thereafter.

THE NEED FOR JUSTICE

Mercedes became even more obsessed after the separation. She stopped sleeping. She began following her husband during the day and stalking his apartment at night. She would throw rocks at his window to wake him up, and scream at him. Needless to say, this did not change his mind and persuade him to come back home.

As the divorce process continued, Mercedes deteriorated further. Walker became more concerned about her erratic behavior and tried to get her to stop doing destructive things such as watching her husband. She persuaded her to hire a detective instead, a professional who could not only monitor her husband's activities but also provide some protection. So the private investigator joined the team along with the attorney, and they would have meetings with Mercedes to plan their campaign.

Walker finally secured permission to speak with Mercedes' former psychiatrist, a request that Mercedes had previously denied, saying that she hated the guy too much because of his failure to believe her story. Walker wanted to get not only more relevant background but also information about any medications that had been helpful.

These events happened about 15 years ago, so there was much less known about diagnoses and medications that might be helpful. Looking back on things, Walker realizes that Mercedes was probably showing evidence of post-traumatic stress disorder, as well as of bipolar disorder. But at the time, this was not clear; all Walker knew for certain was that Mercedes needed to be protected—from her husband and from herself.

The psychiatrist was not willing to become involved in the case again, nor did he think that medication would be particularly useful to this patient. It was also clear that Mercedes had been accurate when she said that he didn't take her reports of abuse seriously. He stated that he had referred the couple to a marital therapist. But after a few sessions the husband refused to continue in treatment, stating it was all his wife's fault and he had no reason to change his behavior.

Meanwhile, almost every week there was some new development in the case with all the information coming in from the investigator and the attorney. The husband was discovered to be having not just one affair, but two—one with a woman, and one with a man.

To make matters even more complex, the husband was also demonstrating erratic behavior. Some days he would berate his wife and tell her he never wanted to see her, or talk to her, again. Other days (even alternating days) he would come to the house and tell her he wanted to reconcile.

These mixed messages were driving Mercedes absolutely crazy. At one point, she became so angry she went to his apartment with a sledgehammer and pummeled his Jaguar into a wreck.

Walker listened to the story, biting her lip and trying not to laugh. "You can't do things like that," she told Mercedes, all the while thinking to herself: "You go, girl!" (Although the behavior itself was not appropriate, the fact was that Mercedes' paralysis was lifting and she was more able to let go of the marriage and all her dreams that it would be successful.)

"I know, Lenore. But you know, I don't care. It was worth it!"

Lenore smiled back, knowing that this was important to her client's sense of justice. In fact, this was one of many lessons that Walker learned from Mercedes, and other battered women like her—that the emotional impact from the abuse can be rectified when the scales of justice are balanced. The key was to find more appropriate (and legal) ways to seek retribution. Fortunately, between the lawyer and the investigator, Mercedes had a great team.

LEARNING TO SET LIMITS

Whereas many other people found Mercedes overwhelming, if not difficult, to be around, Walker developed a deep appreciation for her. "Yes, she was dramatic. Yes, she lived in the midst of chaos. She was exhausting. Yet I loved working with her. She really was able to get better over time, and part of that was because she needed somebody who would just be there for her and support her. I was able to provide a looking glass so she could look back at what was happening without the crippling fears. That is how I developed the kind of survivor therapy that I do. I help people look at their strengths. And when I do that, I find that both others, and I, like and appreciate them better."

On a more personal level, this case gave Walker an inside look at wealth and power, and it helped her to give up any illusions about, or desire, for either one. At first, she envied Mercedes' clothes and houses and cars, but then realized how much they kept her trapped.

Mercedes also taught Walker how important it was to set boundaries, not only with clients but in her personal life as well. This required Walker to consistently, and constantly, let Mercedes know that certain things were not okay—such as calling her late at night. Just as she was able to set limits with Mercedes, so Walker found that she could do this in other aspects of her life to protect her privacy.

As for Mercedes, she did eventually separate from her husband, and she was able to go off on her own about six months after the divorce was final. She is now doing well. Walker still sees her occasionally around town, and they give one another hugs.

Chapter 21

BARRY DUNCAN
When Courage Is Enough

The residential treatment center specialized in helping "seriously disturbed" adolescents. This meant that it was a place for kids who had been thrown out by the system or otherwise given up as hopeless cases. These were teenagers who were runaways, psychotic, or seriously suicidal. They had all been abused—emotionally, physically, and sexually. Perhaps even worse, they had been neglected and abandoned.

Duncan was a doctoral student at the time, working in the facility as a way to help support himself. He was a diligent learner and quite respectful toward the authority figures who had been guiding his education and career. This included not only his professors but also his supervisors, who had taught him to follow their lead and trust their judgments. Considering that he felt so inexperienced and naive, it felt good to rely on more experienced mentors. This had been working quite well within the university, but since he had been working at the residential center, Duncan was beginning to have some misgivings.

During his brief employment, Duncan had begun to notice that most of the kids were heavily medicated as soon as they entered the unit, before an accurate diagnosis could be formed. He also observed that Dr. Walken, the chief psychiatrist, ran the facility with an iron hand. It was made clear to Duncan that he was just a soldier in the system, one who should follow orders and do what he was told. Given how inexperienced he was with this particular population, Duncan felt it was reasonable to expect that he would follow the direction of Dr. Walken and the others.

Duncan worked with the teenagers in groups and in individual sessions. Because the environment was so restrictive and depressing, he arranged to take them on field trips as often as possible. They'd visit museums or the zoo, or sometimes just go to a park and hang out. Although the administration only reluctantly approved this "recreational therapy," Duncan persisted in trying to get to know the kids as best he could. In truth, in the few months since he had been working there, he found himself feeling increasingly pessimistic about what he could do to be helpful. The general philosophy of the staff seemed to be to warehouse the kids and keep them as docile as possible.

HEAVY METAL INTAKE

Child psychiatrists were at a premium in those days. When Dr. Walken went on vacation, there was nobody else readily available who could cover for him. With no psychiatrist available to do intakes and admit new patients, the unit operated on an emergency basis. Thus it happened that Duncan was on call when a 16-year-old girl was delivered by the police as a runaway. No known address or relatives.

Tamara definitely looked the part of a rebellious teenager. She wore an army jacket and tattered jeans. Her hair was long, streaked with color, and mostly unkempt. Her initial surly expression turned even more hostile once the interview began.

"So, Tamara? Is that how you say your name?"

She shook her head in disgust.

"Okay, then," Duncan tried again. "Maybe you can tell me how you ended up here."

"Look, Doc. . .."

Duncan started to explain that he wasn't a doctor, just a doctoral intern, when Tamara looked at him even more suspiciously.

"Look, whatever you are," she said. "I've been in places like this many times before." She stopped for a moment and studied Duncan further. "I've probably spent a lot more time in these places than you have," she challenged him.

"Probably so," he said with a grin. He liked this girl. Liked her spunk. Even though she seemed quite angry and uncooperative, he guessed she had reason to be.

"I just want to do my time here, man. Seventeen months, then I'm 18. Outta here. On my own."

Duncan agreed that sounded pretty good. They started to talk about what would need to happen in order for her to gain emancipation and freedom. He asked her about going to school, jobs she had held, and the usual things that were supposed to be covered during an intake interview, but Tamara's answers were restrained at best.

"Is that Iron Maiden?" Duncan changed the subject abruptly, tiring of the dueling back and forth. He was pointing to the picture of the heavy metal band on her T-shirt.

Tamara looked down, puzzled for a moment, then, noticing what she was wearing, started to laugh. "You know this band?"

"Sure," Duncan smiled back. "I listen to heavy metal, too."

"You do? Wow, man, that's pretty cool."

They started talking about music and then other things that Duncan thought might be of interest to her. Eventually, he was able to transition back to her history and current situation. Tamara had been in half a dozen foster homes over the course of her life. She had been sexually abused and physically assaulted, and finally escaped to live in the streets, where things seemed relatively safer. She had been on the run the last few months and found that the best option.

"I'm wondering," Duncan said, "if there's anything I can do to help you do your time here and stop running. I know this isn't exactly a luxury resort or anything, but you gotta admit it's better than the state hospital."

Tamara agreed that she'd be willing to work with Duncan, and so they arranged for daily sessions during the next few weeks.

QUESTIONING LESSONS LEARNED

Tamara was quite cooperative during the initial days. She immediately enrolled in high school and began attending a therapy group on the unit in addition to individual sessions scheduled with Duncan. They spent most of their time talking about music and hanging out on the ward. This was, after all, a residential treatment center, so sessions were usually conducted informally, as part of other activities.

Over a period of weeks, Duncan felt increasingly protective toward Tamara. Her whole life she had been betrayed, if not abused, by so many parental figures, and he felt it was his job to show her that it was possible to trust an adult and not get burned. In addition, he really, really liked her and wanted her to succeed. This was a kid with so much potential and yet she had had so few opportunities.

Duncan had been taught, not only in school but by also his supervisors, that kids subjected to chronic abuse, as well as exhibiting extreme antisocial behavior, were pretty much hopeless as far as treatment is concerned. It had been drilled into him that such children would never be able to recover from the traumas they had suffered. But for the first time, Duncan was seriously challenging these assumptions. He wanted to believe—no, he needed to believe—that there was some hope. If not, what was the point of dedicating his life's work to helping people? Besides, deep in his heart he believed that Tamara really could put her past behind her and begin again. She seemed incredibly resilient, very strong and resourceful, and also was a quick learner. Based on the progress they had been making in a few short weeks, Duncan was beginning to reevaluate the lessons that been drilled into him by his mentors.

Then the chief psychiatrist returned from vacation.

WANDERING HANDS

Dr. Walken may have felt refreshed from his time off, but he operated with the same sort of single-minded devotion to psychopharmacology as he had before he left. Duncan sat in on his first session with Tamara. The doctor seemed annoyed that this patient had been admitted without his approval.

"Okay, young lady," he said after spending ten minutes asking her a few basic questions and conducting a quick mental status. "I've got something for you." As he said this with grim smile, he began writing on a prescription pad.

"What's that?" Tamara said, returning to the surly, aggressive manner that she brought with her on her first day in the hospital. Duncan was dismayed to see the return of this hostility and suspicion. He had been working so hard the previous weeks to earn her trust. And in place of the hardened street kid, a delightful young woman had been emerging.

"Excuse me?" The doctor seemed surprised by the anger in Tamara's voice. He was not used to being challenged by anyone, least of all by a patient.

"I said, 'What's that?' What do you think you're doing?"

Dr. Walken straightened in his chair and gave Tamara his most earnest look. Duncan could see by his tapping foot that she had gotten under his skin. He couldn't help but smile a little to himself. He had always found the psychiatrist a bit pompous, and it amused him that Tamara was taking him on. Nobody else on the unit had the courage to do so.

"Well, my dear," he said, "I am your doctor. And I'm. . .."

"No, you're not."

"I'm not?"

"No," she said, and then pointed to Duncan sitting in the corner. "He is."

Duncan looked startled by the attention suddenly directed his way. It felt like he was sitting in class and had been caught doing something he wasn't supposed to.

Dr. Walken smiled. "Yes, dear, I see. Duncan, here, is a staff member, but I am the attending psychiatrist. And what I think would be best for you would be trials of lithium and imipramine."

"I'm not taking antidepressants. I'm not taking any drugs." She folded her arms to indicate that the discussion was over.

It wasn't clear if Walken was more surprised by the defiance or that this obstinate girl would recognize the drugs he was prescribing. There was a flash of anger on his face, immediately replaced with what he presumed was an understanding smile. From his angle, Duncan thought it looked more reptilian.

Walken stood up and walked to Tamara, standing over her. Rather than giving him the satisfaction of acknowledging that she was literally beneath him, she resolutely stared at his stomach. He strolled around the room a bit, ending up behind Tamara. She could hear him breathing and looked over her shoulder nervously.

"Look, my dear," Walken said, "it seems we've gotten off to a bad start." He placed his hands on her shoulders and started to massage her neck. "You just need to relax a little. You need to trust us. You need to trust me." His hands now began lightly caressing her back, slowly moving up and down.

Duncan watched with increased discomfort. He couldn't believe that this guy was actually touching Tamara. Didn't he have any clue what these kids had experienced in their lives? He didn't know if he should say anything, and before he could decide, Tamara—bless her heart—spoke up for herself.

"I told you, doctorwhateveryournameis, I'm not taking your drugs. And keep your fucking hands off me!" With that, she turned and swatted his hands away. Duncan felt like cheering.

KNOWING ONE'S PLACE

Predictably, Tamara had a setback after the encounter with the psychiatrist. All the trust developed during the previous weeks now seemed in jeopardy. Tamara remained sullen and hostile to staff thereafter, and still refused to take her medications. This was interpreted as being resistant, and she was punished accordingly. Duncan felt helpless watching her deterioration. Finally, he decided to intervene on her behalf with Dr. Walken.

"Doctor," Duncan addressed him as calmly and respectfully as possible, "Tamara was making so much progress. She was. . ."

"Just manipulating you," Walken interrupted, then went back to reviewing case notes while sitting behind his cluttered desk.

Ignoring the comment, Duncan pointed out that she had been doing better than ever before. "She has been attending school—perfect attendance, as a matter of fact. She's been going to group. She's been cooperative on the unit. . ."

"Not that I can see," Walken interrupted again, then went back to his papers. Duncan couldn't be sure he was even listening.

"She's been cooperative in my sessions with her." Duncan decided to stick with safer ground that he could support. "We've been talking about her long-term plans. She's got lots of plans for the future. . ."

"Barry. Barry. It seems clear that there are some countertransference reactions going on here. You seem way too involved in. . ."

"Doctor, we are here to talk about Tamara, not about me." Duncan was surprised he was being so assertive. This guy really intimidated him. But he resented the hell out of what he'd been doing to undo all the work he and Tamara had completed together. And he felt guilty for not standing up for Tamara earlier.

For the first time, Walken looked up from his desk and gave Duncan his full attention. He looked more aggravated, however, than interested.

"It just doesn't make sense," Duncan pressed, "to force her to take drugs that she doesn't. . ."

"So now we let the patients decide what they want? Is this what they teach you at that school?"

"That's not what I'm saying. I'm just pointing out that Tamara has a history of running away. She's already threatened to do so if we make her take the drugs that she says she's already tried before. They make her feel funny. They make her feel like she's not herself."

"I see," Walken said, looking thoughtful. For a moment, Duncan held some hope that perhaps he was getting through to this man. Then Walken said: "What I see is that this girl is blackmailing us—unless we do exactly what she says, she'll engage in her usual self-destructive behavior. This is clear evidence that she is far more disturbed than you seem to recognize."

Walken continued in this vein, lecturing Duncan about the nature of bipolar disorder and all the ways that Tamara qualified as mentally ill. The only thing that would help her, he insisted, was drugs, several of them, in rather large dosages. He scolded Duncan for operating outside of his training and ordered him to obey the rules, or he would find himself without a job.

Without saying another word, Duncan got up and walked out of the office.

LEARNING COURAGE

Duncan wasn't sure what else to do except to reassure Tamara that he would continue to work as her advocate. She listened silently, revealing little of what she was thinking. The next day she went to school, then ran away as she had originally threatened to do if she was forced to take medications. Days went by without hearing a word. Duncan worried incessantly about all the horrible things that might have happened to her.

When she was finally tracked down by the police and returned to the unit, Duncan's worst fears proved to be true. While Tamara had been roaming the streets, she had been picked up by a group of guys and gang-raped brutally and repeatedly. By the time she was discovered, she was beaten, drugged, and unconscious.

Tamara regained awareness about the time she arrived back on the ward. She was screaming hysterically, pleading to be left alone. Instead, several attendants held her down while she was forcibly injected with an antipsychotic medication. "There I was," she told Duncan later, "bruised and battered after getting the shit kicked out of me and fucked into a stupor, and what do they do to me when I get back here? They hold me down, pull down my underpants, and then give me more drugs. To tell you the truth, I don't know which gang rape was worse." She laughed as she said this, but it was a hoarse sound, devoid of any humor.

"Jeez," Duncan said, shaking his head, completely at a loss for words. He was trying to hold back tears of frustration and anger.

"Hey, Barry," she reassured him, "don't worry about me. I've lived through far worse than this before."

Here was a 16-year-old girl, his client, trying to take care of him in the midst of her own crisis. If he thought Tamara was strong-willed up until this point, he hadn't seen anything yet. During the ensuing weeks, Dr. Walken and his assistants kept trying to keep Tamara as medicated and docile as possible. Yet for every attempt they made to feed her drugs, she figured out a way to block them. She was, by now, an expert at hiding the pills, tonguing them, spitting them out unobtrusively. Duncan could only shake his head in amazement at her spirit; he felt weak and spineless by comparison.

It was time for Duncan to take a stand. He could no longer stand by and watch this wonderful girl be broken systematically by the medical establishment. He started doing his own research on psychopharmacology. This was many years ago, before a whole lot was known about these drugs and how they operate on the nervous system. In reviewing all the outcome studies on tricyclic antidepressants and lithium, he could not find a single study in the literature that supported their use for children and adolescents. Given their prevalent use with kids, both on his unit and elsewhere, he couldn't believe this was possible, figuring he hadn't done a proper search. He tried again, this time with the assistance of research staff at the library. Again he came up with the same result: no demonstrated evidence of effectiveness. It seemed that everything he had been told about the rationale for using these medications for childhood mental illness was simply not true, or at least based on little empirical support.

Duncan accumulated and organized the data into a brief report summarizing the evidence to date. He made an appointment to see Dr. Walken, who was less than happy to see him in the office again. Duncan was extremely anxious about this meeting, so he made every effort to be as obsequious as possible. He very calmly presented what he found, mentioning that he was concerned about the ways that Tamara and other children on the unit were being medicated (or, rather, overmedicated). He concluded his presentation by saying he couldn't find a single study that showed such drugs were effective with patients this young.

Dr. Walken listened—with complete attention for a change. He steepled his hands into a prayer position, the tips of his fingers thoughtfully touching his lower lip. Then he folded his hands on his desk and looked Duncan right in the eyes. "Just who the hell do you think you are, young man?" he said. "You've got just about five minutes to get out of this office, pack your things, and get off this property. You're fired! And how dare you question my judgment!"

FINAL HUG

Duncan did manage to see Tamara one more time before he left. He told her what happened and that he was on his way out.

"Hey, that's great," she said with a smile. "At least one of us gets out of here."

Duncan smiled back, though he felt more sick than proud. Yes, he had done the right thing, but now he was abandoning Tamara and the other kids.

Reading his mind, she again came to the rescue. "Don't worry about me," she said. "I'm a survivor."

"Yes, you are," he agreed.

"I'll do just fine now. I really appreciate all your support. Nobody's ever done that for me before."

They hugged, and then Duncan walked out the door for the last time.

Tamara taught Duncan never to be complacent or complicit again, as a function of virtue or ignorance. Her resilience and determination and pure out-and-out courage were just about the most inspiring thing that he had ever witnessed. Here was this 16-year-old kid able to stand up to all these arrogant doctors. She had been beaten and raped and abused and humiliated, and yet she found a way to fight back without losing hope or her dignity. She really believed that she could transcend all this unpleasantness; somehow she would overcome it all.

Duncan figured that if someone like Tamara could do this, then anyone could. This is what led him down the path as an advocate for patient rights. "This was the defining moment in my career," he recalled. "I no longer believed the things I had been taught, just because they came from so-called experts. From that point onward, I started questioning things, and some of my teachers and supervisors didn't care for that much."

Until this point, Duncan had some idealistic, and in some ways naïve, beliefs, about the way things work in the mental health system. He should have known better, coming from lower-class roots, but he had been awed by the confidence of his mentors. After his experience with Tamara, however, he was shaken to his core.

"Here I had this grand image of being a helper and what a noble enterprise it was to want to be a helper. I really, really wanted to help people. Now I realized that such good intentions could actually hurt people when they were accompanied by certain assumptions. This led me to begin questioning and challenging everything rather than just accepting what I was told. Nothing was the same for me after I lost my job. I lost my innocence. I felt humiliated. But I also felt humbled."

FOLLOW-UP THREE YEARS LATER

Duncan eventually heard from Tamara again, when she was 19 and finally on her own. She was taking classes at the community college and had a new baby. Life was still hard for her, but she was doing well. In the brief note she sent, she wanted him to know that she was still grateful for all he had done for her. Duncan wished he could have told her how much she had helped him as well.

Chapter 22

LEIGH McCULLOUGH
The Lady Cloaked in Fog

Leslie had been in therapy for over 25 years. She described herself as a "therapy junkie," someone who wanted to keep the sessions going her whole life. One reason for this was that she had been so neglected as a child, and thus was much too easily hurt by others, so that she had eventually withdrawn from family and friends and was almost completely isolated. She was severely depressed and acutely suicidal. She had been hospitalized five times for acute episodes of serious intent to harm herself.

Her previous therapist had moved out of town, which was just about the only way their relationship would have ended. Leslie was referred to McCullough, who had served as a consultant to the previous therapist over a number of years.

It took some time for Leigh to discover how to help this severely depressed patient who was so challenging to work with. For years, Leslie had described herself as a "toxic waste dump" who didn't matter to anyone. Given how long this woman had been feeling this way, and how intense her feelings of worthlessness were, McCullough wondered how she could possibly make a dent in her depressed and lonely life. After a while, Leigh decided that if Leslie felt that she did not matter to anyone, it was crucial for her to learn that she did matter. And since she was estranged from most of the people in her life, Leigh decided that the "mattering" had to start within their relationship.

It was several months into the relationship when McCullough finally decided to explore this issue with Leslie more directly and focus on the feelings of mattering: "If you feel like you don't matter," she asked Leslie, "what do you think I feel about you? Do you think you matter to me?"

Leslie seemed puzzled by the question, as if she had not considered this before. "I don't know," she said finally. "I guess I don't expect that I do matter to you. After all, I am just one of your clients. We're not friends."

"No, we're not," Leigh agreed. "This is a professional relationship. But does that mean that there are not real human feelings here? You have people whom you work with. Don't you have feelings for them?"

This was a question that Leslie couldn't begin to answer. It was apparent that in her previous years of therapy she had never been asked to talk much about the immediacy of her relationship with the therapist. Finally, she shrugged and looked down, unable, or perhaps unwilling, to answer.

"So how do you think I might feel about you?" Leigh knew better than to say directly that she cared about her. She also knew that saying that Leslie mattered to her would be dismissed out of hand. The analogy she thought of was that instead of giving her a fish, she was trying to teach Leslie to fish inside of herself, to see if she could resonate with what her therapist might be feeling. In fact, Leigh was feeling very close to Leslie, who was suffering so much. She was greatly concerned that this vulnerable woman would indeed end her life someday.

Seeing the difficulty that Leslie was having trying to put her feelings into words, Leigh decided to press further. "If you look at my face, how does it seem to you that I am feeling toward you?"

Leslie looked up for a moment, made eye contact, then looked down again.

McCullough took a deep breath because she was feeling anxious herself, wading into new waters, and said even more gently, "If you look at my face, what do you sense that I might be feeling?"

In her therapy model, Leigh believes that it is important to expose the client to warded-off feelings, but in this particular case, she felt it important that the therapist also be emotionally present or "exposed." She was quite uncomfortable during this process, inviting her client to examine her.

After some time, Leigh asked again, "So, what do you see? What do you sense in my eyes?"

Leslie hesitated, then nodded—just a little nod, but still it was an acknowledgment. "Yes," she said in a whisper.

"Yes, what?"

"Yes, it does seem that I matter to you."

"And what's that like for you?"

"It makes me nervous." As she said this, Leslie cringed and shifted in the chair.

McCullough could see that Leslie was indeed terrified by the feelings. She thought it might be useful to do some desensitization, gradually exposing Leslie to these feelings until she could tolerate them without running away. They spent the rest of that session doing exactly that, slowly exposing Leslie to caring feelings that were uncomfortable for her, but that also were a beacon of light—from one person to another— that she could learn to respond to and take in.

"This isn't as deep as we can go...," Leigh commented at one point. She could feel tremendous warmth between them. "But it is very pleasant, isn't it?"

Leslie, now less burdened, smiled, her eyes still closed.

"From one person to another, from one woman to another, how does this feel between us?"

"I feel. . .I feel like a virgin," Leslie answered.

"Like a virgin..."

"It feels like you are peering deep inside me. And I feel scared."

McCullough thought about exploring sexual feelings at this point, since she knew that Leslie had had sexual relationships with women. However, her problems had not been with sex, but with isolation and alienation from others, so Leigh thought it more important to stay with the theme of closeness in their relationship. If the sexual feelings had continued to emerge and get in the way, she would have addressed them, because closeness and sexual feelings are closely linked. But at this point she wanted to keep things relatively simple.

"How does it feel," Leigh asked, "inside your body right now, to have these feelings of closeness with someone?"

Leslie placed her hands on her chest. "I feel it here," she said, "and here." She moved her hands to her stomach, then they balled into fists. "It feels like a strong-self kind of place. It's okay. I feel okay." She smiled.

Leigh could feel something shift. She sensed that at that moment, for the first time in a long, long time, Leslie felt okay with herself as a human being. In that moment, she no longer felt like a toxic waste dump.

For the next few minutes, the two of them just smiled at one another. Then, Leslie began to feel anxious.

"What's going on?" Leigh asked.

"I just can't bear this." Leslie broke eye contact.

"Tell me what you're feeling right now. Stay with it."

"I'm not... I can't hold the feeling about being cared about and that I don't matter. I can't hold those two things."

"Uh-huh. Just say that again. 'I can't hold....'"

"I can't say I don't matter if I let myself know you care about me."

"That's right!" Leigh was feeling excited that the previous exposures were now making it easier for Leslie to let go of her defenses and to acknowledge that she was worthy of being loved.

"Well," Leslie sighed, "it doesn't make me want to stay right here forever, but I'm not in a real rush to go home to be alone and play computer games."

"Well, then, I wonder if you can take me with you, take these feelings with you." McCullough was thinking that this was, after all, the crux of therapy—to help clients take in the positive feelings from their therapists and use them to find other intimacy in their lives.

"Yeah, that would be nice," Leslie agreed with a wistful smile.

"You not only have me with you, but also your previous therapist, and your sister and your best friend. You can keep us with you all the time." McCullough was pressing home the point that Leslie could generalize from the session to other aspects of her life.

"I guess," Leslie agreed, not at all sure she could do this.

"After all, it would do you no service if this was the only place you could feel cared for. You'd be coming here forever. And that isn't the goal here. We need to set you free...but not without these feelings." Given Leslie's previous strong attachments and dependency on her previous therapists, McCullough was trying hard to generalize these positive feelings to other situations outside of therapy to emphasize independence and resourcefulness whenever possible.

"Right."

"We need to set you free, but without all the misery you carry around within you."

Again, Leslie nodded. She seemed to get it.

"I'm wondering if you are ever able to let yourself feel like this when you're at home. Letting yourself feel safe and good."

Leslie's whole face lit up with understanding, and she smiled. "Oh, yeah!"

"It feels good to hear you say that."

"It does."

"Where, exactly, do you feel it?"

Leslie paused for a moment, thoughtfully, then held her fist at her midsection. "It's not up here (touching her chest), it's more down in my belly, more in the center."

"What good feelings are in there, in the center?"

"Power," Leslie said immediately. "Like the Buddhist chakra."

"You're feeling strong," Leigh reflected.

"Yeah," Leslie grinned. "It's kind of nice, I've got to admit. I'd like to hang out in that place more often!"

McCullough waited for a bit and just let this sink in. After the long struggle, it felt wonderful to just sit there together.

"You know," Leslie said finally, "it feels like I've been in a fog my whole life. And now you're the harbor light that is beaming me in to shore."

"Yes, but there are others there, too," Leigh responded, and then immediately regretted it. She recognized that she was being given a lovely gift by being referred to as Leslie's "harbor light," and she had minimized the compliment instead of savoring it. She was being perhaps a little too vigilant about dependency concerns—and somewhat nervous herself. "Certainly I am helping to guide you," she added, "but I'm not the only one who has these feelings for you."

Leigh immediately felt relieved that Leslie had not been offended or put off. She realized that she had tried to push her away because of her own anxiety about intimacy. She was delighted to see that her patient was not angry with her.

"That's true," Leslie agreed, "you're not the only harbor light. But you do shine brighter than the others. You're shining real bright."

"Especially during a storm," McCullough added.

"Right. Storms. But it's fog that's bothering me the most right now."

"It's less stormy than it used to be." Leigh chose to focus on the positive as much as possible.

"Yeah. Sometimes when I'm in the boat alone, it doesn't feel like I have any oars. But it feels so nice right now, that if I just poke my head up out of the fog, I can see your harbor light somewhere out there, guiding me in."

When the session ended, Leigh felt elated with the progress they'd made. It had been a difficult, challenging experience for her, exploring the feelings between them, but the outcome appeared to justify the risk. Leslie seemed positively transformed, and more significantly, the results lasted long after the session ended.

They spent the next six months after this breakthrough working on ways to help Leslie restructure her life. She began to make friends. She joined a book club. She enrolled in graduate school. She developed a love relationship with a woman she had met; they began living together (and still were together the last time she made contact with Leigh). The suicidal thoughts all but vanished once Leslie broke through the fog of isolation. And throughout these dramatic changes, Leigh remained the guiding light. It had all begun with the metaphor of the harbor light in the fog.

PERSONAL REFLECTIONS ON THE EXPERIENCE

"When I first became a therapist," McCullough recalled, "I wasn't sure what emotional intimacy was all about. I was taught to be a caretaker and be good to people, and to be generous. Be a good listener. I went into the field because I was empathic and knew I made people feel better. But I had never learned how to express really tender feelings or reveal myself in emotionally intimate ways."

Leigh mentioned that it wasn't until her children were in their twenties that she apologized to them for not being as tender a parent as she should have been. Her children initially reassured her, but they, too, became more aware of the emotional distance that they had earlier taken for granted. Yet just as The Lady Cloaked in Fog came out into the light and warmth of human contact, so it felt to Leigh as if she were following her own beacon of light, one that involved much greater personal contact with others.

"This was all kind of new ground for me. I began trying to change my interactions with my children. I changed the way I responded to close friends. These were just things I didn't know about, and I have to say that well into my forties I was still learning. I continued to learn from my patients as I did with this special woman."

Leigh paused for a moment, feeling teary-eyed thinking about how much richer her relationships have become in later years. She expressed how grateful she feels to her patients, and to her colleagues, for teaching her how to become more intimate. In this very moment, as she talked about what she had learned from her therapeutic encounters, she felt flooded with feelings to the point that she needed time to compose herself.

"This has all been such a huge gift to me. Growing up, I never knew this level of human contact with others. Now I have that not only with my patients but also in my personal life. I now see this as a crucial area of therapy that is so often overlooked and so rarely dealt with. I know what I am saying now could make other therapists feel uncomfortable—as it did me at first. We therapists don't often talk about this, do we? And we need to."

Chapter 23

PATRICIA ARREDONDO
The Client Who Inspired
Her Therapist

Sandy was Arredondo's very first client upon becoming licensed, a woman who needed to talk to someone about some family conflicts. As a first impression, Sandy appeared both depressed and helpless; she was the kind of person who practically invited you to take care of her. Although she had obtained a paraprofessional degree in civil engineering, and worked hard in her job, she talked about herself as a complete failure. Of particular concern to her was a very conflicted relationship with her mother, who was suffering from emphysema.

Arredondo was a bit nervous working with her first client, so she mentally reviewed everything she had learned about women's psychological development, especially those relational and feminist theories that were more gender-sensitive. One thing she noticed right away was that she couldn't help but identify with her client's strict Catholic upbringing that emphasized clear roles for women as selfless caretakers in their families. Arredondo recognized easily that this was a probable source of Sandy's guilt and frustration.

Although estranged from her sick mother, as well as from one of her brothers, Sandy reported a good relationship with her father. He had been the one who had done things with her when she was a child, and mentored her throughout her early adulthood. So much for basic family background. Sandy had one best friend, a high school chum in whom she confided and who recommended that she seek counseling.

HOPING FOR A MAGIC WAND

"You just have to help me," Sandy pleaded in a manner that reminded Arredondo of a puppy. "You've got to get me out of this situation."

Arredondo nodded her understanding, but inside she was panicking. What was she supposed to do with this woman who was expecting that she would be the savior who had all the answers?

"That's why I'm here," Sandy repeated, "I was told that you could help me."

"And what is it, exactly, that you are expecting I will do for you?" Arredondo dreaded the answer, but she had to ask again to be sure.

"Just that you'll tell me what I need to do."

"Let's look at your options then," she responded, hoping to put the responsibility back on her client. "You can continue to visit your mother at home on the weekends. You can even start going to see your mother more often on the weekdays, if that will make you feel any better. What else can you do?"

Sandy just shrugged helplessly.

"Well, you could just call her on the phone."

Again, a helpless shrug. Arredondo couldn't tell if this was indifference or just not knowing what she wanted to do. One thing for sure was that she was not liking this role of trying to fix the problem by telling her what to do. She realized that she was only reinforcing Sandy's helpless role that she needed someone to give her the answers, to be an authority figure in her life.

"I sense your frustration," Arredondo tried again. "But I really can't give you the answers you are looking for. I can't do the work for you, but I want to help you think about what makes sense for you."

"Okay," Sandy said, clearly disappointed.

"You work five days a week, right?"

Sandy nodded.

"You live about a half-hour away from your mother."

Another nod.

"You've said that every time you go to see her, you feel worse about the visit. You don't feel good about yourself, and you don't feel like you are being responsible to your mother. Is that right?"

"Yes."

"I want to help you to change some of your "bad habits" of giving yourself away so that you can feel better about yourself, as well as what you're doing for your mother to support her."

Reluctantly, Sandy agreed that this seemed like a reasonable plan. She was still feeling disappointed that Arredondo didn't have a magic wand that could simply fix everything all at once.

FAMILIAR PATTERNS

In the next few sessions, Sandy talked about her loneliness. She was single and had not been in a good relationship with a man for some time. She kept picking men who were unavailable. Even now, she was involved with a man who had recently separated from his wife and didn't have much to offer in the way of availability or commitment.

"Sandy," Arredondo confronted her, "it seems like you are taking care of John just the way you take care of your mother."

"What do you mean?"

"Well, let's look at the similarities. With both John and your mother, you are giving a lot to the relationship and getting back little in return. John keeps telling you he wants your support, your patience, your under-standing. He wants you to be there for him—but only when he is available. Yet you aren't getting what you want in return. Does this sound familiar?"

"Yeah," Sandy agreed with a laugh, "but what am I going to do about it?" She looked at Arredondo with the familiar puppy-dog look that said: "Tell me what to do!"

Arredondo ignored the usual request for advice and instead helped Sandy to look at the ways she was setting herself up for disappointment and making herself crazy with guilt. When John didn't call her as she had hoped, she would go into a funk and tell herself she was worthless. When her mother had a bad day, Sandy would blame herself for the setback. These self-defeating, toxic thoughts were cumulative to the point that she felt totally worthless.

Sandy also complained about the way she was treated at work. Although she was working as a civil engineer, because she was a woman in a male-dominated world, and because she had only an associate de-gree, she felt just as worthless during the day as she felt in her social and family life.

"So," Arredondo pointed out, "again we are seeing the same thing that you do with your mother and John."

Sandy said she didn't understand, but that was her usual response.

"You are always the good girl," Arredondo said. "You are the good daughter. You are the good employee. You are the good girlfriend. You do everything that everyone else expects of you, always putting your own needs on hold. You cover for everyone else. You take responsibility for everyone else's problems."

"You mean like at work when they don't appreciate me?"

"Exactly. You've said you work your butt off there. You cover for everyone else, but nobody seems to acknowledge that. It is as if it's just expected of you."

"They're just not warm people," Sandy said, half as a defense, half as acknowledgment.

"I see. So because they are engineers and civil servants, they are entitled to be rude and take advantage of you?" Sandy smiled, getting the point. "Yeah, they all make more money than me. They go out for long lunches while I sit in the office and do their work. And they act like that is what I'm supposed to be doing. They don't show any gratitude."

"Like your mother. And like John."

Sandy nodded, her head down, tears in her eyes.

"So there are three different areas of your life that are all out of control, and all pretty much following the same pattern."

Sandy looked up and met Arredondo's eyes, then nodded her agreement.

"You've got so many 'shoulds' in your life," Arredondo pressed further. "So many demands that you think you have to meet, impossible demands that you could never meet to anyone's satisfaction. That's why you feel like you keep letting everyone down, including yourself."

Working in a women's treatment center, Arredondo recognized this pattern as very familiar among her clients who were working in male-dominated professions. She let Sandy know that she was not alone, that many, many women were struggling with similar concerns, trying to earn respect and equal treatment in the workplace.

A GIFT

Arredondo saw Sandy weekly over a period of many years. She was her very first client, and also the one with whom she worked the longest, two reasons why she had such an impact on her. Arredondo also felt a lot of caring and respect for Sandy because she worked so hard in therapy, just as she did in every other area of her life. She was utterly determined she was going to make things better for herself in spite of all the challenges she faced, and all the people in her world who were determined to keep her at their beck and call. She would come to sessions during her lunch hour, because it was the only free time that she had not allocated to take care of others.

Sadly, just when Sandy had been making significant progress in her growth, she was diagnosed with cancer. This was a huge trauma for her, and for Arredondo personally, who had never known anyone with a life-threatening illness. It felt as if a member of her family was in danger, and that's exactly how Sandy felt to her after all those hundreds of hours they'd spent together in such intimate contact. Arredondo started feeling helpless that there was little she could do for Sandy.

Looking back on the relationship, Arredondo now feels that Sandy gave her such a gift. All throughout her chemotherapy and treatments, she showed such courage and resilience, such a determination to survive. Whereas before the cancer, Sandy had been willing to put herself last and take care of everyone else, the prospect of death finally got her attention in ways that nothing else had before. She showed a will to live that was remarkable.

Sandy inspired Arredondo to start a support group of women who were struggling with self-esteem issues and relationship problems. Sandy became the star of the group, the one who inspired everyone else to take more active, assertive stances/positions in their personal and professional lives. The cancer was a ticking bomb inside of her, and she simply was not willing to waste a single precious moment of her life any longer.

The members of the support group became a surrogate family for Sandy. It was also during this time that she met a man at work who seemed very different from the men she usually met. At first Arredondo felt protective of Sandy because she was so vulnerable and gullible, but it turned out that this man really was as good as he appeared to be. He took Sandy to nice places around town, and they traveled together in and out of the country. And then they got married. Everyone in the group attended the wedding, including Arredondo.

Sandy decided to retire from her job, another gift she gave herself. After all, life is too short to waste it as a drone in a meaningless job with people you don't care for. She and her husband moved to Florida, where he had contracts for his consulting work and Sandy could take care of her health. This was a dramatic act of independence for her, one that opened a new chapter in her life.

Once settled in Florida, Sandy worked for the local cancer society until her cancer returned. It was about this time that Arredondo went to visit her. Although Sandy was quite ill, Arredondo was amazed at the transformation: this woman positively glowed with spiritual energy. She seemed at peace. Arredondo was delighted to see that Sandy and her husband had built a beautiful life together and enjoyed a solid relationship. They were happy. And she was living life to the fullest.

Not long afterward, Arredondo received a phone call that Sandy had died.

ESCAPE FROM OPPRESSIVE SYSTEMS

Arredondo had been taught to maintain certain boundaries as part of her training, yet Sandy, her first client, taught her another lesson: that her humanity had been most realized once she had given up an arm's-length posture. She had learned since then, in her work with many other women, that it was important to see, and be seen, as a person, not just as a professional. There were times when she abandoned her role as a traditional therapist in order to make contact with Sandy on a more personal level.

As we will see in many other stories throughout this book, opening one-self up like this changes both parties in the process.

Arredondo could easily identify with Sandy's issues because so many of her own struggles had been related to the rules of responsibility, "shoulds" about what she was supposed to do. She learned, just like her client, that you can't always play by the rules of the workplace; you can lose yourself if you do. While watching Sandy losing herself by subordinating her needs to those of her coworkers, it hit Arredondo square in the face that she was doing the same thing.

Arredondo had been working as a professor at an elite university on the East Coast. When she had accepted the job, she hadn't realized that no junior faculty had received tenure in the department in many years. It was while working with Sandy that Arredondo finally saw the writing on the wall: she would probably not earn tenure either. To add to her pressure, she had just gone through a divorce.

In listening to herself guide Sandy on a journey toward greater empowerment, Arredondo couldn't help but apply the same principles to her own life. She realized that she was no more satisfied in her job than Sandy had been in hers. Just as Sandy had been feeling battered within an oppressive system, so, too, was her therapist. And just as Sandy was working to free herself of this system, Arredondo decided that it was time for her to find a more healthy work environment.

Arredondo's own insights and resolutions that evolved as a direct result of her work with Sandy were never openly discussed in the sessions. In fact, it wasn't until after their therapeutic work ended that Arredondo realized the source of her impetus to make personal and professional changes. To this day, she feels grateful to her first client for the courage and commitment she demonstrated. Sandy never realized the strength of the impact she had on her therapist, how her resourcefulness and commitment inspired Arredondo in ways that might never have otherwise been possible.

Chapter 24

HOWARD KIRSCHENBAUM
A Flood of Feeling

"It's about my brother," the woman began without much preamble. She was a counselor herself, so she knew how things worked and what her new therapist might be looking for to get started.

Kirschenbaum nodded, encouraging her to begin any way she felt comfortable. As the biographer of Carl Rogers, the father of client-centered therapy, he was accustomed to allowing clients to structure sessions the way they wanted. He would wait to hear her story, to get a sense of what was going on, before he interrupted or intervened much.

"I was very close to him," Wendy said in a soft voice. "So close."

Kirschenbaum learned that Wendy had a very close-knit family. They talked to each other a lot and enjoyed the intimacy between them. This made it particularly surprising when Wendy learned from a friend that her brother, Scott, had been seen around town soliciting money on behalf of some shadowy religious group that seemed more like a cult than a legitimate charitable organization.

Wendy's parents were understandably distressed upon learning this news, and they asked her to see what was going on. Nobody had heard much from Scott for some time, and this was not at all like him.

Wendy eventually tracked her brother down and found him very thin, as if he hadn't been eating properly for some time. Sure enough, he was indeed living in a communal situation with a group that kept him under tight control.

As Wendy was relating this story, Kirschenbaum noticed that there was very little affect in her voice, as if this were all matter-of-fact and well rehearsed. It was when she started to describe her visit with Scott that some of her feelings began to emerge. "They led me into this room," she said, her voice cracking a little. "Before I even got the chance to see him, they told me that we would only have a short time together."

"'They' being. . . ?"

"His keepers," she quickly said with a short laugh but no smile. "The leaders of this. . .this cult. . .this group."

Kirschenbaum nodded his understanding.

"So I sat down and they brought Scott in. I was just so shocked when I saw him. He was just so. . .so. . .I don't know. . . .He didn't look like my brother at all. He was so skinny. His cheeks were sunken, and he had almost no color in his face. He looked sick, kind of like a zombie or something. It was like he was. . .I don't know. . .not there."

"So he barely resembled the brother you had known. It was like he was someone else?"

Wendy nodded. She explained that when she told him about her concerns, about how worried their parents were, he just responded in a robotlike voice that he was fine. "He kept saying that over and over, that he was fine. But the more he kept saying it, the more upset I was becoming. It was pretty obvious that he wasn't fine at all!"

She paused, seemingly lost in the memory.

"What happened then?" Kirschenbaum prompted. "Did you say anything?"

"Yeah, I did. I asked him to come home with me. I told him that he didn't have to come back permanently, just to visit. I wanted to get him the hell out of that creepy place and away from those people. But he just kept saying that he was fine, that he wasn't allowed to leave, and that was fine, too."

"Did you sense he was making his own choice to stay there?" Kirschenbaum asked, sensing where this might be heading.

"I suppose. But it didn't feel that way. It seemed like he wasn't able to make choices like that. It was like they'd brainwashed him or something."

"So he wouldn't leave with you?"

Wendy shook her head. "No. I tried to convince him, but he insisted he was fine and he wasn't going to leave. There was. . .there was nothing I could do." It was at this point that real emotion was coming into her voice and tears were pooling in her eyes.

Wendy reported to her family what had happened. They consulted attorneys who told her that she had no legal standing, that her brother was of the age where he could make his own choices. They decided that she should try again, so she waited a few weeks and then returned to the commune to try and pry Scott loose from the clutches of the cult.

As soon as she saw her brother, she realized that he had deteriorated significantly since their last visit. Now he was beyond thin—he looked like the emaciated inmate of a concentration camp. He had little energy; his movements and speech were listless. He looked like he was dying.

Wendy's arguments were no more persuasive this time. Scott hardly even seemed to believe his own assertions that he was fine; yet he was still unresponsive to his sister's pleas. She begged him one more time to come with her, but he didn't seem to hear her. He just sat on the chair, his posture slumped, staring into the air. After a short time, two members of the cult came to take Scott away. The last thing Wendy managed to say before leaving was how much she loved her brother. Just before he disappeared down the hallway, he turned to face her, and at that moment, Wendy knew that this was the last time she would ever see her brother. That vision of him haunted her. A few weeks later they heard that Scott was dead.

As Kirschenbaum listened to this tragic story, he had a sense that there were much deeper feelings than those Wendy had expressed so far. He could feel the oppressive weight of her sadness—and the suggestion of guilt—that she was carrying around inside of her. When he reflected this to her, Wendy seemed to collapse.

"He was dying," she said in a voice that could barely be heard. "And there was nothing I could do to help him." She was crying freely now, without restraint.

"You couldn't help him," Kirschenbaum repeated, reflecting what seemed to be a theme of recurring importance to her. She had said it earlier, and she was saying it again. He repeated, "There was nothing you could do."

Wendy looked up at him and met his eyes. "I couldn't help him!" she screamed in a voice that startled both of them. "He was dying, and I couldn't do a damn thing to save him."

It was as if a crack in the dam that had been holding back all her rage and despair finally split open. Wendy began to sob with a depth that was agonizing to watch. Howie couldn't even imagine what it must have felt like to carry around all those feelings inside of her for so long.

"That must have been so awful for you," he responded, "that you felt so helpless that you couldn't do anything."

"I just couldn't help him," Wendy moaned over and over. "I couldn't help him. . .I tried. . . I tried!. . .But I couldn't help him. I couldn't. . .." Then great wracking sobs drowned out her words, as if the flood of emotion was building in intensity.

Ten minutes of this went by, which felt to Kirschenbaum like hours because it was so intense. Finally, as suddenly as the rush of emotion had begun, Wendy stopped. She had accumulated handfuls of tissue, soaked with her tears, in her lap. She stared down at the wad as if shocked that so much water could pour out of her eyes.

Kirschenbaum waited for another few moments, watching her carefully, then asked how she handled all those feelings that she had been carrying around for so long.

Wendy shook her head, indicating clearly that this was not a place where she wanted to go just then. After a pause to regain her breath, she started sobbing again with a power that was almost frightening to see.

Kirschenbaum backed off completely at this point. There was no point asking any more questions, or reflecting any more feelings, until his client could take in what was being said. For now, she was in a place where all she could do was grieve.

GOING DEEPER INTO FEELINGS

"Picture me as your brother," Kirschenbaum suggested to Wendy several minutes later when she regained her composure. "Okay?"

Wendy nodded with a smile. She seemed a little embarrassed by her lengthy outburst but now appeared to be back in control. The counselor training inside her seemed to realize that she had to do something with all of this emotion that had been accessed; it wasn't nearly enough to express it just once.

"Okay, so I'm your brother," Kirschenbaum repeated, inviting Wendy to join him in a reenactment. "Remember me in that room when you saw me for the last time."

Wendy closed her eyes for a moment, concentrating on the scene she had described earlier. She was breathing deeply as a means to keep herself focused and avoid surrendering to the feelings all over again. Finally, she nodded, indicating that she was envisioning the scene.

"There I am," Kirschenbaum said in a hypnotic voice. "I'm sitting there, hollow, slumped, tired, empty. Right?"

Wendy nodded.

"Now I am turning around to say good-bye to you for the last time. I'm. . ."

Before he could go any further, Wendy cried out in a strangled scream, "No. NOOO! Please, no. Don't go, Scott! Please, Scott. Come with me. Scott. Scott!" And then her screams strangled in her throat and she began to sob once again.

Kirschenbaum leaned forward in his chair, moving closer. He reached out and took both of Wendy's hands into his own. He recognized that someone who was so deeply distressed from a trauma desperately needed a connection to the here-and-now. "I want you to look at me, Wendy. Can you do that?"

Wendy struggled, her eyes flitting back and forth between the pillow of wet tissue in her lap and her therapist's eyes. She made contact for only a moment and then seemed to drift back to the scene with her brother.

"Wendy," Howie said more firmly, squeezing her hands, "I want you to look at me. Look into my eyes." He waited until she gulped in some air and could look at him without turning away.

"He was dying," Wendy repeated like a mantra. "He was dying, and I couldn't help him. I couldn't save him." And then she pulled away from Kirschenbaum, literally pulled away from his hands and leaned back in the chair to cradle herself like an injured animal. The noises she was making indeed resembled the moans of someone dying from a mortal wound.

Again the cycle repeated itself with Wendy sobbing, repeating to herself that she couldn't help her brother. Kirschenbaum just waited, unsure what else to do, and yet convinced that this was what she needed to be doing right then.

A few more minutes passed, enough time that Kirschenbaum was convinced that surely Wendy had expressed the full extent of her loss. Now they could move to explore those feelings more objectively. But just when he tried to redirect the conversation toward some sort of understanding, Wendy would fall back into her sobs and feel the need to tell the story all over again.

Catching the pattern that was developing, Kirschenbaum also started over, pretending that they had just begun. "I understand you had a brother," he said in a cheerful, innocent voice, inviting her to describe all over again what happened. He was doing this for far more than to merely desensitize her to the pain. He believed that such distressing emotions needed physical release. Wendy needed to let go of all the hurt and anger and guilt and sadness. Until she could let the feelings go, there was little chance she could move forward.

Over the course of several more sessions, they began each time as if they were meeting for the first time. Howie would always begin with the apparently naïve invitation: "I understand you had a brother." That would be the signal for Wendy to tell the story all over again and release the accompanying flood of feelings.

Each time she described what happened, Wendy would repeat over and over again that her brother was dying and she could do nothing to help him. She kept resonating with this sense of helplessness and powerlessness.

At one point, after a half-dozen rounds of this, Kirschenbaum asked a clarifying question to encourage Wendy to explore her possible guilt. But she just shook her head in impatience: that was not a place she was interested in going just yet, especially if it involved moving away from her feelings to the intellect. Instead, she wanted to keep telling the story, adding more detail and layers to it. She ended with the declaration "There was nothing I could do."

Kirschenbaum noticed immediately that this was a very different statement than: "I couldn't help him." Previously, she had been saying she couldn't accept what had happened. She remained obsessed with the image of watching her brother die before her eyes without her being able to intervene in any way. Now, however, she was telling the story with a different twist: Yes, her brother had died of neglect, but there was nothing she could have done to stop it. She and the family had done all they could.

Wendy made the transition from helplessness and self-blame to acceptance almost seamlessly. She seemed to acknowledge that there was nothing she could have done, or should have done, differently. If ever there had been an issue of guilt—and surely there must have been—it never came up. It was as if she had discharged all the negative energy in the flood of feeling. She still felt a sense of loss, of course, but she now accepted what happened, and how it happened. She could never forget what happened, but now she could live with it.

Never in his life had Kirschenbaum witnessed, or experienced, such depth of feeling, whether related to grief or anything else. The level of horror, the emotional torment, the anguish that Wendy expressed were stronger than he had known in any previous client or personal relationship. He certainly knew a great deal about the Holocaust and other acts of extreme human cruelty. Many relatives he had never met had died in the death camps. He had been involved in the civil rights movement in Mississippi at a time when three coworkers were brutally murdered. Yet he had never had such a direct, intimate, and intense contact with emotional expression as he experienced with Wendy.

"I was awed by what happened," Kirschenbaum remembered. "I had witnessed something that profoundly affected my understanding of emotion and the depth to which it can be experienced. This was a kind of grief that was beyond anything I had ever known personally. I don't know how to attach any deeper meaning to it other than to say that it was like having a kind of religious experience, or seeing one of the greatest works of art, or witnessing the birth of a baby—I had that sense of awe . This was certainly not one of the most pleasing or beautiful parts of life, but it was still part of human experience. I was profoundly grateful for what Wendy shared with me."

Professionally, Kirschenbaum learned that there are some problems in people's lives that simply can't be fixed. There are some things that one just has to come to terms with and accept the reality that there is little else you can do. This was not only Wendy's therapeutic task, but also Kirschenbaum's: he learned about the limits of his own healing powers. He couldn't bring back Wendy's brother, nor could he take away her painful memories. All he could do was help her to live with them in such a way that she was no longer debilitated. She would carry around her profound loss for the rest of her life, and he couldn't do anything about that. All he could do was to be with her, to stay with her in the moment, and that had to be enough. In one sense, it was enough.

On a far more personal level, Kirschenbaum was able to gain access to greater depth of his own emotions after his work with Wendy. At this point in his life, he had not experienced the loss of a loved one. That is one reason why he was so moved by what he had witnessed; it was totally beyond what he had ever known.

"My lucky streak ran out before too long, and I began experiencing loved ones becoming ill and dying. I believe that I have been able to more fully experience and acknowledge the grieving process and loss than I did before as a direct result of what happened with Wendy. If I feel the need, I can now ask a trusted family member, friend, or counselor-colleague to hear my story. I can now unburden my hurt in ways I could not have done before. I now know about the power of acceptance by others to help me to heal."

Since then, Kirschenbaum has been able to generalize this learning to other emotions and contexts. "If someone close to me is angry at me, I am more able to allow them to be angry without feeling I have to get defensive or get angry myself. I recognize that in many instances they just want to express their feelings, and they don't need me to respond by justifying myself or trying to make them feel better. They just want to get it out for their own sake, and maybe they want me to hear how angry they are. This has helped me in so many areas of life—anger, fear, physical pain, and of course loss."

Kirschenbaum paused for a moment in our conversation, realizing that something had happened very recently in his life that had direct relevance to what we were talking about. His father died last year, at age 95, after a long, slow, progressive battle with Alzheimer's disease. Howie had been there for him throughout this long journey—he was with him in a way that might not have been possible without his own increased comfort with emotion. He was able to grieve the loss of his father gradually over the years. Last year, when his father fell and was hospitalized, and then went into a nursing home where he began a precipitous decline, Howie visited him and was shocked that his father could barely speak or recognize him. When the nurse was washing his father, Howie went into the adjoining room and wept with huge sobs. The nurse, clearly uncomfortable hearing a grown man cry, tried to reassure him and get him to stop. Howie explained that he was fine, that he just needed to cry. Over the next two weeks, before and after his father's death, he grieved in this way several more times. In the end there was not a lot of accumulated hurt built up inside. He had acknowledged and expressed these feelings as the need arose throughout the years, and especially in the intense last month.

Just last week, Kirschenbaum and his family held a one-year memorial service for his father in which the gravestone was unveiled. In the presence of friends and relatives, he led the ceremony in which traditional prayers were said and those present shared some of their remembrances. Howie wept just a little at one point, allowing his tears to honor his father's memory and all the things they had shared together. But he was also there to support his mother and aunt and other relatives whose shed and unshed tears were palpably present. Their grief did not restimulate his, because his had been thoroughly or at least sufficiently expressed.

Accompanying Wendy into and beyond the depth of her enormous grief played a significant role in helping Kirschenbaum to access the depth of his own emotions over the years—to experience them, to accept them, and to let them go.

Chapter 25

HOW CLIENTS CHANGE THEIR THERAPISTS
with Mary Halunka

We have added one more member to our team in order to bring our journey to an end. We have been practicing therapy for over three decades, and doing interviews like those found in this book for the past five years; Mary is a graduate student and relative neophyte. We thought it important to consider the implications of these stories not only for experienced practitioners, but also for those who are just beginning in this field. After all, the messages we received when first starting out—essentially that therapists don't change in therapy, and if they do, it is only because we have been negligent and naughty in not maintaining appropriate boundaries—are in marked contrast to the themes that you have just read in this book. Not only do our field's most prominent theoreticians feel changed by their work, and especially by some of their clients, but they appear to be quite grateful for these interactions. This is not at all merely within the domain of countertransference, in which therapist changes are framed as projections or inappropriate personal reactions.

FOR SOME, IT IS FORBIDDEN GROUND

A reader could get the impression from this book that therapists' admitting personal transformations is a frequent occurrence. Some of our interviewees were downright casual and matter-of-fact in sharing their stories. A few were so disclosing, open, and vulnerable that it would lead one to believe that this is common practice. It assuredly is not.

One theorist we contacted for this study (who shall remain name-less) wanted very much to contribute a story. We interviewed him for about 30 minutes, about half of our allotted time. Try as he might, he couldn't think of a single instance in which he had been changed by a client. Not one.

"What about in your teaching?" we asked him. "In all of your years in the classroom, surely there have been students who have impacted you in enduring ways."

"You mean, like, contributed to my intellectual development?"

"Ah, no," we said. "Not exactly. We mean changed you personally."

He thought for a long minute, then apologized. No, after more than 30 years as a clinician, supervisor, and teacher, he still couldn't think of a single instance.

"Not one?" we repeated again, stalling. This was the most unbeliev-able response we'd had so far. It seemed inconceivable to us that it is possible to spend so much intimate, intense time with people and not be changed by those interactions. Could it be that he was changed but just didn't know it?

"Wait a minute. Wait a minute," he said after another pause. "I have been changed by some things I've read over the years. Especially poetry. There was this one poem. . ."

So here was a guy who couldn't even imagine being personally influenced or changed by clients. He admitted that he deliberately chose his specialty of cognitive therapy because of its clear boundaries in the therapeutic relationship (at least as he conceived of them) and because it stressed intellectual discourse rather than the sort of "messy" stuff that might lead to unnecessary complications.

It is easy to scoff at this response, but this is a very well-respected thinker and writer in the field, and a first-class clinician. He was not delib-erately trying to be resistant or evade our questions. He was not coerced to participate in this study; he actually volunteered. And he also tried his best to give us what we were looking for. But it just wasn't part of his way of being to allow himself to consider personal changes in his work.

We would like to think this is an extreme peer reaction, but unfor-tunately there are many in our field who have been trained to avoid all mention of therapists' personal reactions, except as they may interfere with treatment. We were puzzled, at first, by those therapists who seemed so reluctant to talk about how clients changed them. These are some of the answers supplied by those who turned down the invitation to partici-pate in this project:

"It's embarrassing to admit that you are not all together."

"I don't want to appear self-serving and exploitative."

"I think it is unethical and unprofessional to allow yourself to be changed in the ways you suggest."

"People might think I'm unstable or crazy or weak. We've got too much of that in the field already."

"This is just too personal for me. I don't feel comfortable."

"I just have a mental set that has been ingrained in me that my job is to change the client, not the other way around."

Each of these stated reasons is legitimate. We respect the points of view of our colleagues who don't share our strong belief (and experiences) related to reciprocal changes in therapy. We have offered the stories in this book as a counterpoint to this perspective.

IDENTIFYING THEMES

We have examined the stories in this book in order to identify some key themes of how and why the therapists are changed. Upon reading and rereading the stories, such themes began to emerge. Some of them are rather obvious, even stated explicitly by the contributor. John Gray, for example, clearly recognized that the parallels between his marriage, and that of Marilyn and Nathan, were so strong that he forever changed the way he viewed communication between men and women. Not only did his marriage improve, but he was able to apply what he learned to hundreds of other couples.

Steve Lankton attributed some of the changes he experienced to "continual reminder incidences," which he explains as the messages that some clients give their therapists about an area of their own lives that is in need of upgrading. "During the pep talks that we give to people in these circumstances," Lankton says, "we might sometimes recognize that we are speaking to ourselves as much as to them."

Given all the public discourse in the media and our professional codes about all the potential ways that therapists can harm their clients, especially if they cross established boundaries, it is very refreshing to read about the mutually rewarding relationships that are possible between client and therapist. We are by no means suggesting that therapists should be deliberately meeting their own needs in sessions, nor should they be collapsing boundaries that are critical for maintaining safety and predictability in the therapeutic relationship. Rather, we hope the stories in this book have offered some illumination about the reciprocal benefits that take place in this type of work. Therapists almost can't help but change as a result of spending so much intimate time in the company of others who are working so courageously on their growth.

CORE THEMES

The stories in this book are so genuine, multifaceted, and meaningful that it is difficult to compartmentalize the essence of each transformation. In our efforts to "code" and classify the core themes that emerged from the stories, it became evident that several contributors mentioned issues that fall into more than one thematic category. During your own first reading of the narratives, it may have struck you, as it did us, that a half-dozen or so themes consistently stand out.

- A number of therapists (Gray, Lankton, Love, Arredondo, Pittman, Marlatt, Keeney, Duncan) were changed by the personal connections with their clients. They each lived a life parallel to that of their client, one that was enhanced by the bond they shared. This resulted in a lifelong impact.
- Some therapists (Carlson, Oaklander, Ellis, Keeney, Scharff, Arredondo) journeyed with their clients for several years and were forever touched by the intimacy forged during their time together. Still others (Ellis, Love, Hardy, McCullough, Kirschenbaum, Carlson, Neimeyer, Scharff, Duncan, Kottler) experienced states of intense emotional arousal. They were often overwhelmed by what they experienced. Whether the stories took place when the contributors were new to the field (Oaklander, Pittman, Scharff, Hardy, Murphy, Pedersen, Duncan, Arredondo, Ellis, Keeney, Brown, Lankton, Love, McCullough), or welcomed the lessons into all facets of their lives (Carlson, Oaklander, Keeney, Gray, Murphy), all of these contributors allowed themselves to be vulnerable and open to the possibility of change.
- It is a given that therapists need to be healthier than their clients. It is generally a good idea for us to have worked through issues before we attempt to help others do the same. This is not a luxury of the profession, but rather a mandate that we should practice in our own lives what we preach to others (Kottler, 2003).

- In the sections that follow, we review some of the core themes (see Table 25-1), after which we each talk about how we were changed by hearing these stories.

EMPATHIC TRANSCENDENCE

Several therapists (Gray, Lankton, Love, Arredondo, Pittman, Marlatt, Keeney, Duncan) reported experiencing moments that went far beyond just being present with the client. Pat Love described her experience through tears as she recalled the pain Loretta shared with her. Love is

TABLE 1   Themes of Change

THEMES	CONTRIBUTOR
Empathic transcendence	Gray, Lankton, Love, Arredondo, Pittman, Marlatt, Keeney, Duncan
Intimacy	Marlatt, Keeney, Love, Brown, Carlson, Oaklander, Ellis, Scharff, Arredondo, Lankton, McCullough
High emotional arousal	Ellis, Love, Hardy, McCullough, Kirschenbaum, Carlson, Neimeyer, Sharff, Duncan, Kottler
Letting boundaries down	Keeney, Lankton, Brown, Love, Walker, McCullough, Arredondo, Carlson, Neimeyer, Murphy, Pittman, Marlatt, Sharff, Murphy, Krumboltz, Duncan
Impressionable	Oaklander, Pittman, Scharff, Hardy, Murphy, Pedersen, Duncan, Arredondo, Ellis, Keeney, Brown, Lankton, Love, McCullough
Validating cherished ideals	Oaklander, Marlatt, Ellis, Yapko, Walker, Pittman, Love, Carlson, Lankton, Pedersen, Keeney, Gray, Murphy, McCullough, Brown
Beyond challenged	Carlson, Neimeyer, Ellis, Scharff, Hardy, Murphy, McCullough, Lankton, Pedersen, Walker, Duncan
Witness to profound change	Carlson, Oaklander, Neimeyer, Marlatt, Sharff, Lankton, McCullough, Arredondo

still moved by this experience. She carries the depth of the connection she experienced with Loretta into every subsequent therapy session. She is fully attuned to her clients' needs, and has developed the ability to allow herself to be vulnerable and feel their pain.

Barry Duncan also experienced something beyond the traditional therapeutic relationship that he was trained to abide by. Rather than following the orders of his supervisors, Duncan began to care personally about Tamara. He felt Tamara's pain, and today allows himself to experience the client where he or she is, without making assumptions. In each of these cases, the therapist not only empathized with his or her client, but also shared an understanding that cannot be expressed in words.

Feeling a need for a "tune-up" in one's personal life also played a role in the magnitude and intensity of the client's impact. Brad Keeney discovered something he had been longing for, the use of techniques that went beyond talk. Keeney sought to implement imagination, creativity, spiritual awakening through rituals, and opening new realms of transformation. He wanted his clients to experience something more powerful than the stifling limitations involved in formal talk therapy. He got his chance with Sven and his parents. Keeney had the opportunity to move Sven's family in new directions, beyond what they could have ever imagined. They become more attuned to each other, and Keeney discovered that he could better trust his instincts. Keeney forged a special bond with Sven and his parents that surpassed even his imagination.

One additional example of empathic transcendence is found with Pat Arredondo's client, Sandy. She has been the impetus for many of the positive choices Pat has made throughout her life. Sandy's strength, originality, and dedication inspire Pat to this day. So we are talking about a kind of "deep" empathy that goes far beyond what is usually talked about in the literature; it is a state of communal connection in which both participants are profoundly affected by the experience.

INTIMACY

The inherently intimate nature of therapy suggests that all therapists experience a closeness with their clients during their encounters. Yet, some therapists (Marlatt, Keeney, Love, Brown, Carlson, Oaklander, Ellis, Sharff, Arredondo, Lankton, McCullough) talked about the profound change experienced as a result of the relationships they developed with their clients. At one end of the continuum, Laura Brown exemplifies openness to this intimate interchange that too many therapists deny, and perhaps fear (sometimes for good reason). She talks about how many of her clients have managed to change her in some way, but none like Ellen. This client challenged her to look inside of herself as part of their relationship. Laura resisted at first, concerned about dangers related to more permeable boundaries, but she later allowed a part of herself to emerge that she had fought to control. The authentically genuine relationship that developed between Ellen and Laura not only helped Ellen to heal, but also allowed Laura to confront her fears of deep intimacy. These changes helped both women live more authentic and fulfilling lives. This is where the theoretical orientation of the practitioner would inform and guide (and judge) the appropriateness of such flexible relationships. A psychoanalyst (such as Scharff) is most likely going to have a more formalized structure than that of a feminist (such as Brown).

Several therapists (Carlson, Oaklander, Ellis, Keeney, Sharff, Arredondo) enhanced the intimate relationships with their clients as a consequence of spending several years working with them. Jon Carlson spent over five years with Max. Their time together culminated in tremendous change for both of them. Jon witnessed tremendous alterations in Max, from his appearance, to his physical health, to educational and professional achievements. Jon's relationship with Max challenged all of his preconceived beliefs about what it meant to be crazy. As a result of their intense relationship, innumerable changes occurred in Jon's professional and personal life.

Likewise, Violet Oaklander spent years watching Molly develop into a young lady and forged a connection with her that was more special than any before, or after. Keeney stayed in touch with Sven and his family for several years. Sandy and Pat Arredondo remained close for many, many years, and although Sandy has since passed away, she will always have a special place in Pat's heart. It seems that after spending several years with a client, the intimate connections that are forged result in changes that last a lifetime. We do not think that this can be taught in any counseling textbook.

HIGH EMOTIONAL AROUSAL

High emotional arousal can cause increased heart rate, anxiety, and even impaired cognitive functioning (Kaufman, 1999), but other studies have found that there is often an increase in awareness and acuity (Levine & Burgess, 1997). For some therapists (Ellis, Love, Hardy, McCullough, Kirschenbaum, Carlson, Neimeyer, Sharff, Duncan, Kottler, Pedersen), the intensity of emotions experienced during specific therapy sessions with their clients forever changed them. Pat Love personally experienced Loretta's pain, not for herself, but for Loretta; she had never experienced such a genuine connection prior to this one. Ken Hardy had to face unimaginable circumstances, not only in attempting to get through Joey's racist barricade but also in coping with the realization that his colleagues did not recognize their own denial of the prejudice Hardy was facing. Hardy managed to move beyond this incredible challenge and devote his career to uncovering the history of slavery, and to becoming a preeminent therapist.

Howard Kirschenbaum's experience opened his eyes to the intense pain involved in losing a loved one. Wendy's ability to pour out her pain, right there in front of Howie, was an undeniably transformative moment for him. The intensity of her emotions shed light on what would come to be a new era for her therapist. Howie learned about the truth behind being there for the client and how to cope with future losses in his own life.

Several therapists (Carlson, Neimeyer, Scharff, Hardy, Duncan) reported initially feeling overwhelmed by their clients. Carol posed what appeared to be an impossible situation for Bob Neimeyer. During their very first meeting she appeared catatonic and painfully dissociated from reality. Neimeyer helplessly observed Carol for three sessions before she even spoke a word. The realization of Carol's painful existence caused Bob to question how he operated as a therapist. He became acutely aware that her case was far more complex than any other he had encountered. In time, he managed to reach Carol, and she, in turn, managed to reach him. Bob developed a new sense of self and purpose, and, because of Carol, was able to communicate in a new language—the language of caring. This was quite different from the overly logical mode he had been operating from prior to their encounter.

Experiencing emotional arousal is highly stressful, just as it can be exhilarating. At the time, we are often thinking: "Whoa, I want out of here!" But once the feelings are worked through, by both participants, the effects often last far beyond what could have taken place under calmer circumstances.

LETTING BOUNDARIES DOWN

The maintenance of strict boundaries allows therapists to remain objective and impartial, and to protect both clients and themselves from impropriety (Chadda & Slonim, 1998; Herlihy & Corey, 1997). Such prohibitions are absolutely critical to prevent exploitation of clients, as well as to clearly demarcate the limits of the relationship. Especially with more disturbed clients, the enforcement of strict boundaries often becomes the essence of the treatment. But can allowing boundaries to blur sometimes aid in the healing process?

As a result of following their instincts and not maintaining strict boundaries, many of the contributors (Keeney, Brown, Love, Walker, McCullough, Arredondo, Neimeyer, Murphy, Carlson, Pittman, Marlatt, Sharff, Duncan) found that their clients benefited. There were, in fact, no instances of boundary crossings that resulted in any apparent harm to the client. These therapists chose to be moved, to connect with their clients on a new dimension, and to allow their clients to see them as human beings. Laura Brown shared herself with Ellen and, in turn, learned how to share herself with others in her life. She also discovered that when it is appropriate for the client, self-disclosure can be beneficial and even healing.

Pat Love shared Loretta's pain and wept with her in shared companionship. For the first time, Pat was able to be totally present, and realized that shedding tears with a client did not have to be anything other than expressing how attuned she felt. Of course, we can imagine many similar situations that could have a very different outcome. I (Jeffrey) remember one time I was with a client immediately after my father had a stroke. (Why I was seeing clients in this circumstance is a good question.) During the session, when the client mentioned his father, I suddenly broke into tears. This was not a good thing at all; in fact, it turned out to be very distracting and disturbing for the client. Rather than bringing us closer, it pushed us farther apart. So context is everything.

Lenore Walker, stepping out of the role of a traditional therapist, became part of a team to help Mercedes separate from an abusive relationship. In the end, both women were more empowered than ever before to conquer obstacles in their lives.

Some of the therapists (Carlson, Neimeyer, Pittman, Marlatt, Keeney, Scharff, Murphy, Duncan) trusted their instincts and used new techniques while treating their clients. Keeney used imagination. Neimeyer pushed aside his tradition of using cognitive-behavioral therapy and embarked on a deeper level of communication through the use of metaphorical language. Alan Marlatt rejected the disease model of alcoholism and encouraged Tina to try something new: meditation. Their journey resulted in a lifetime of change for both of them. Tina became empowered and conquered her demons. Alan, too, became empowered. He was able to stand up to his critics and discover aspects of himself that he had long neglected. Barry Duncan refused to follow the tradition of heavily medicating and severely restricting the patients at the adolescent treatment center where he worked. His encounter with Tamara taught him the importance of relating to clients on a personal level. Once he gained Tamara's trust, and showed her how much he genuinely cared for her, she was able to open up and allow Barry into her world.

Trusting their instincts, and allowing their humanness to dictate who they are during therapy, helped these therapists to connect with their clients and discover new avenues of treatment. Again it should be noted that these particular cases were related specifically because they had positive outcomes. We are in no way advocating for all therapists, in all situations, with all clients, that they do anything other than follow the ethical code of their profession.

IMPRESSIONABLE

A good number of therapists featured in this book (Oaklander, Pittman, Scharff, Hardy, Pedersen, Duncan, Arredondo, Ellis, Keeney, Brown, Lankton, Love, McCullough) were impressionable. They opened themselves up to change and allowed themselves to be vulnerable with their clients. Many of the expert therapists reported being changed in their early or initial cases. This makes us wonder if they have a "beginner's mind," and with time operate on automatic pilot, no longer as aware of the impact.

Even after 20 years, Violet Oaklander has not forgotten the gift she received from Molly. "I've learned how to be more accepting and patient with myself. I remind myself of this every day. Molly also taught me to be more optimistic and hopeful, not only with my clients but with myself."

It may have been their youth and inexperience that allowed many of the therapists to be changed in unimaginable ways. Frank Pittman made his own path and decided for himself that the prevailing ideas of the time, more than 40 years ago, were not all they were chalked up to be. He forged a new destiny, for himself and for the many clients who followed Roger.

Ken Hardy was new to the field and shocked into reality by the racism he encountered, both in the therapy room and behind the one-way mirror. He realized that what he had been taught in school was not representative of the harsh realities of the real world.

Sandy was Pat Arredondo's very first client (and who does not remember their first client?). She posed the biggest challenge to Pat, and yet became someone very important and close to her heart.

Tamara was one of Barry Duncan's first clients. She instantly piqued his curiosity and taught him the true meaning of courage, determination, and compassion. Barry emerged from his relationship with Tamara a changed man. He was able to discern the difference between what he was taught and what was real. Tamara inspired him, and, as he describes it, "This led me to begin questioning and challenging everything rather than just accepting what I was told. Nothing was the same for me after that."

Paul Pedersen's experience is unique. He was not conducting personal or family therapy when he came to the realization that nothing had been what it seemed. He was in Japan, on a mission to enhance cross-cultural communication. Early in his career, he had an idealistic image of what would take place during the meetings he attended. Pedersen came away with a profound sense of humility and a new way of perceiving the message from "so-called experts in the field."

VALIDATING CHERISHED IDEALS

Many of our contributors (Oaklander, Marlatt, Ellis, Yapko, Walker, Pittman, Love, Carlson, Ellis, Lankton, Pedersen, Keeney, Gray, Murphy, McCullough, Brown) held deep beliefs about how best to conduct therapy. Violet Oaklander used play therapy with Molly. Her imagination, training, and ability to meet Molly on her terms enabled Violet to work magic. Through sand play, art, and role-playing, Violet helped Molly break through her pain. Molly also taught Violet some valuable lessons about patience and self-acceptance.

Bob was inspired to meet with Michael Yapko because of Michael's prior work as a staunch critic of memory recovery. Yapko was so moved by Bob's experience as a result of his daughter's manipulation at the hands of an abusive therapist that he devoted himself to changing the way the world viewed recalled memories. The misinformation that was out at the time was giving untrained therapists a ticket to practice their own style of memory recovery. After meeting with Bob, Yapko helped to start a movement that has changed the field of hypnosis and memory recovery as we know it.

As we mentioned before, by following his instincts and sticking to what he felt was right, Alan Marlatt helped Tina overcome her battle with alcohol and an unhappy marriage. Alan guided Tina down a path of inner strength and wisdom. At the same time, he was guiding himself down the same path. The choices that Tina made for herself, and the choices they made together, strengthened Marlatt's feelings and ideas about treating addiction. Marlatt's journey with Tina put him back in touch with his spirituality. He has since evolved a new sense of being, as a Buddhist psychologist, and as a result has had the ability to successfully treat many more clients suffering from addiction.

Similar to Marlatt, several therapists (Lankton, Keeney, Brown) discovered, or rediscovered, their spiritual side. Jane led Lankton to rediscover the Holy Spirit in his life. Lankton was forever moved by the experience of being with Jane as she allowed herself to feel the depth of her spirituality and self-acceptance. Working with Sven and his parents reinvigorated Brad Keeney's faith in shamantic rituals, beliefs, and use of imagination. Likewise, Laura Brown rekindled her spiritual faith while working with Ellen. Brown has since maintained a strong connection to her faith, while also practicing the art of authenticity, something she feared prior to working with Ellen, with all those with whom she comes in contact. This has benefited not only her professional life, since she is more in tune with her clients, but her personal life as well. Greater spiritual awareness is so inimitable that when a person experiences a true awakening, it can often be life-changing.

BEYOND CHALLENGED

Many of the therapists interviewed (Carlson, Neimeyer, Ellis, Scharff, Hardy, Murphy, McCullough, Lankton, Pedersen, Walker, Duncan) developed courage as they watched their clients face difficult, and at times insurmountable, challenges. When Carlson initially met Max, the man was actively psychotic. Even after five years and the many strides they made together, Max never did stop believing that there was a microchip in his brain.

In Neimeyer's case, Carol had been in and out of the hospital, a victim of abuse and suicidal. She was catatonic and unable to speak during their first few meetings, leaving Bob with few options. He had never faced a task as daunting as helping this particular client. But, as a result of this overwhelming task, he learned how to connect with Carol on a new level. This gave him hope about possibilities for the future.

Albert Ellis was pelted with hateful words from Natalie, who never ceased to "crawl under" his skin. Oddly enough, Natalie's hateful berating of Ellis actually helped him (but Al would make the best of any situation). Ellis became stronger, more accepting, and more patient. He not only had to deal with Natalie during this time; he was also defending REBT as a therapeutic technique. Natalie's attacks did not diminish, but she did get better—and Ellis, too, got better. He improved his methods, grew as a therapist, and proved to the world that REBT was a useful method.

John Murphy was faced with a young boy who came from tragic circumstances and who, like others, was not willing to speak at first. As a matter of fact, Murphy was able to utilize the silence to create an enduring bond between him and Michael. "I had been a behaviorally oriented, solution-focused therapist—and I still might describe myself this way—but Michael taught me not to fall in love with my solutions or try to impose them on others, because to do so carries the risk of running roughshod over the more important task of establishing and maintaining a respectful relationship with clients. In the case of Michael, this required me to shut up, listen, and be present. As has been the case with most of the powerful lessons I have learned throughout my career, this one came from the greatest of all teachers—the client."

The changes Murphy experienced transcended his professional life and entered into his personal life, teaching him how to be present for friends and family. This is a theme prevalent in many of the cases reviewed.

WITNESS TO PROFOUND CHANGE

Several therapists (Carlson, Oaklander, Neimeyer, Marlatt, Scharff, Lankton, McCullough, Arredondo) were surprised by what people can become, by how much of our nomenclature for understanding is limiting and rooted in viewing the pathological. Many reported that they developed very different views of their clients, and of their profession.

The changes in themselves often resulted from the impact of witnessing profound changes in their clients. Max went from a psychotic, overweight, lifeless "blob" to an able-bodied, successful husband. Carlson was forever moved by the unbelievable changes that Max was able to accomplish during their time together. Violet Oaklander watched Molly go from a broken, fearful, tortured child to a vibrant young teenager. She watched the light of life reenter Molly and transform her into someone she deserved to be. Leigh McCullough guided Leslie through her transformation from a suicidal and socially inept woman to a resourceful and empowered woman. Leslie taught McCullough how to truly use emotional intimacy in therapy. With those tools, and witnessing the undeniably positive changes in Leslie's life, Leigh herself transformed into a more loving mother and caring therapist.

The gift of aiding someone in need, the power to heal, and the satisfaction of a job well done may all contribute to the unimaginable gratification of witnessing profound change in a client. Sandy has passed away, but as we mentioned before, she will always be in Pat Arredondo's heart. The changes Sandy made, the strength she showed, and the inspiration that she brought to Pat's life will never be forgotten. Pat, too, transformed herself, and with undeniable fortitude embarked on an entirely new adventure in her life, one with the love and respect she had been lacking and always deserved.

Being a part of someone's resurrection in life, watching them hatch from their shell of pain, invariably has a profound impact on the partner, the teacher, the therapist. We have been given the opportunity to share in the miracle.

HOW JON HAS CHANGED

I (Jon) was again encouraged by how willing people are to share their experiences. This is our fourth book in which we have asked leading therapists to be open and honest about their practices and lives. It was refreshing to hear how exciting therapy is for the therapist and how much each one of the experts enjoys what he or she does. It helped me realize, or at least re-realize, how much I like what I do, and how privileged I feel each day as people come to me with the goal of living a more satisfying life. I not only work hard at helping my clients directly, but I also feel compelled to try just as hard to make sure that I am living a healthy life and that I am practicing what I am advocating. I have a tremendous responsibility to help others, and I take it seriously. I had not realized how important this is to me and how much it drives me.

I learned to become more honest regarding the depth of the changes that have occurred in my life. Many of these changes have their origin with my clients. I am aware of how I struggle with issues that did not bother me until one of my clients presented that issue as one that was challenging him or her.

I looked forward to each interview and wondered just how each expert was going to report being changed by a client. I noticed that most of the changes were consistent with the theoretical model that the therapist followed. I am not sure if this was done to support the therapist's model or if the expert's theory is so much a part of his or her own personal way of explaining change.

I was surprised to realize the difference between men and women. The women seemed to have gone deeper into more intimate and emotional areas. The men were more comfortable working in the areas of changed beliefs and behaviors. I often realized through my clients, and those in this book, some of my buried emotions. I am sure there are many more to be unearthed as I go into each new area of personal relating. It seems that this "peeling the layers off the onion" is a lifelong process.

Maybe we need to talk more about therapist change in our training programs. Maybe this needs to be highlighted. Many of the therapists stated that rather than exploiting clients through their personal changes, it was the therapist's change that was in the best interest of the client. It was the therapist's change that made it possible for the client to change.

It might be time for us to sanction the therapist's change and learn to ensure that is done in the best interest of the client. Denying the existence of this mutual change would seem to be unprofessional, if not a distortion of reality. Therapists need to accept the fact that change is reciprocal, and is healthy as long as it is not harming our clients. Many of the experts felt that therapist change is a necessary component for effective therapy.

WHAT JEFFREY HAS LEARNED FROM THIS PROJECT

Unlike Jon, who still has a very active practice, I see only a few clients these days and spend most of my time teaching, writing, and lecturing abroad (Jon does these things, too). As I write these words, I am preparing for my next trip to Nepal, where I have been working to develop programs for improved health care in rural areas. I devote not only a significant amount of time to this project, but as much money as I can afford.

I have been thinking about why I am spending my time doing this, when I could be doing other things (surfing, for one). After reading the stories in this book, I realize why so many of us devote ourselves to service and altruistic pursuits that have little to do with helping others and everything to do with helping ourselves. I am not talking about the "helper's high," in which physiological changes in the body have been documented when people reach out to others in a significant way. Rather,

I am referring to the ways that we grow and stretch as a result of joining others on their journeys of self-discovery.

Reading and reviewing the stories in this book makes me feel so proud that I am a member of a profession with so many dedicated, passionate members. The contributors to this book are not only our colleagues but also our friends. They inspire us, just as we hope they do you. I may disagree with what many of them are doing in their sessions (because I have a very different style of practice), but I can't possibly question the devotion they feel to their work—no, not their work, their calling.

I feel humbled by the stories in this book. Always a bit insecure, I can't help but make comparisons between what these great therapists have done, and how I might have proceeded differently. Granted, these cases represent their most memorable clients, but still, I would never have had the courage or the foresight or the creativity to think of the amazing things that they have tried. So these stories inspire me to take more risks in my work—not the sort where I put my clients or students at risk, but those that force me to get more outside my comfort zone and try things I've never tried before. When you've seen as many clients as I have, and taught as many classes, it gets harder and harder to reinvent yourself every time. Yet I do know that the best work I've ever done takes place when it feels as if I am doing something for the very first time.

THE LESSONS THAT MARY HAS BEEN TAUGHT

This is truly an unprecedented look into the personal transformations of more than two dozen distinguished therapists. Their stories offer insightful revelations about what actually happens within the walls of the therapeutic sanctum and inside the therapists themselves. And, more important, the stories reveal that personal transformation of the therapist can occur without detriment to the client.

I am grateful for the therapists' candid accounts in this book. They have revealed their secrets, their personal journeys, and their souls. I am touched and somewhat surprised by their revelations. Every theory of psychotherapy includes a theory of how change takes place in the client. I have yet to read about the changes that a therapist may experience. In fact, I have been under the impression that the therapist is not supposed to be impacted by the client. The therapist is to remain a stoic participant who provides empathy when appropriate and is always listening. Is it okay for therapists to be changed by the client? All of my previous experience told me otherwise.

As a graduate student, I have been taught that I must maintain strict boundaries or risk losing my license and my credibility. I have been taught about the various theories of psychotherapy, all of which offer the appropriate techniques to change the client. I have received mixed messages: "Be there for the client, be genuine," yet "Remain detached, and do not reveal anything about yourself to the client."

In my training, I have learned how to avoid any dual relationships and extensive intimacy, and how to remain completely detached. I have learned that the slippery slope of impropriety is inevitable once the therapist allows the client to penetrate the professional shield. Any mention of the therapist benefiting from the therapeutic relationship implies unscrupulousness by the therapist. The paramount message is that the therapist is not to benefit from the relationship, and to do so means that he or she is exploiting the client.

In therapy the client is encouraged to reflect, be insightful, and change. The client's change is lauded as courageous and magnanimous. The client develops, while the therapist remains an impartial facilitator. Anything beyond mere facilitation of the client's change by the therapist is self-serving and beyond the scope of his or her duties. Opposition to change on the part of the client is "resistance," and is viewed as unhealthy. As Pedersen points out, "Ethical codes presume that all learning is one-directional...we know that is not true. There are times when the therapist, or the teacher, learns even more than the client or student." Widely held therapeutic principles tell us that change in the client is essential, while change in the therapist is, paradoxically, objectionable.

The stories by the theoreticians in this book have been truly eye-opening. Change happens to everyone, every day, as a result of every interaction. Laura Brown's statement about therapist change struck me as particularly poignant. "Anyone who meets us, changes us. Every encounter we have, transforms us. How could we be therapists and not be transformed profoundly in all kinds of ways?"

I noticed that the therapeutic alliance in all of the stories appeared to be horizontal rather than hierarchical. A horizontal relationship is one in which neither party is an expert on the other's experience. The therapist is an expert on psychological theory, process, and intervention, while the client is an expert on his or her own experience. They are equal in the encounter. This egalitarian theme seemed to set the stage for the ensuing reciprocal influences between therapist and client.

I have a feeling that the stories in this book are a drop in the bucket of the mutual influences that occur during each therapy session. The changes that occur invariably imbue the therapist with wisdom and increase his or her effectiveness with future clients. As Jeffrey testifies, the relationships that develop as a result of hours, weeks, and months of intimate conversations are inherently transforming. Immunity to change is impossible to imagine upon considering all of the intricate details, traumas, and narratives disclosed during a therapy session.

I look forward to entering what appears to be an immensely rewarding field. I believe that I will be able to help people in need, and look forward to growing as a therapist and a human being along the way. I cannot imagine what it will be like to have an encounter even close to any of the ones mentioned by the fine therapists in this book. I only hope that I will be able to provide the same kind of caring for my clients—and for myself—that they have. I feel scared of the possibilities, but am also tremendously excited. Will I be able to help? Will I break down under the pressure? Will the client see that I am lost? As apprehensive as I am, these stories have provided me with comfort. I am inspired to help, to be empathic, to be authentic and attuned to my clients' needs. I am here for the long haul, and look forward to someday being on the other end, telling about my personal transformation, about my finest hour!

ABOUT THE
CONTRIBUTORS

PATRICIA ARREDONDO is an associate professor of psychology and education at Arizona State University in Tempe. She has published several books, including *Counseling Latinos* and *La Familia: A Practical Guide and Multicultural Counseling Competencies.*

LAURA BROWN is a professor of psychology at Argosy University in Seattle. She has written a number of books, including *Subversive Dialogues: Theory in Feminist Therapy, Recovered Memories of Abuse,* and *Diversity and Complexity in Feminist Therapy.*

JON CARLSON is distinguished professor at Governors State University and psychologist at the Wellness Clinic in Lake Geneva, Wisconsin. Among Carlson's books are *Time for a Better Marriage, The Intimate Couple,* and *Bad Therapy.*

BARRY DUNCAN is a trainer and therapist who practices in Boca Raton, Florida. His best-selling books include *The Heroic Client* and *The Heart and Soul of Change: What Works.*

ALBERT ELLIS is a psychologist in New York City and the founder of rational emotive behavior therapy. Some of his best-known books are *Reason and Emotion in Psychotherapy, A Guide to Rational Living,* and *How to Stubbornly Refuse to Make Yourself Miserable About Anything.*

JOHN GRAY is a columnist, lecturer, and author of many books, including the best-selling *Men Are from Mars, Women Are from Venus.* His most recent book is *The Mars and Venus Exercise and Diet Book.* He lives in Mill Valley, California.

KEN V. HARDY is the director of the Center for Trauma in the Family at the Ackerman Institute for the Family in New York City. Dr. Hardy has published many articles and book chapters, and developed an award-winning video on the psychological residue of slavery.

BRADFORD KEENEY is vice president of Ringing Rocks Foundation and a cultural anthropologist living in Tucson, Arizona. Keeney has written many books, including *The Aesthetics of Change*, *Everyday Soul*, and *American Shaman*.

HOWARD KIRSHENBAUM is on the faculty at the Warner Graduate School of Education and Human Development at the University of Rochester in New York. Two of his most popular books are *The Carl Rogers Reader* and *Values Clarification: A Handbook of Practical Strategies for Teachers and Students*.

JEFFREY KOTTLER is professor and chair of the Counseling Department at California State University, Fullerton. Jeffrey has written over 60 books, including *On Being a Therapist*, *The Last Victim*, and *Making Changes Last*.

JOHN KRUMBOLTZ is professor of education at Stanford University. He has been instrumental in the promotion of learning theory and behavioral counseling, and is the author of a number of books, including *Planned Happenstance*, *Behavioral Counseling*, and *Changing Children's Behavior*.

STEPHEN LANKTON is a leading Ericksonian therapist and trainer who lives in Phoenix, Arizona. He has written many books, including *Practical Magic*, *The Answer Within*, and *Tales of Enchantment*.

PAT LOVE is a family therapist and consultant who lives in Austin, Texas. Pat has written several best-selling books, including *Hot Monogamy* and *The Truth About Love*.

ALAN MARLATT is a professor in the Department of Psychology at the University of Washington. Among his best-known books are *Relapse Prevention*, *Assessment of Addictive Behaviors*, and *Harm Reduction*.

LEIGH McCULLOUGH is an associate clinical professor and director of the Psychotherapy Research Program at Harvard Medical School. Her books include *Changing Character: Short-term Anxiety Regulating Psychotherapy for Restructuring Defense* and *Treating Affect Phobia*.

JOHN J. MURPHY is associate professor at the University of Central Arkansas. He is the author of *Solution Focused Counseling in Middle and High Schools* and *Brief Interventions for School Problems*.

ROBERT NEIMEYER is a professor of psychology at the University of Memphis. He has published many books, including *Constructivism in Psychotherapy* and *Lessons of Loss: A Guide to Coping*.

VIOLET OAKLANDER is a psychotherapist and play therapist in Santa Barbara, California. Her best-known work is the book *Windows to Our Children*.

PAUL PEDERSEN is visiting professor at the University of Hawaii in Honolulu. He is one of the leaders in the multicultural counseling movement and is author of *Counseling Across Cultures* and *A Handbook for Developing Multicultural Awareness*.

FRANK PITTMAN is a psychiatrist in private practice in Atlanta, Georgia. His best-known books include *Turning Points: Treating Families in Transition and Crisis, Private Lies*, and *Grow Up*.

DAVID SCHARFF is a psychiatrist in Chevy Chase, Maryland. He has written several books in the field of object relations therapy, including *Object Relations Family Therapy, Object Relations Couples Therapy*, and *Scharff Notes*.

LENORE WALKER is a professor at Nova Southeastern University's Center for Psychological Studies, and coordinator of the clinical forensic psychology concentration, in Davie, Florida. She has written 12 books, including the now classic *The Battered Woman*.

MICHAEL YAPKO is a psychologist and consultant who has written several books about treating depression by using an integration of clinical hypnosis and cognitive and strategic therapies. Among his most popular books are *Breaking the Pattern of Depression* and *Hand-Me-Down Blues*.

REFERENCES

Aeschylus. (1926). *Prometheus bound* (H. Smyth, Trans.). Cambridge, MA: Harvard University Press.

Campbell, J., & Moyers, B. (1991). *The power of myth*. New York: Anchor.

Chadda, T., & Slonim, R. (1998). Boundary transgressions in the psychotherapeutic framework. *American Journal of Psychotherapy*, 52(4), 489–500.

Freud, S. (1910). The future prospects of psychoanalytic therapy. *Standard ed., 11*, 3–55.

Goldfried, M. R. (Ed.). (2001). *How therapists change: Personal and professional reflections*. Washington, DC: American Psychological Association.

Herlihy, B., & Corey, G. (1997). *Boundary issues in counseling: Multiple roles and responsibilities*. Alexandria, VA: American Counseling Association.

Kahn, S., & Fromm, E. (Eds.). (2001). *Changes in the therapist*. Mahwah, NJ: Lawrence Erlbaum.

Kaufman, B. E. (1999). Emotional arousal as a source of bounded rationality. *Journal of Economic Behavior and Organization*, 38, 135–144.

Kottler, J. A. (2003). *On being a therapist* (3rd ed.). San Francisco: Jossey-Bass.

Kottler, J. A., & Carlson, J. (2003). *The Mummy at the Dining Room Table*. San Francisco: Jossey-Bass.

Levine, L. J., & Burgess, S. L. (1997). Beyond general arousal: Effects of specific emotions on memory. *Social Cognition*, 15, 157–181.

May, R. (1992). *Cry for myth*. New York: W. W. Norton.

Rogers, C. R. (1972). My personal growth. In A. Burton & Associates (Eds.), *Twelve therapists: How they live and actualize themselves*. San Francisco: Jossey-Bass.

Spiegel, D. (2001). In S. Kahn & E. Fromm (Eds.), *Changes in the therapist*. Mahwah, NJ: Lawrence Erlbaum.

Yalom, I. (1989). *Love's executioner and other tales of psychotherapy*. New York: Basic Books.

Yalom, I. (2002). *The gift of therapy*. New York: HarperCollins.